Studies in International Performance

Published in association with the International Federation of Theatre Research

General Editors: Janelle Reinelt and Brian Singleton

Culture and performance cross borders constantly, and not just the borders that define nations. In this new series, scholars of performance produce interactions between and among nations and cultures as well as genres, identities and imaginations.

Inter-national in the largest sense, the books collected in the *Studies in International Performance* series display a range of historical, theoretical and critical approaches to the panoply of performances that make up the global surround. The series embraces 'Culture' which is institutional as well as improvised, underground or alternate, and treats 'Performance' as either intercultural or transnational as well as intracultural within nations.

Titles include:

Patrick Anderson and Jisha Menon *(editors)*
VIOLENCE PERFORMED
Local Roots and Global Routes of Conflict

Elaine Aston and Sue-Ellen Case
STAGING INTERNATIONAL FEMINISMS

Christopher Balme
PACIFIC PERFORMANCES
Theatricality and Cross-Cultural Encounter in the South Seas

Susan Leigh Foster
WORLDING DANCE

Helen Gilbert and Jacqueline Lo
PERFORMANCE AND COSMOPOLITICS
Cross-Cultural Transactions in Australasia

Helena Grehan
PERFORMANCE, ETHICS AND SPECTATORSHIP IN A GLOBAL AGE

Judith Hamera
DANCING COMMUNITIES
Performance, Difference, and Connection in the Global City

Alan Read
THEATRE, INTIMACY & ENGAGEMENT
The Last Human-Venue

Joanne Tompkins
UNSETTLING SPACE
Contestations in Contemporary Australian Theatre

S. E. Wilmer
NATIONAL THEATRES IN A CHANGING EUROPE

Forthcoming titles:

Adrian Kear
THEATRE AND EVENT

Studies in International Performance
Series Standing Order ISBN 978–1–4039–4456–6 (hardback)
Series Standing Order ISBN 978–1–4039–4457–3 (paperback)
(outside North America only)

You can receive future titles in this series as they are published by placing a standing order. Please contact your bookseller or, in case of difficulty, write to us at the address below with your name and address, the title of the series and the ISBN quoted above.

Customer Services Department, Macmillan Distribution Ltd, Houndmills, Basingstoke, Hampshire RG21 6XS, England

Worlding Dance

Edited by

Susan Leigh Foster

First published 2009 by
PALGRAVE MACMILLAN

Palgrave Macmillan in the UK is an imprint of Macmillan Publishers Limited, registered in England, company number 785998, of Houndmills, Basingstoke, Hampshire RG21 6XS.

Palgrave Macmillan in the US is a division of St Martin's Press LLC, 175 Fifth Avenue, New York, NY 10010.

Palgrave Macmillan is the global academic imprint of the above companies and has companies and representatives throughout the world.

Palgrave® and Macmillan® are registered trademarks in the United States, the United Kingdom, Europe and other countries.

ISBN-13: 978-0-230-20594-9 hardback
ISBN-10: 0-230-20594-1 hardback

This book is printed on paper suitable for recycling and made from fully managed and sustained forest sources. Logging, pulping and manufacturing processes are expected to conform to the environmental regulations of the country of origin.

A catalogue record for this book is available from the British Library.

A catalog record for this book is available from the Library of Congress.

10 9 8 7 6 5 4 3 2 1
18 17 16 15 14 13 12 11 10 09

Printed and bound in Great Britain by
CPI Antony Rowe, Chippenham and Eastbourne

Contents

Acknowledgements

We would like to thank the faculty, staff, and graduate students in the Department of World Arts and Cultures, and also the Dean of the School of the Arts, Christopher Waterman, for their support of this project. We are also indebted to Harmony Bench for facilitating the organization of our meetings, and most especially to Yehuda Sharim and Ana Paula Höfling for assisting with the editing of the text.

Notes on Contributors

Ananya Chatterjea is Associate Professor and Director of Graduate Studies in the Department of Theater Arts and Dance, University of Minnesota. She is also Artistic Director of Ananya Dance Theatre, a dance company of women artists of color working at the intersection of artistic excellence and social justice (www.ananyadancetheatre.org). Her book, *Butting out! Reading cultural politics in the work of Chandralekha and Jawole Willa Jo Zollar*, was published by Wesleyan University Press in 2004.

Susan Leigh Foster, choreographer and scholar, is Professor in the Department of World Arts and Cultures at University of California, Los Angeles. She is the author of *Reading Dancing: Bodies and Subjects in Contemporary American Dance* (University of California Press, 1986); *Choreography and Narrative: Ballet's Staging of Story and Desire* (Indiana University Press, 1996); and *Dances that Describe Themselves: The Improvised Choreography of Richard Bull* (Wesleyan University Press, 2002). She is currently working on a study of the terms 'choreography,' 'kinesthesia,' and 'empathy.'

Lena Hammergren is Assistant Professor in Dance Studies at the Department for Musicology and Performance Studies, Stockholm University, Sweden, and Visiting Professor at University College of Dance, Stockholm. She is currently involved in a research project together with scholars from Denmark, Finland, and Norway, with the title 'Dance in Nordic Spaces: The Formation of Corporeal Identities.'

Anthea Kraut is Assistant Professor in the Dance Department at the University of California, Riverside, where she teaches courses in dance history and theory. Her book, *Choreographing the Folk: The Dance Stagings of Zora Neale Hurston* (University of Minnesota Press, fall 2008), recovers the history and traces the influence of Hurston's stagings of black diasporic folk dance in the 1930s. Her articles have been published in *Women & Performance: A Journal of Feminist Theory*, *Theatre Journal*, *The Scholar & Feminist Online*, *emBODYing Liberation: The Black Body in American Dance*, and *Theatre Studies*.

Marta Elena Savigliano is the author of *Tango and the Political Economy of Passion* (Westview, 1995) and *Angora Matta: Fatal Acts of North-South*

Translation (Wesleyan, 2003). *Angora Matta*, a tangopera-thriller developed in collaboration with composer Ramon Pelinski, choreographer Susan Rose, and animator Miguel Nanni, premiered at the Teatro Presidente Alvear, Buenos Aires, in December 2002 (www.angoramatta. com). She is co-director of/ GLOSAS / (Global South Advanced Studies), Buenos Aires (www.glosas.org), Professor Emeritus of the University of California Los Angeles' World Arts and Cultures department, and Visiting Professor at the University of California, Riverside's Dance Department.

Jacqueline Shea Murphy is Associate Professor in the Dance department at the University of California, Riverside. She is author of *'The People Have Never Stopped Dancing': Native American Modern Dance Histories* (University of Minnesota Press, 2007), and co-editor of the collection *Bodies of the Text: Dance as Theory, Literature as Dance* (Rutgers University Press, 1995). Her current project, of which the chapter in this volume is a part, looks at the political, historical, and institutional interventions that contemporary Indigenous choreographers in the United States, Canada, and in Aotearoa/New Zealand, are making.

Priya Srinivasan is an Assistant Professor in Dance at the University of California, Riverside. Srinivasan's research intersects with Asian diaspora studies, performance ethnography, dance historiography, labor, and citizenship. Her current book project is titled 'Dance, Labor, and Citizenship: The "Stages" of Transnational Indian Performers in the US.' Srinivasan has worked as an experimental dance/theatre choreographer in Chicago and Los Angeles, and has extensive training as a professional dancer in Australia. Her recent publications include an article in *Discourses in Dance* titled 'The Bodies Beneath the Smoke' and an article forthcoming in *Women and Performance*.

Yutian Wong is an Assistant Professor in Asian American Studies and Dance at the University of Illinois, Urbana-Champaign. Her research interests include Asian American performance, visual art, and popular culture.

Worlding Dance – An Introduction

Susan Leigh Foster

We convened in Los Angeles, what Saskia Sassen and others have identified as a 'global' city – home to massive numbers of diverse immigrants from across the globe, who, pressured by the uneven flows of capital and ideas, are working to get ahead and co-exist within a myriad of distinctive values, ethics, and practices (Sassen, 1994).[1] In this moment of global awareness, and at a time when even our small field of dance studies has grown to connect scholars from every continent and many countries, we met in Los Angeles to think collectively and with global perspective about something called 'world' dance.[2] Our meeting was inspired by conversations over the past ten years in the Working Group in Choreography and Corporeality sponsored by the International Federation for Theater Research that brought together an international group of scholars to consider how dance studies is expanding and diversifying throughout the world.[3] The department at UCLA that sponsored our meeting is called 'World Arts and Cultures,' and it has offered courses called 'world dance' practices. Many of us teach in programs where courses in various dance traditions are offered under the rubric 'world dance.' To what does this term refer? How and when was it implemented? How might contemporary theories of colonization, nation formation, diaspora, and globalization help us to conduct an inquiry into the term and its effects?

At UCLA the title World Arts evolved out of an earlier nomenclature 'Ethnic Arts,' which in turn grew out of, and was allied with, curricular interests in 'Folk Arts.' Whereas departments of Music, Art, and, eventually, Dance established classically oriented canons of study, faculty felt the need also to recognize the populist and quotidian practices of the folk that were otherwise excluded from these arts curricula. Thus, as early as the 1930s the Women's Physical Education program at UCLA

1

offered 'Folk Dancing' courses along with 'Dancing' courses. And with the establishment of the Department of Dance in the 1960s various nomenclatures were introduced, including 'Creative Dance,' 'Ethnic Dance,' and 'Dances of Specific Cultures.' Partially in response to its Los Angeles location, UCLA's Department of Dance promoted more intensively than many other US programs the study of a variety of dance forms from around the world. The course entitled 'History of Dance,' however, reflected the orientation more typical of US curricula by focusing on the Western tradition from 'Primitive to Renaissance' and 'Baroque to 20th Century.' 'Ethnic Arts,' an interdisciplinary program that attracted faculty from all of the arts departments plus folklore and anthropology came into existence in 1972. In the early 1990s it fused with the Dance Department to become the Department of World Arts and Cultures.

The substitution of 'world' for 'ethnic' at UCLA and in various labeling practices, such as the music industry and arts programming, has worked euphemistically to gloss over the colonial legacy of racialized and class-based hierarchizations of the arts.[4] Ethnic dances – envisioned as local rather than transcendent, traditional rather than innovative, simple rather than sophisticated, a product of the people rather than a genius – are resuscitated and transformed into products of various cultures from all around the world. The term 'world dance' intimates a neutral comparative field wherein all dances are products of equally important, wonderfully diverse, equivalently powerful cultures. The titling of art as 'world' also promises maximum exposure to a cornucopia of the new and exotic.[5] Yet through this relabeling, the colonial history that produced the ethnic continues to operate. For example, the brochure for the 2007–08 season of Cal Performances, the annual series of performances sponsored by UC/Berkeley, lists in the category 'Dance' six ballet companies and three modern companies.[6] Of the 12 press photographs included in the brochure, Alvin Ailey's American Dance Theater and the Guangshou Ballet offer the only photos with non-white dancers. Another category, entitled 'World Stage,' offers concerts by two Latina singers and four African music ensembles, Arlo Guthrie, the Moiseyev Dance Company, and Perú Negro (Cal Performances, 2007–08). On what basis is 'Dance' constituted as exclusively ballet and modern? Why does the 'Dance' category consist overwhelmingly of white artists, whereas artists of color dominate the 'World Stage'? How is it that the Moiseyev Dance Company, described as 'the greatest of all folk dance groups, and Perú Negro, 'offering an intoxicating mix of traditional and new [...],' dance their way onto the 'World Stage' but are not 'Dance'?

In our first discussions about 'world dance,' we focused on the effects of these kinds of categorizations. We examined the legacy of Western dance history – and the violence against dancing wrought by various rubrics of categorization, such as the 'primitive,' that have created complex hierarchies of value and worth. We likewise examined the contemporary status of the world's dances as they have become uprooted from their various locales and commodified and spectacularized for the global stage. We contemplated our own pedagogical investments and predicaments – teaching courses that help to perpetuate ethnocentric classificatory systems even as we work to envision new frameworks for comparing and analyzing dances. Over a three-year period of regular meetings, we came increasingly to address how authors and their subjects are implicated in relations of power that produce both subjection and privilege. We affirmed the need for new models of history writing that could provide alternative narrative structures. And we realized the need to recognize our own complicity in the project of 'worlding' dance.

As Edward Said (1983) has argued, any text lives within and partakes of a world. In order to interpret that text, the critic must consider the text's 'historical contingency' and 'sensuous particularity,' determining how to engage with that world as part of the text.[7] What world has been constructed for dancing through the use of the term 'world dance'? What kinds of worlds do we as scholars create for a given dance when we undertake to describe and analyze it? What effects do our analytic frameworks have upon dance as the object of our study?

This volume, the product of our collective reckoning with these questions, endeavors to make new epistemological space for the analysis of the world's dances. The chapters challenge the very foundations upon which the terms 'ethnic' or 'world' dance were created. They examine the exclusionary processes of collection and classification through which the world-building of various dance practices takes place, and as a result, how they acquire relative value and meaning. The chapters implement a global perspective in order to examine the local – tracing how dances have developed in specific localities, migrated, and transformed alongside and in response to political and cultural pressures. They work to reflexively interrogate the embodied status of the researcher. And they 'choreograph' new approaches to the writing of history that respond to the exigencies of our global political moment.

Sachs's legacy

This volume is certainly not the first or only effort to think about dance in global perspective. In 1937 German musicologist Curt Sachs wrote

A World History of The Dance, a radical attempt to collate and compare dances from around the world and through time. For Sachs dance is a pan-human phenomenon that originates in the experience of the 'effervescent zest for life' that animates the body, and reaffirms its spiritual as well as social vitality. Regardless of the form the dance takes, its power resides in this primal urge to connect with the divine rhythms of the universe. In conformance with cultural histories of that period, Sachs organized his history to reflect the various developments and refinements of that primal motivation.[8] He examined, first, evidence of Stone Age dances, then summarized the evolution of dance as spectacle in the 'Oriental Civilizations,' and finally, regressing back in time to the Greek and Roman Classical period, he traced dance's evolution through the Renaissance, the eighteenth century, the age of the waltz (nineteenth century) and that of the tango (twentieth century). In this approach Sachs presumes that contemporary exemplars of Stone Age dances endure in the 'tribal' rituals of communities such as the pygmies. He likewise assumes that dances of Asia have remained unchanging for thousands of years. Thus, for Sachs, the only dance forms to have evolved through time are those practiced in Western Europe.

Sachs's narrative depends upon several assumptions that continue to haunt the practice of dancing and the study of dance. Foremost among these is Sachs's assertion that dance in its most original and ontological form is the product of an ecstatic subjectivity. As Sachs describes the process, the dancer is possessed by the dance: 'Delivered then from his will, the dancer gives himself over to the supreme delight of play prescribed by custom [...].' In this conceptualization of dance, the autonomous individual is guided by culturally specific customs to produce a distinctive expression of a universal experience of transcendence. Cultures look different on the surface, but their underlying structures reflect the contours of the human predicament. Similarly, dances manifest in a vast diversity of forms, yet they are unified by their common function of providing an ecstatic alternative to quotidian life.

While much dance scholarship over the past 20 years has contested this assumption, as well as the allied notions of authenticity, spontaneity, and the general trope of the natural, dances categorized as 'ethnic' or 'world' forms continually fall under its influence. In the classroom and on the global stage, dances from Europe and the US are received as choreographed, contrived or arranged as representation, and those from other parts of the world are treated as more fervent and immediate, and therefore capable of offering an unmediated glimpse into the cultural distinctiveness of their respective communities. Thus, according to the Cal Performances brochure, the Moiseyev Dance company offers 'exuberant evocations of traditional dances,' whereas Mark Morris's 'combination of lyricism and astounding precision [...] marks the emergence of an instant classic' (Cal Performances, 2007–08: 5, 3). The Moiseyev evokes a way of life, whereas Morris's choreography achieves the standards of excellence necessary to become a classic. Similarly, the highly popular culture clubs at US universities that deploy dance as the principle expressive medium within which to assert diasporic identity are typically removed from, and non-aligned with, departments of dance. 'Art' dance or 'concert' dance dwells in the unmarked realm of aesthetics, removed from both the social and the political, whereas 'culture' nights use dance as marker of, and integral to, a way of life.

Whether spontaneous or contrived, the assumption that dances share a common universal origin enables them to be compared, one with another, using standard categories of analysis. For Sachs, these standardized systems of measurement included simple positions of the body, such as bent or straight knees; actions, such as stamping or turning; motions, such as expansion or convulsion; and configurations of dancers, such as serpentines, rounds or choral dances. In these comparisons, Sachs privileged the shape of the body, conceptualized as a geometry with angles, straight lines, a center and a periphery, and whose direction of motion likewise leaves a trace with geometric attributes – curved or straight. The seemingly neutral implementation of geometry obliterates indigenous senses of value and meaning in the dancing, uprooting the dancing from its local habitat and relocating it to an unmarked space where it can be evaluated and compared with other forms.

Beginning in the 1960s, a team of researchers led by anthropologist Alan Lomax resuscitated Sachs's approach in their development of the 'choreometrics' project, a rating system for the comparative study of dances using analytic frameworks corollary to Rudolf Laban's systems of movement analysis. Envisioning dance as 'a representation and reinforcement of cultural pattern,' they observed postural and movement flow patterns in films of dances from around the world, determining a strong correspondence between features of the movement repertoire utilized for purposes of subsistence and those invoked in dancing. These researchers found that the bodily stance and style of transition, whether 'cyclic, angular, rotated, or looped,' among others, assumed while dancing correlated strongly with the 'rubbing, digging, or chopping,' and the like entailed in food production (Lomax, Bartinieff and Paulay, 1968: 240–1). Not only does Lomax's approach implement universal categories that provide standards of measurement against which all dances can be analyzed and then compared, but it also implies a hierarchy of cultures, similar to Sachs's, that moves from more 'primitive' to 'complex' social organizations.

Both Sachs's and Lomax's projects are undergirded by a classical and linear narrative of continual progress and the invention of new forms. 'Proper' histories, in Hayden White's nomenclature, they are founded in the moralizing impulse to embrace all human activity as unfolding with greater and greater complexity in a single plan that the studies themselves help to reveal (White, 1980). Dance's history, they suggest, can be understood through the chronological study of its development over time, using classificatory rubrics that prove one dance's influence upon another.

More recently, Pegge Vissicaro and a team of computer scientists have developed an ethnochoreological comparison that, although it refrains from any implicit or explicit ranking of cultural systems, subjects the dancing body to a similar set of universal criteria for movement analysis. Their study focuses on the changing distances between parts of the body and the concomitant alteration in their silhouettes as well as the distance among dancers and their paths through space (Golshani, Vissicaro and Park, 2004: 90). Using technologies at the Multimedia Information Systems Laboratory at Arizona State, they have 'extracted' these measurements from films of dances by dividing the image into segments and detecting edges of shapes so as to track their changes over time (2004: 92). They envision the new information processing potential of computer systems as more adequate to the task of parsing dance's complexity. However, the process of extracting that information from the dancing body through the construction of abstract, geometric principles remains the same as in Sachs's and Lomax's approaches.

Sachs's assertion that dance originates in the ecstatic psyche, and his use of seemingly neutral frames of analysis, constituted dance as an object separate from the operations of power. Although it might reflect a political hierarchy, a competition, or a division of labor, dance stands apart from the 'real' workings of society. Lomax's theory integrated dance into social organization as a styling of the body and movement that resonated with other physical practices. Calling dance an 'information system,' Vissicaro and colleagues likewise conceptualize dance as a complex event affecting both practitioners and viewers through multiple sensory channels. Whether as a representation of individual or cultural states of being, however, dance, as a fundamentally ephemeral and transitory event, can only reflect cultural value and meaning. In all three research projects, it does not actively participate in the construction of such meaning.

In contrast to this legacy, the chapters in this volume examine dance, not as a reflection of individual or cultural values, but *as* culture. As culture, dance is in(sinew)ated with power relations. Built bone-deep into the dancing body and permeating its practice and performance, these structurings of power both discipline and pleasure the body. And this cultivation of the corporeal takes place within and as a part of the power relations that operate throughout the body politic.

Body memories/bodyscapes

Contemporaneous with Lomax, sociologist Pierre Bourdieu began conducting his fieldwork among the Kabyle of Algeria in the 1960s. Not unlike Lomax, he envisions bodily attitudes and ways of moving as a pervasive repertoire of patterns that circulates throughout the social (Bourdieu, 1980). Unlike Lomax, Bourdieu endows this 'habitus' with the capacity actively to participate in the construction of cultural meaning. He posits the body as a repository of forms of cultural memory that have never been documented in history. For Bourdieu, however, this form of memorizing and commemorating is fundamentally conservative: the body's movement repertoire retains and holds on to the past. Even when improvising, its actions are limited to a rule-governed range of responses that serve only to rediscover and renew traditions of thought and action. Bourdieu thereby casts the body in the role of a vehicle for tradition. In so doing, he, like Lomax, identifies the body as a vehicle for channeling culture rather than creating culture, as expressing culture rather than as expressive in and of itself.

Bourdieu's theory of the habitus also presumes that culture is relatively stable, cohesive, and distinct. Subsequent studies in ethnography, such as those by James Clifford and George Marcus, have argued that boundaries defining cultural difference are inherently porous and unstable (Clifford and Marcus, 1986). They constantly reconstruct themselves, produced partially by the physical responsiveness of the ethnographic encounter and the equally physical act of writing an ethnography. More recently, Homi Bhabha has argued for the in-between status of culture, and Arjun Appadurai has suggested that not only is culture a messy and unstable aggregate of practices, but also that these practices are themselves in motion (Appadurai, 1996, 2001; Bhabha,

2004). Culture thus configures as the synergistic encounter between 'process geographies' and 'scapes,' such as those contoured by media, technology, or economic practices.

For her chapter in this volume, Lena Hammergren adapts these concepts, following sociologist Paula Saukko's expansion of Appadurai's 'scape' to include the bodyscape (Saukko, 2003). For Hammergren, the bodyscape functions as a set of corporeal vectors that intersect with other systems of values, likewise in motion, to construct meaning. She accounts for the complex reception of Ram Gopal's performances of Indian dance in Sweden by examining it as the frictive encounter between the ever-changing conglomerates known as India and Sweden, but also the evolving Swedish notions of classicism and modernism and the nation's relationship to the emerging formation known as the United Nations.

The notion of bodyscape could also be useful in examining how certain social pressures, such as those embedded within the Euro-American museum, work to exclude physical forms of signification. In her analysis of the new Native American Museum in Washington, DC, Jacqueline Shea Murphy elucidates traditional assumptions about a museum's function and contents through comparison with a Native perspective on corporeal forms of knowledge. As Shea Murphy argues, Native dance and ceremonial practices form a central means of knowledge production and transmission that refuses categorization within the typical boundaries of the museum. Such practices are not stored in some kind of container called the body as a form of memory. Rather, they re-member knowledge through their movements as the body acts.

Diana Taylor has identified this capacity of physicality to re-create and reinvigorate memory as the repertoire, placing it in dialectical tension with the archive – systems of documentation that, although still ephemeral, endure with greater permanence (Taylor, 2003). For Taylor this repertoire of movements, through which history is summoned up and reinvoked, does not necessarily perform the conservative, retentive function that Bourdieu envisions for the habitus. The repertoire can also salvage histories repressed by colonial or dictatorial domination, and it can network with other repertoires to construct new alliances or affiliations across cultural differences. As Cynthia Novack has persuasively demonstrated in her ethnographic study of contact improvisation, the repertoire can serve to invent and/or subvert cultural values (Novack, 1990). Furthermore, the same actions can embody multiple, and even contradictory, values.

Decolonizing dancing

As we convened in Los Angeles, we aspired to construct inquiries into dancing that would acknowledge and celebrate the complexity of any given dance's significance while simultaneously locating it within a global perspective on dance. Specifically, we worked to imagine new rubrics of analysis that do not depend upon the kinds of universal categories invoked by Sachs, Lomax, and Vissicaro as a means to convoke relatedness. And we hoped to complicate the procedures through which dance is written into history, similar to the way that Dipesh Chakrabarty identifies options for post-colonial historians to rewrite their colonial pasts (Chakrabarty, 2000).

Examining the legacy of Western history and its use of universal terms, Chakrabarty characterizes Western historical time as 'godless, continuous, and homogeneous,' a construct exempt from supernatural forces, Gods, and spirits that creates a bottomless sack into which any number of events can be stuffed (2000: 73). He argues that time, as a natural category against which all experience is to be measured, must be contested. Concomitant with this use of time, Western history depends upon the split between public and private selves and upon the assertion of a secular worldview. As a result, post-colonial historians struggle with the dual mandate to implement a public and secular perspective while at the same time interrogating that framework as part of the colonizing and civilizing process to which their ancestors were subjected (2000: 93).

Thus, rather than merely succumb to Western conventions for history writing by using its conventions to tell the stories of previously unrepresented peoples, Chakrabarty advocates a form of history that documents the contradictions inherent in the confrontations between distinctive worldviews. This is not to say that all cultures can tidily be separated into cohesive units and their contacts with one another carefully recorded. Nor is it justification for the distinction between 'emic' and 'etic' points of view, a framework that perpetuates the possibility of cross-cultural comparison using standardized categories of analysis. Instead, Chakrabarty argues for the need for new models of translating experience that do not depend upon a middle term that functions as a universal. As example, he cites the way that the symbol denoting the chemical constitution of water, H_2O, stands as the universal for water, even though its name is water in English and 'pani' in Hindi (2000: 75).

Chakrabarty proposes that historians search out these new forms of translation by writing the confrontation between one model of history and another occur, and he urges us to conceptualize these confrontations as knots in time, or in Hindu 'granthi,' a term that references all manner of jointed articulations such as those that compose the skeleton. 'Granthi' are dense with potentials to move in multiple directions. They both register the influence of forces exercised upon them and actively channel or direct those forces. This approach does not expand traditional modes of history writing to include new subjects, previously ignored or repressed. For Chakrabarty, writing history as knotted, is not a form of cultural relativism, but rather a project of conceptualizing history as contradictory, plural, heterogeneous.

Continuing our discussions of what it might mean to embark on writing about dance with these concerns in mind, we found ourselves embarked on the vertiginous project of calling into question many of the fundamental terms of our discipline. For example, is the notion of 'form' one that already demands of dancing the exhibition of certain aesthetic principles or features that make its structure visible? When we speak of dancing's form, to what features are we referring? Do all dances have a form or formal properties? Does the discussion of a dance's form partition the practice from the practitioners? And what might be the consequences of this separation? When we trace the migration of (a form of) dancing from one location to another, on what basis can we draw comparisons?

A similar set of questions arises around the concept of technique: Is there any generalized conception of 'technique' that dance practices share? Could 'training' the body mean the same thing in different geographies? Dance scholarship has already called into question whether any specific criteria can be used to assess technical competence. But what if implicit in the notion of technique itself are different attitudes toward the body and its relationship to subjectivity? Can technique be separated from spirit? from pleasure? or from moveability?

Can we distinguish between the dance and the space surrounding it? Do dances occur in space? Do they create space? How has space, similar to Chakrabarty's critique of the Western notion of time, come to function as a blank, neutral container for dancing? What effects does such a conception of space have on the teaching of dancing?

And can we separate a dance's choreography from its performance? Three of the chapters in this volume tackle this question by looking at the ways choreography has been conceptualized in different artistic and scholarly practices. Anthea Kraut examines how copyright policies have impinged upon and been influenced by prevailing conceptions of choreography in the early twentieth century. My chapter considers the evolution of choreography from its eighteenth-century meaning to the early twentieth century, noting how the term has functioned to categorize traditions of dancing. And Marta Savigliano looks at how the term has been used to suture together distinctive epistemological inquiries into the value and meaning of dancing.

Writing about a subject in motion while in motion

Each of the chapters in this volume wrestles with the knotted quality of history writing. They resist efforts at comparison based on universal categories, and instead envision the project of translating dance to the written page as a labor of identifying and examining the complexities of the project. They work to excavate subjugated knowledges and also to construct new forms of narration.

Many of the chapters examine the mobility of dancing bodies and practices across national boundaries. Yutian Wong tackles the identity of Michio Ito as an 'international artist' whose fame was based, in part, on his status as an exceptional person who transcended national boundaries. She further exposes the kinds of racial bias that enables a category such as that of international artist in the first place. Similarly, Hammergren examines Ram Gopal as a kind of international artist whose reception so clearly altered from one country to the next. Priya Srinivasan looks at the disparate functions enacted by the Bharata Natyam concert as it is performed by the professional artist in Chennai and by the adolescent NRI (Non-Resident Indian) in southern California. And Savigliano traces the migration of the very term 'world dance' across multiple archives and knowledge bases.

Several of the essays make use of the writer's own physical experiences and situatedness to inform their analysis. Srinivasan places her own body as a central node through which multiple discourses from both past and present, Chennai and southern California pass. Her essay weaves back and forth between the object of history and the historian's own life, so that each illuminates the other. Hammergren constructs a genealogy that works backwards from her own study of Indian dance, showing how alternative frameworks of classification can be constructed. Shea Murphy observes her own physical responses to the museum alongside those of other visitors and the staff. And Ananya Chatterjea stitches a quilt-like narrative that includes patches from her own history of dancing 'folk' dance and 'expressive' dance in Kolkata.

And each of the chapters crafts a distinctive narrative style, one that foregrounds the kinds of documentation with which they are working.

Kraut, for example, extrapolates from copyright law as well as rumor in order to forge an argument about racialized power relations under-writing the transformation of dance into a form of intellectual prop-erty. Wong and Chatterjea emphasize the absences in documentation that have been produced through operations of the nation-state. And Srinivasan performs as an unruly spectator whose inability to keep focused on the dancing body yields important insights concerning the labor that produced it. Taken together, the chapters offer a tool-box of tactics that, far from constituting a revisionist world history of the dance, will hopefully promote ongoing debate over the worlds that dances create and the worlds that we create for them.

Notes

1. For additional perspective on Los Angeles history and culture, and the diver-sity of dance practices it supports, see Hamera.
2. For example, the joint conference of the Society of Dance History Scholars and the Congress on Research in Dance held in June 2007 at the Centre National de la Danse, Paris, brought together 500 scholars from 30 different countries on five continents.
3. Lena Hammergren and I co-founded this Working Group in 1998, and it continues to meet at all FIRT conferences.
4. As Tim Taylor has shown, the phrase 'world music' came into widespread use in the late 1980s in response to the overwhelming popularity of musical genres from West Africa and South Asia. Realizing that these musics could not be sold as 'ethnic,' producers devised a new category to compete with 'classical,' 'pop,' 'jazz,' and so on (Taylor, 1997: 1–3).
5. For example, consider this enthusiastic description of courses offered through UCLA's student center under the headline 'Grades/Groove: Students can release stress, get moving and get units in a variety of classes from hip-hop to salsa': 'Forget the days of forced country line-dancing lessons in the elementary school gymnasium with partners plagued by two left feet and country music crackling through an outdated stereo system. The John Wooden Center and the world arts and cultures department offer cultural dance classes that provide students with an alternative way to work out and learn about world cultures through movement and music' (Cohn, 2008: 1).
6. My selection of this brochure is purely arbitrary and intended only to point towards the generalized use of the category 'world.' I want also to clarify that the programming by Cal Performances is unrelated to the activities of the Department of Theater, Dance, and Performance Studies at UC/Berkeley. As at UCLA, the season of performances presented by the campus received little or no input from the faculty and is entirely separate from departmentally sponsored events.
7. Said writes that the text's 'worldliness, circumstantiality, the text's status as an event having sensuous particularity as well as historical contingency, are considered as being incorporated in the text, an infrangible part of its

capacity for conveying and producing meaning. This means that a text has a specific situation, placing restraints upon the interpreter and his interpretation not because the situation is hidden within the text as a mystery, but rather because the situation exists at the same level of surface particularity as the textual object itself' (1983: 39).

8. See Youngerman (1974) for a robust critique of Sachs' approach, one that locates his efforts within the historical context of scholarly inquiry into folk materials.

1
The Power of Classification

Lena Hammergren

[...] war dances, swan dances, Bharatanatyam, dances included in this list, Manipuri, dances you see from the third row, *Dixit Dominus*, Jewish dances, classical dance, Indian dance, *Pieces of me*, imageless dances, dances you have only read about, Ram Gopal, multicultural dance, *To the flower people*, dances that have just finished [...]

This listing above of different dances and dance related items is, in Michel Foucault's words, a 'linking together of things that are inappropriate' (1973: xvii). One can marvel at the manner in which Foucault develops his ideas on classification in *The Order of Things*, based on his reading of a passage in a book by Luis Borges. What occupies Foucault's thoughts is a fictitious entry on animals in a Chinese Encyclopedia. He interprets the Chinese taxonomy created by Borges as 'thought without space [...] words and categories that lack all life and place,' located in a geographical site that the West conceives as a 'vast reservoir of utopias' (1973: xix).[1] Utopia should be understood here as a non-space, lacking order. In Foucault's reading this taxonomy does not categorize things in a manner that enables us to name, speak, and think.

Contrary to Foucault, I consider my list of dances adequate, filled with thought, space, and life. The list is so, because it is saturated with power. Of course, it does not look like the categories of dances we are familiar with, in the sense that they should all share coherence and reflect a consensus in the ordering code with which they are linked together. According to Foucault, if a common locus does not exist, 'things are "laid," "placed," "arranged"' in sites so very different from one another that it is impossible to hold them together (1973: xvii–xviii). However, from a historical point of view, the common locus of this list of dances exists in the idea and practice of a history of world dances that over time has come to include the classification and comparison of diverse forms, and also the identities and psychological profiles of the dancers performing them.[2] Thus, my list could be described, in Foucault's terminology, as a heterotopia, which is a realized utopia based on a subverted order that allows incompatible things to meet. The question then follows: which functions or effects can this particular heterotopia have?

In answer to this, I will begin my chapter with reflections on cross-cultural and multicultural dance studies, a field of research in which comparison, commensurability, and thus classification have been key operations. Then I will shift to an analysis of how three choreographers/dancers with different connections to India perform identity and choreograph politics in a Northern-European context. Both areas address the problems that occur while trying to perform the practice of distinguishing the Same from the Other.

Diversity versus difference

What kinds of meaning and power reside in the category of 'multicultural' forms of dance? In a textbook on multicultural dance targeted at college and university students, Pegge Vissicaro explains the term 'multicultural' as something that is similarly experienced by people all over the world: 'we see ourselves as living in a culturally heterogeneous world, or one with "many cultures"' (Vissicaro, 2004: 3).[3] She is hereby describing a kind of global consensus, the 'we' who see ourselves living with many cultures. The choice of the term 'multicultural' is further outlined in connection to globalization. Vissicaro states that 'global dance or world dance does not exist, nor can it happen since cultural knowledge is and always will be context specific' (2004: 104). It is easy to accept the positive notion of the need to acknowledge dances' various contexts, although one must question the use of the global 'we' as a kind of trans-cultural world-subject, free to discover and appreciate dance cultures around the world. After all, we live in a time of global apartheid, experiencing the protection of ethnic differences by a separation that is maintained with techniques ranging from language tests for immigrants seeking citizenship, to the construction of fences along national borders.

Embedded in Vissicaro's argumentation lies another problematic conceptualization, one that could be described as the contrast between cultural diversity and cultural difference. To her, the word 'multiculturalism' embraces diversity, and this, it is argued, must be studied cross-culturally with the help of comparative methods. Homi Bhabha has criticized the use of the term diversity, by juxtaposing it to difference. He argues that in applying the concept of cultural diversity as an analytic tool, one risks producing separate, local, and stable cultural systems which are linked to ideas of 'pre-given ethnic or cultural traits' set in a fixed historical tradition (2004: 3). Furthermore, he sees the term as belonging to a 'category of comparative ethics, aesthetics or ethnology' (2004: 50). For Bhabha the concept of diversity produces negative effects, such as liberal notions of multiculturalism and policies of cultural exchange, and he argues that the time for such cultural communities has definitely passed.

Bhabha prefers the concept of cultural difference, whose analytic focus is directed toward the processes of naming, knowing, authorizing, and differentiating cultures. Hence, he locates culture as the 'cutting edge of translation and negotiation, the *inbetween* space' of enunciation (2004: 56). With the word 'enunciation' he means the possibility and the acts of articulating knowledge about culture and difference, that is, the positions from which we speak and write. These articulations are embedded discursively as well as in time and space, thus we cannot locate meaning solely in the statement itself but must also engage in the 'indeterminacy of intertextuality' (2004: 48). Applying his arguments to dance, it becomes clear that even if dances are contextualized, the intertextual dimension makes the exterior forms of these contexts appear ruptured. Important in such a case is that context would not be used to explain a dance phenomena, but to make it more complex and reveal different aspects of how it is constructed and understood. This approach means that we do not simply put a dance in a context, but rather articulate a chosen connection *between* 'different elements, under certain conditions' (Dilley, 1999: 37).

Vissicaro's views on this point are not so easily detected. One of her key concepts is a theory of dynamism, with which she argues that the only constant in the universe is change. Thus, cultures, societies, and individuals manifest continuous change. However, she does not provide methodological tools for the study of these changes from a discursive and socio-historical perspective. A poignant example of this is found in her discussion of race and ethnicity. The concepts are investigated according to their potentiality as tools for dance classification, that is, she discusses their applicability (in both negative and positive terms) as universal categories for describing dances.[4] Because of this emphasis, issues of fictional and other forms of discursive racial classification elude her attention, and it becomes difficult to interrogate how these acts of power are played out. Post-colonial theorists have convincingly argued that race and ethnicity are cultural and historical rather than biological and a-historical phenomena, thus the terms need to be put in context and analyzed as social constructions, since both *retain their discursive power* (see, for example, the entries 'Ethnicity' and 'Race' in Ashcroft, Griffiths and Tiffin, 1998: 80–4, 198–206).

What seems to be at stake in the ideas of Vissicaro and Bhabha respectively are two very different views on culture. As I have discussed above, Bhabha locates culture in the powerful field of translation and negotiation, which places culture in a moving, ambivalent and ever-changing structure of meaning-making. Vissicaro mediates between two different modes of locating culture that include her definition of ethnicity. On the one hand, she argues that in some parts of the world, life and dancing exist in specific ethnic form, regardless of external influences (Vissicaro, 2004: 76). On the other hand, she notices a contemporary shift in perspective where ethnic identification is made difficult 'due to intermarriage and population shifts' (2004: 76–7). Thus, some dance cultures are static, and some are undergoing change.[5]

Bhabha wants us to resist 'the attempt at holistic forms of social explanation' (Bhabha, 2004: 248), because cultures are too incommensurable to be placed in one system – and this is an explicit critique of cross-cultural comparisons. One could argue that it is impossible to do without any comparativist methodologies in studies of cultures in different locations, and I would agree on a general level. But is it necessary to use the kind of pre-given, fixed set of micro features, so typical of many cross-cultural dance comparisons? I would, instead, hope to see emerging methods departing from more dynamic models, which both order, and are ordered by, the objects and events as we move through them. The problem with Vissicaro's argument, as I see it, is that she strives for diversity through the use of a multicultural perspective, but she ends up, unwittingly, with a fixed system of how dance cultures persist or change. Vissicaro is undoubtedly not a follower of Curt Sachs's outdated methodology, but unfortunately her argument looks quite similar to his use of the *Kulturkreislehre*, which states that cultures do not change unless they come into contact with other forms of culture through, for example, migration (Sachs, 1937).[6] Instead of this argument, one could claim that seemingly 'ethnic dances,' that is, dances from ethnically distinct groups of people (Vissicaro's definition) participate in an unstable system of cultural reference and possibilities of enunciation. Furthermore, ethnic dances are involved in structures of power on a local as well as global scale. In my opinion we have access to theoretical tools which could help us in working along this line of thought.

Arjun Appadurai, who has worked extensively on the topic of globalization, offers pertinent insights, in particular his concepts 'process geographies' and '-scapes' (Appadurai, 2001: 1–21; Appadurai, 1996). Appadurai discusses scholars' traditional thinking of area studies (e.g., American, Asian, or Scandinavian studies), which are based on a cultural coherence of immobile 'values, languages, material practices,' and rely on an assumption of durable historical boundaries (2001: 7). Instead, Appadurai wants to think of areas as in motion, as bringing about actions and interactions. Thus, process geographies regard areas as 'initial contexts for themes that generate variable geographies, rather than as fixed geographies marked by pregiven themes' (2001: 8). Appadurai takes as his examples areas of human organization such as trade, travel, colonization, and so on, which he considers shifting geographies, each highlighting variable assemblages 'of language, history, and material life' (2001: 7–8). His term 'scape' works in tandem with the concept of process geographies. Scape refers to spheres of life (economy, media, technology, people, etc.) that, in a flowing movement, connect to different places and relate different places to one another. Paula Saukko has expanded Appadurai's original list of scapes, and she has used bodyscape (referring to corporeality) in her analysis of multi-sited research on dance (Saukko, 2003: 180–7).[7] Both concepts focus on the connections between global and local experiences and expressions, and both challenge a traditional system of classification.

Indian dancing – in Sweden

To conceive of Sweden as part of process geographies, and as an initial site that brings on actions and interactions reaching beyond the nation-state, has been a productive starting point for my research on Indian dance in Sweden. It must be stressed here that the choice of Sweden as example in a discussion about multicultural perspectives is not intended as a typical geography that can provide analyses for widespread use. But, there is a shortage of texts on these matters from European countries that have not been marked by colonial practices to the same extent as, for example, France and the United Kingdom. The latter nations have formed a kind of 'canonical' collection of illustrative examples. I find this situation runs the risk of diminishing our understanding of potential variations in a context of globalization.

Moreover, the idea of a bodyscape has helped focus the ways in which Indian dancing is intertwined with local human experiences and discourses as well as global socio-cultural structures of power. These perspectives have made relevant Homi Bhabha's theories of the power of enunciation, and the questions they pose concerning how definitions, classifications, and discourses are formulated, how they are expressed, and in what contexts.

Ram Gopal – an exponent of classicism

To be able to speak about Indian dance in Sweden, one would initially have to investigate what has been defined as 'Indian' dancing in this geographical location. This act of articulation or enunciation appears to be one of the central considerations of the topic, and its manifestations can be found in discourses concerning guest performances starting in 1948 by Indian dancer Ram Gopal and his company in the Scandinavian countries. Ram Gopal was born in Bangalore in the 1910s, and undertook training in Indian classical dance forms during the 1930s, before touring in India as well as abroad. His two tours to Sweden in the 1940s were both privately sponsored, and the first happened unscheduled after the company had been stranded in London, due to disagreements between two impresarios (Westman, 2006: 89). After Gopal's second visit to Sweden in 1949, a dance critic wrote a lengthy newspaper article on the effects of his performances, bringing up a debate on the authenticity of both Gopal's dances and dancers (Idestam-Almqvist, 1949). In that critic's opinion Gopal's dances are not authentic, but also this criterion itself is deemed unproductive, because of the fact that the dances are being performed within a Western theatre tradition. Another argument he makes is that Indian dancing is a mixture of several local cultures; hence, Indian dance is too multifaceted to be adequately represented by any one coherent and common dance form. In order to emphasize his statement, the critic compares Indian dance to classical ballet. Although different from one another, both build on a variation of expressive forms, have roots in different folk dance traditions, and neither should be conceived of as anthropological museum displays, but rather as free, innovative, artistic creations. As such, they demand the mastery of virtuoso dance techniques rather than the display of authentic dancing. In one swift move, the critic awards Ram Gopal an artistic autonomy and makes him an exponent of classicism, which exists universally without specific ties to region or nation, or to authenticity.

In my interpretation, the context for this assertion is not limited to Sweden; it is better conceived of as a locally situated articulation of events occurring in India as well as in the United States. After World War II, the independent Indian nation-state was constituted, and the

1930s Indian renaissance in dance was integral to this development of nationalism. Here, ideas of classicism were created, but in a manner different from those articulated in the Swedish context where artistic autonomy, inventiveness, and virtuosity were emphasized. One can also notice the apparent ease with which the Swedish dance critic rejects any need to establish an authentic Indian dance form – and this is of course in stark contrast to contemporary Indian dance discourse. In India, claims to ancientness, authenticity, and the organization of an approved repertoire are important features (Erdman, 1996: 288–305; Chatterjea, 2004: 143–56). The factor that links these two ideas of classicism to one another is that they both deal with the construction of a cultural modernity in corporeal form – a bodyscape. In the Ram Gopal example, it is the transnational dissemination of this cultural modernity that creates a multi-sited geography.

Invoking a transnational perspective, it is important not to lose sense of the different local discourses that are produced with regard to modernity in the different geographical sites. So, what is particular about the cultural modernity that is articulated in the Swedish context? At the end of the 1940s, Sweden had a different political agenda than India, which was in the initial stages of its post-colonial development. There are a few passages in the Swedish article about Gopal that I find of particular interest, and that reveal an awareness of the contemporary political situation outside of the critic's own country. The first is the mentioning of the recently formed United Nations (which happened in 1945), through which 'our eyes are opened to the necessity of increasing our awareness of other countries and peoples' lives in order to create collaboration and peace on earth' (Idestam-Almqvist, 1949, my translation). Indeed, a naive declaration from our current perspectives, but central to that particular place in time. Sweden had not been at war, but during the early post-war years it was made public how the government had allowed the transportation of Nazi troops on Swedish railroads, and also how the Swedish Bureau for National Security had returned German refugees to their homeland during wartime. Sweden can thus be said to have had a particular interest in supporting dreams of 'peace on earth', in order to change and better the collective national image that had been tarnished by functioning as a Nazi collaborator. Perhaps another example of this drive towards obtaining redress was the election of the Swede Gunnar Myrdal as General Secretary of the United Nations Economic Commission for Europe in 1947. Myrdal had been an explicit critic of German politics during the war. The reference to the United Nations in the article about Gopal discursively affects the other important feature in the text, in which the comparison is made between classical ballet and Indian dance. The critic is arguing that Ram Gopal presents a modern Indian 'ballet' which, in technique and expression, can compete with Western ballet. The cultural modernity that the Swedish context embraces seems to be in need of the establishment of dance forms of equal, global artistic value, mirroring the image of a world of united and equal nations. Gopal's Indian dance is fittingly conceived of as an expression of independent India, and as a new independent style of dance.

Nevertheless, the set of criteria by which Ram Gopal is so favorably judged is typical of a Western modernity (universality, innovation, autonomous high art), and one could ask: where does this leave Ram Gopal and his artistic ambitions? Should we see him merely as a Westernized Other, or did he find ways of putting his cultural resources to different uses? In the Swedish discourse, at this particular historical point in time marked by its immediate post-war experiences, Ram Gopal is actively contributing to the shaping and development of a cultural modernity, because he is revealing what an individual subject and singular nation within the world of united nations can achieve – Ram Gopal and India are perceived as agents of change.

However, one should not overemphasize the statement in the newspaper article that 'all cultures are equal'. According to Bhabha, this attitude would be an example of cultural pluralism, in which different cultures are placed in the same time, which is an ethnocentric form of cultural modernity that contemporizes cultural difference. In so doing, minorities are deprived of liminal space from which they might have the chance to articulate their own agendas. The use of European ballet as the norm for comparison is certainly proof of such cultural pluralism, but on the other hand, the Swedish critic does describe a creative artistic force, originating in a defined geographical location, yet not constituting an ontological and racially defined Indianness. He points out how the many different dance forms in India invalidate the use of a common label. I consider this a fairly progressive idea given its time and place, especially if I compare it to the objective of some of today's cross-cultural, comparative studies, which aim at defining and classifying 'that which is comparable,' through creating a basis of 'similarities and differences' (Vissicaro, 2004: 23). If we accept the statement that cultural knowledge is context specific, and therefore that enunciatory conditions are different from one another, how then can we find that which is comparable? This analytic approach appears to build on a system of filiations in which dances are connected serially and seamlessly with one another, in a kind of kinship system for movements, while the Swedish critic instead adopts an affiliate reading in connecting Gopal to the social force of nation building, that is, conditions that are affecting how Gopal can perform, and how different audiences receive his dances.[8] The Swedish discourse from the 1940s also differs markedly from the way in which Ram Gopal, at the time of his death in 2003, was described in several obituaries as an artist who had tried to convey 'an essential Indianness to western audiences' (Venkataram, 2003).

The struggle over the power to classify does not end here. In Ram Gopal's autobiography, published in 1957, he comments on his position in between different cultures: 'I am happy to be "Westernized" as some Indians childishly accuse me [...] I am [...] bridging the gap between the East and the West [... it has to do with the] harmony of being a complete human being' (x). In this declaration, he is resisting other enunciatory conditions than he had faced on his early tours in the 1940s. In India the dance revival had continued, but Gopal, by this time having settled in England, had a diasporic identity to grapple with, and had to find a defense against being declared 'not authentic enough' by his former homeland.

This oscillating movement between representing India and being Westernized, one that Ram Gopal probably performed many times during his life, can be understood as the workings of the translation aspect of culture. Gopal could easily be considered universalistic, appearing to neutralize differences, but being on tours around the world, and later on as a migrant, he claimed his right to 'difference in equality' (the Marxist philosopher E. Balibar on transnational citizenship, qtd. Bhabha, 2004: xvii), and his artistic as well as social identity had to be continuously redefined in answer to the various limitations of recognition and institutional indifference that he and his dances encountered.

A woman's perspective – race matters

Ram Gopal was never referred to as not himself being Indian by birth, but the debate on authenticity involved both his dances and dancers. In the newspaper article from 1949, the critic briefly remarked that he had questioned the nationality of the dancers, and Gopal had responded that two of the dancers were in fact Europeans rather than Indians. However, he did not find this piece of information necessary to put in advertisements of his performances. Instead, Gopal argued: 'That is of no importance. Do not non-Russians dance in the Russian Ballet?' (Idestam-Almqvist, 1949, my translation). A congenial answer, the critic agreed, since it supported his own statement about the problems of authenticating or classifying Indian dancing.

For the 1948 and 1949 tours to Europe and Sweden, the young dancer Lilavati Devi was a member of the Gopal dance company. A couple of years later she married the Swedish impresario of the tour and settled in Sweden, where she performed, choreographed, and taught, and she was for several years my teacher in Bharatanatyam. Internationally, she is perhaps best known for being the dancer for whom Kurt Jooss created his last choreography, the solo dance *Dixit Dominus*. The narratives about her biographical background have remained enigmatic throughout the years, and I will discuss them not in order to present the true facts about her birth and early years, but as a discursive result of the social, political, and cultural relations within which she lived.

In some of the first, longer articles about her life, from 1958, a certain narrative begins to take form, and I will summarize it briefly.[9] To begin with, her exact age was presented as unknown due to the lack under British rule of a functioning birth registering system in India. She was born in Kolkata, and her father, Sudhir Chandra Bose, born in Bengal, was a doctor of music and a tabla player. He was also reported as having played for Anna Pavlova and the Indian dancer Menaka (Leila Sokhey). Bose, who was present during one interview, tells the reporter that he introduced Pavlova to Uday Shankar, and even introduced Shankar to dancing, a statement that contradicts information in later sources where it is argued that the initiative for the meeting between Pavlova and Shankar came from the Indian composer Commalata Bannerjee (Money, 1982: 324). Lilavati's mother is simply described as a native of Kashmir. Lilavati started dancing early and during the war years, being in her teens, she was sent to a school in England. After some years, she returned to India as a field artist and danced for the Indian military troops in Burma and India. After the war she became a student at Ram Gopal's school in Bangalore, studying with Krishna Rao, and in 1947 she joined the Gopal company and moved to England.

Over time, rumors within the Swedish dance community have circulated that Lilavati was English and Jewish rather than Indian, and in a recently published book about her husband it is remarked that she was probably born in London, that her mother died soon after giving birth but that no facts are really known about her, leading to the author's speculation that this mystery may be linked to the Indian caste system of the time, and hence that Lilavati may have been born out of wedlock (Westman, 2006: 136). In contrast to this story, Lilavati herself sometimes described childhood memories from India, including an image of how her mother performed early morning rituals in front of the house altar (Ulvenstam, 1984). The European link is also stressed in an advertisement for the Ram Gopal British Commonwealth School of Dance, Drama and Music placed in *The Dancing Times* in 1963, when Gopal tried to establish a school in England. In a promotional mode the text declares: 'The Ram Gopal System, based on his own method [...] has produced the outstanding dancers Shevanti, Kumundini [...] and the Europeans, Lilavati Raphael Hager' (*The Dancing Times*, 1963).

This insistence on authentic origin, on the establishment of a 'bloodline,' and of relating an unclear ancestry to the caste system (as if questions of lines of descent are absent in Western societies) are all articulations of tensions emanating from a site of integration, the national policies of which Sweden was just beginning to formulate in the 1950s, and in particular were motivated by the need for labor immigration. The 'political' process of integration presumes change, and consequently an initial classification of racial, ethnic, or national identity is needed – otherwise change cannot be measured. The lack of closure in the narrative about Lilavati's background disturbed this process, and opened up a dormant space for conceptual hostility in a seemingly social-democratic, equality-boosting society. This, mostly disguised, antagonism lived side by side with the willingness to perceive Lilavati as a representative of India and Indian dancing in different public formats – a professional persona that she herself strongly supported. She was among the first artists in Sweden to undertake outreach programs with a repertoire of Indian dances in schools and workplaces, for political, humanitarian, and entrepreneurial organizations. She has seldom received credit for this community work in national dance histories, which instead is given to the Swedish modern dance movement of the 1970s, when artists started performing contemporary European dance in similar venues.

Being a woman and with her particular background, Lilavati had to act upon and within intersecting fields of power, oppressed because of her gender, race, nationality, and also religion since 'her' narrative includes traces of Hindu and Jewish filiations. It is from within this nexus of powers that one can understand her process of identity formation. In a newspaper interview from 1958, she describes the severe discipline and hierarchy that surrounded the young female dancers in Gopal's company, and declares that, although she appreciated the experience, she would have become a slave had she stayed on in the company (*Dagens Nyheter*, 1958). She also expresses her worry and shock, while visiting India earlier the same year, when she realized how the traditional temple dance seemed to have lost its religious essence in some places. Here, we see simultaneously a will to break with a nationally located, patriarchal practice and the reinstating of a past with deep roots in religion and nation. Stuart Hall has described this doubling as two kinds of identity; as both oneness, seeking a shared essence and continuity with the past, and as rupture, a positioning stressing discontinuity and transformation (Hall, 1994: 393–4).

Lilavati's own choreography and solo performances address these same issues in a more implicit manner. For her choreography she chose a wide variety of subject matters and production partners. In 1968 her solo dance for a contemporary Swedish dancer, *Till blomsterfolket* (To the Flower People), was broadcast on national television, and contained references to the flower-power movement. In the same year she worked with three Indian musicians who had played with the Beatles, and was suggested as choreographer for their upcoming movie. In 1969 she choreographed *Scheherazade* for a ballet company in the south of Sweden, casting jazz dancer Doug Crutchfield in the role of the slave, and in 1970 she choreographed *Skapelse* (Creation) for a church-opera company, braiding the African-American dancer Clifford Fears's Horton-technique with Indian-derived movements. In tandem with these dances – which rely on a 'cosmopolitan' consciousness typical of the time – Lilavati presented her own solo performances, in which she kept more strictly to Indian dance forms, usually a combination of Bharatanatyam, Manipuri, and Kathak dances.

Throughout this period journalists tried to capture the mix of identificatory politics implicit in her choreography and dancing: 'Lilavati is a poetic combination of Asian exoticism and Western modernism. Representing fragile femininity in an unprejudiced and socially engaged female gestalt. Performing the 2000-year-old dance tradition to audiences she locates in workplaces, industrial sites, and schools [...] in everything Lilavati does, the break between new and old springs forth' (*Göteborgs Sjöfarts- och Handels Tidning*, 1968, my translation). The rhetoric reveals the traditional Eurocentric troping of a deep divide between a modern, socially engaged West and an ornamental, exotic East, and in the process fails to understand the specificity of Lilavati's artistic and existential agenda. To her, it did not seem to be a divide between old and new. For example, she stressed how her social engagement did not stem from experiences in Europe, but from encountering poverty and inequality among servants in her own home in India, as well as when she performed for the military troops in Burma and India. Moreover, she connected her socio-political commitment to the Bose family's long history of political work (Ulvenstam, 1984).

In contrast to Ram Gopal, Lilavati never spoke of being Westernized as a result of a diasporic identity. Instead, she continued to build upon an increasingly stronger Indian persona, not only in her biographical narratives but also in her artistic work. Several times during her professional career, she traveled to India and continued taking dance lessons and learning new repertoire. This agenda also became explicit in her view on teaching. We had many conversations about why people from the West wanted to learn Indian dancing, and what Lilavati aimed at with her teaching. She always considered this interest as part of a way to learn about a culture, but was usually suspicious about non-Indian students who wanted to professionally perform Indian dances in 'original' form. This point of view was general, and once having visited Japan, she found it equally disturbing to see the Western classics, such as *Swan Lake*, performed by an all-Japanese cast. In her response to both non-Indian students and Japanese ballet dancers, the particular enunciatory conditions reveal how race has managed to retain its discursive power, both as a threat to, and in defense of, identity-formation through dancing.

Multi-vocal dancing

About a year after Lilavati's death the dancer Rani Nair (with Indian father and Swedish mother) performed the Kurt Jooss and Lilavati solo *Dixit Dominus* that Lilavati had premiered in 1977 in Mumbai. Nair described the dance as inherited from Lilavati, with permission to perform it given by her husband Bengt Häger. Even so, Nair's inclusion of the solo in her repertoire cannot simply be interpreted as a strengthening of an Indian identity. Nair's version was performed in 2003, as part of a concert called *Solos of the Century*, including international and Swedish dances from the 1920s to contemporary times. Several dances were reconstructions and recreations of avant-garde choreography from the 1970s and 1980s, a feature that was part of a broader interest in returning to one's own earlier work among contemporary Swedish choreographers. Before the concert in 2003, Nair had experience of performing with Shobana Jeyasingh and the Imlata Dance Co, and her choreography *Slängt!* (Thrown!) had been the winning contribution at a festival in Stockholm. At times, she expressed dissatisfaction over the manner in which her winning choreography made critics singularly speak about the Indian qualities of the work. She was a contemporary choreographer, and wanted criticism to address aesthetic issues in that same way. Given the two artists' different stances towards their own identities, it is interesting to draw some comparisons between the versions of *Dixit Dominus* danced by Nair and by Lilavati. This comparison might seem strange in relation to my earlier argument, but it is not based on the idea of comparing a fixed set of micro features of the dance. Instead, the investigating lens is directed at how their performances articulate the different positions and identities of different times.

According to Jooss, the solo depicts a kind of sermon, the warnings of a poet *cum* philosopher against war, greed for power, and violence. It is also a prayer that mankind shall awake to awareness while there is still time for change. Despite her youth, Rani Nair appears as a more mature persona in her performance. She is an individual who has seen and experienced everything, and reflects upon this with calm and control. Throughout the dance, she reveals this quality in some signature jumps, executed with a striking, effortless elevation, and in the virtuoso manner in which her movements relate to the music. Against the curvature of the melodic lines in Handel's music, she performs the syncopations of Indian-based footwork, allowing the viewer to, for a second, feel the rupture between two rhythmical systems, before she makes them dependent on one another. In contrast, Lilavati cultivates a more diverse persona, expressing emotional qualities – at times playful, at times fragile, naïve, or vengeful. The elevated signature jumps are turned into light skipping; the split between rhythms is not controlled so much as used as an external force affecting the expression of emotional content.

In a particular section, which, according to Lilavati, Jooss had already used in *The Green Table* in 1932,[10] Death slaughters humans, and Lilavati performs the movements with a heavily weighted step pattern, with strong, bound arm movements, all wrapped up in an intense kinesthetic projection of doom. In Nair's contrasting interpretation of the same movement sequence, the strong image of death is absent; instead the body designs and rhythmical footwork are made more technically distinct. Moreover, in Lilavati's version, the *Ausdruckstanz* elements are subsumed under the presence of the dancer's Indian persona, and both movement vocabularies are merged into one. This integrative manner performed in movement mirrors Lilavati's stress on her 'singular' ethnic persona in other public formats such as interviews and television documentaries. In Nair's performance both vocabularies are given equal weight, and she performs the solo as a dialogue between aspects of two worlds that are never fully joined together – as if addressing the issues of multiculturalism versus integration, which were hotly debated in Swedish politics and media at the time. Nair's performance of *Dixit Dominus* sharpens her excellence as a dancer, and her virtuoso technique creates a dramaturgy based more on expressive form than on narrative. Based on this performance mode, I see her choice of dancing the solo as congenial with a wish to be in reflective conversation with her contemporary affiliations, rather than as a search for a seamless link to an inherited culture. In 2004 this attitude is further explored and articulated in her solo *Pieces of me*, in which she explicitly wanted to present a multi-vocal portrait of herself. This time, critics seemed to understand the intentions, and avoided any essentialism regarding questions of ethnicity. They either wrote about her skills as an artist, and her ability to work in different media (video, scenery, speech, poetry, dance, lighting), or about the ideological message concerning the problematic definition of terms such as 'multiculturalism.' Difference was thus established as something that not only happens between people but also within individuals.

Indian dance in Sweden – a heterotopia

The history I have presented has not been multi-sited in terms of geography so much as in historical space. On the surface, global socio-cultural structures have changed only marginally over the decades from Ram Gopal's tours in the late 1940s, Lilavati's settlement in Sweden in the 1950s to Rani Nair's performances after 2000. But, in looking closer at the local contextual factors during this period, several important changes occur in how global and local factors interweave with and affect individuals' choices of action, and their public, discursive effects.

Lilavati's entrance into Swedish society happens at a time when social welfare programs are being developed, and processes of integration are beginning to be defined. The outer world that earlier, via Gopal's performances and imaginations of a modern world of united nations, could be positively embraced, has suddenly settled inside the nation and made modernity and its effects into a social problem to be solved. Both Gopal and Lilavati encounter diaspora conditions, but respond differently. Gopal articulates an oscillating movement between East and West, and when he declares himself Westernized, it is in this sense that this has come to influence his manner of presenting Indian dances. However, in his autobiography he presents this mode of working as something that had originated already in his early years as a dancer and choreographer in India. He recounts a discussion with a professor of Sanskrit, who had told him: 'you love something that is dead,' the dances of today are mechanical, lifeless, and tiresome. Gopal had answered that this was the reason why he had to 'prune traditional dances of all repetitive movement' – he wanted to create something that was understandable to Indian audiences in terms of today (Gopal, 1957: 52–4). The anecdote begs for a questioning of Westernization as the key to innovation and change. Even though Gopal seemed eager to partake of the artistic innovations occurring in Europe, he might have felt that the 'modern' spirit was Indian as much as European. To Lilavati it became increasingly more important to reconnect to India and an image of its rich and ancient dance traditions once she had made a living in Sweden, and especially when aspects of integration made her vague background a problem. Initially, she had to achieve a break with her professional filiations, in separating from Gopal and creating an independent career as a female performer. But later on, assimilation's colliding forces of particularization and homogenization might have necessitated the suturing of the particular wound being inflicted by this separation. It is possible to interpret the different phases of her artistic career in light of these colliding forces. Her earlier work with several intercultural projects later became overshadowed, and even replaced by the return to a slightly mythologized India-as-origin.

Hybridity is a disputed term, particularly in the ways in which it has been said to mask cultural difference. Nonetheless, in Rani Nair's work I see a hybridity that does not neglect the specificity of local difference. To some extent her performance *Pieces of me* can be said to work fully only in a Swedish context, in particular regarding the sections with spoken text. Born in the south of Sweden, Nair speaks a particular Swedish dialect that immediately confronts a Swedish-speaking audience's desire to categorize her as 'Indian.' On stage, it becomes a theatrical identity politics intimately linked to geographical space, and as such it works against either/or assumptions. In performing *Dixit Dominus*, Nair repeats this intercultural pedagogy, by both inviting and rejecting a clear-cut reading of ethnic belonging. She performs in a subtle manner, as if wanting to contradict the much louder, more overtly political voices of the Swedish debate, in which competing analyses of ethnic and structural discrimination, and of the effects of integration, stand firm against one another.

Ram Gopal's, Lilavati's, and Rani Nair's artistic work can only with great difficulty be classified as belonging to the same category of Indian dance. Moreover, the 'India' they perform and relate to is also not the same. Given the importance of intertextuality when it comes to locating cultural identity (cf. Bhabha), and Foucault's argument concerning the need for coherence in classification, the analytic perspective makes us realize that definitions of coherence are hard to achieve. So, an important insight that the concept of heterotopia can contribute in this context is that the problem does not lie in the 'things' being incompatible, but in the assumed common locus for classification, since the topos itself is always shifting. The understanding of a topos in continuous motion is also pertinent to Appadurai's definition of process geographies and scapes. Not only does 'Sweden' as a socio-cultural and lived geography change over time, but so does 'India.' Thus, neither India nor Sweden can stand as a fixity or structural center ordering the classification of the flow of dances – the bodyscapes – that have been brought, only momentarily, to rest in this history.

Notes

1. Foucault uses Borges's taxonomy to identify 'the pure experience of order and of its modes of being' that form the region between 'ordering codes and reflections upon order itself' (Foucault, 1973: xxi). In other words, he investigates the rules by which the development of classificatory systems is assumed as knowledge.
2. In Curt Sachs's world history of dances, psychology is used for distinguishing between peoples who perform image or imageless dances. Respectively, they are described as extrovert, sensory, empirical, and 'bound to the body' versus introvert, imaginative, capable of abstraction, and 'free of the body.' The argument continues by explaining how a middle zone develops where the two types interweave due to 'interbreeding [...] and migrations' (Sachs, 1937: 60–1).
3. I have chosen Pegge Vissicaro's book for critical discussion because of its educational focus. In addition, it seems to build on a methodological consensus within cross-cultural studies, which adds to its usefulness in debate.
4. Vissicaro is explicit in rejecting race as a classificatory tool for comparative purposes (Vissicaro, 2004: 74).
5. If ethnicity is defined as a social, interpersonal category rather than a fixed physical substance or 'object,' and constituted through a group of actors' modes of distinguishing themselves from other groups, we get a better understanding of the term. For this use, common among anthropologists of today, see Hylland Eriksen, 1993.
6. Curt Sachs's book was highly influential for a long period of time, but his analytic methods were criticized in the 1970s, initially by the anthropologist Suzanne Youngerman, 1974. In this review she describes and criticizes Sachs's use of the *Kulturkreislehre*.

    Vissicaro does, however, offer an additional perspective on change in her discussion of 'enrichment,' which can also happen 'spontaneously, through internal development' as in opposition to external forces (2004: 28), although it is not clear how this distinction between so-called internal and external forces can be studied. It seems to build on a notion of locality as completely stable, instead of conceiving it as 'primarily relational and contextual' (Appadurai, 1996: 178), as something that is always a transformed consciousness of its other.

7. The research Paula Saukko discusses with the help of the concept bodyscape is Marta E. Savigliano's book on tango (Savigliano, 1995).
8. For a discussion of the terms filiations and affiliations, see Edward Said, 1983.
9. For this information I have combined information from articles and interviews in *Stockholms-Tidningen*, 16 and 17 October 1958; *Dagens Nyheter*, 29 December 1958; *Svenska Dagbladet*, 17 October 1958.
10. Lilavati performed the solo in New York, in the autumn of 1980, and during the rehearsals and performances I worked as her assistant. During this work she discussed various aspects of Jooss's choreography and his intentions. The dance was broadcast by Sveriges Television, in December 1977.

2
Mobilizing (in) the Archive: Santee Smith's *Kaha:wi*

Jacqueline Shea Murphy

Dancing in the archive

I arrive at the National Museum of the American Indian theater (NMAI), on the mall in Washington, DC, just in time for the first night's presentation of Haudenosaunee[1] choreographer Santee Smith's evening-length *Kaha:wi*. The 50-minute contemporary dance piece in 16 scenes, with nine dancers, tells a story of the lifecycle, life and death and birth and life again, of Haudenosaunee people. Its set depicts trees evoking the Tree of Life, which gave entry to the beginning of life on Earth.[2] The dance begins with life emerging into physical form, and includes coupling, death, and birth scenes that foreground women's sensuality, and joyfully celebrate Haudenosaunee ways of being and knowing. It shows a world animated with human and spirit beings. It uses space – both the way bodies move through the stage space (circular floor patterns, movements in the four directions) and the spiraling movement of bodies in that space – to confirm Indigenous spatial understandings. It incorporates specific Haudenosaunee dance steps into its choreography. With hymns sung in Mohawk and Cayuga, and gorgeous music commissioned from Indigenous musicians, the music makes you want to move and sing, which the two older women sitting next to me in the theater do a little, under their breaths, hey ya a hey hey yah, laughing when they catch me smiling at them as we file out.

The next day, echoes and images from *Kaha:wi* settle in with me: the swirling women, the Ancestor Spirit pulling the Grandmother's breath out of her, the Young Woman at the end, so full of life and pleasure, the Mohawk-language hymns. But before I see it again that evening, I decide to check out the new museum. I am excited to be here, to see the architecture and exhibits, to see if it is as different as they say from

Natural History museum-type 'American Indian' dioramas. I wander around and mingle with the mix of museum goers marveling at Ben Nighthorse Campbell's stunning jewelry and reading the placards around exhibits on the different floors. The museum's first three levels present breathtakingly beautiful examples of material culture, elucidated by accompanying texts that provide background to each object's place in a broader community. Gourd Dance regalia hangs behind glass, beads, baskets, and other exhibits on various communities and their worldviews and philosophies. On the fourth floor, the 'Our Peoples: Giving Voice to Our Histories' exhibit tells a different part of the story: colonization, dispossession, destruction, loss. Here I find exhibits of treaties, guns, and of Bibles translated into Indigenous languages: a Sioux Bible with beautiful glass beadwork, an Inupiat New Testament, Bibles in Apache, Cree, Cherokee.

As the day goes on, with my attention to moving, living bodies heightened by the dancing I came to this archive to see, I catch my focus turning away from the glassed-in exhibits and toward the comings and goings on around me. I notice the young museum guides, with dark hair and fashionable glasses, keeping people in line for a multimedia presentation. I see others ushering tour groups around, pointing out the treaties, rifles, and Native-language Bibles in glass cases as 'three colonizing forces used against us.' I watch them, these guides, next to these glassed-in archives, performing their very alive, young, modern, hip selves alongside and against this official history, their own bodies and movements performing a different part of the story than the guns and treaties and Bibles tell. I linger as they pass by, and take in the mass of tribal names projected on one wall around the words 'WE ARE THE EVIDENCE.' Then 'Look! There's Pima!' a young woman next to me shouts out, pointing to a spot up high, and she and her companion beam up at it. The rest of us look to find 'Pima' too; her excitement is contagious.

How do these bodies' mobilizations throughout the museum complicate the history of colonization held in the maps, Bibles, guns, treaties, and other documents in this museum's collections? In what follows, I explore dual trajectories: the ways that watching *Kaha:wi* shifts attention to the people moving throughout the museum and not just the objects in it, and the ways that these museum movements help elucidate Smith's sensual, joyful performance of Haudenosaunee dance, culture, and history. *Kaha:wi*, an alternative mapping of the museum's archival documentation, presents complex Haudenosaunee epistemologies and ideologies, including ways of knowing and of accessing knowledge, ways of understanding death, gender, and sexuality, ways of negotiating familial and political relationships in the world.

How might these moving, dancing mappings complicate the history represented in the artifacts held in most 'American Indian' museums? And might attention to these bodily mobilizations as an alternative archival space in turn provide a model for rethinking 'worlding dance' practices that, like the conventional museum, have often contained and collected dances for easy student/viewer consumption? The Indigenous philosophy enacted throughout the NMAI – including its production of *Kaha:wi* – calls for viewers and scholars' not (only) to collect knowledge, but to pay attention to the stories, histories, and ideologies in contemporary dancing practices, and to the complexities of our viewing (and dancing) relationships to them.

Remarking the archive

First, however, a brief foray into the legal history of Haudenosaunee land which became the Six Nations of the Grand River, Ontario, reserve. The documents in this history recount a narrative of pervasive territorial loss. In 1784, the governor of Quebec, Frederick Haldimand, proclaimed a parcel of land, described as six miles deep on either side of the Grand River beginning at its mouth at Lake Erie, as belonging to Mohawk leader Joseph Brant (Thayendanegea) and his followers. This Haldimand Proclamation was made, in part, as a way of recognizing the Six Nations' loss of land in their alliance with the British Crown during the American War of Independence (and of quelling fears of their anger should the British now appear to abandon them); it provided the land base for the Six Nations Reserve (Dickason, 1997: 162–4). Over the next century, the tract of land was whittled down to its current 49,289 acres – less than 4.8 percent of the 950,000 acres originally granted (Six Nations of the Grand River: Land Rights, Financial Justice, Creative Solutions, November 2006).[3]

Since the repeal of the Indian Act in 1951 (which prohibited First Nations people from hiring lawyers to bring claims against the Crown without the Government's permission), members of the Six Nations reserve have actively addressed this loss, establishing an Office of Native Claims in 1974, filing hundreds of 'Specific Claims,' working to reform the unreasonably slow claims review process. In 2004, these Six Nations' court cases were put on hold while exploratory talks began addressing out of court settlements to claims that, the Six Nations Council writes, 'seek an accounting and damages with respect to over 200 years of history and transactions.'[4] In November 2006, the Six Nations Council published a dense, 64-page document giving brief overviews of Six Nations land history and claims filed. The map on its cover shows both the Haldimand tract, flanking the Grand River for six miles, and a small red-colored corner marking the current boundaries of the Six Nations Reserve. This resurgence in land claims cases, coupled with a vibrant and visible arts community, marks the Six Nations Reserve as a place actively addressing this colonizing history.

Santee Smith and Kaha:wi Dance Theatre

Santee Smith is a member of the Mohawk Nation, Turtle Clan, from the Six Nations Reserve. Her parents Steve and Leigh Smith are renowned Mohawk ceramic artists, and she has been steeped in Haudenosaunee art, history, culture, and politics since she was born. She is an accomplished dancer and choreographer who trained with the National Ballet School of Canada and at the Aboriginal Dance Program in Banff, Canada, before launching her own stage dance company – 'Kaha:wi Dance Theatre' – in 2005. *Kaha:wi*, danced by five women and four men, toured in the United States. and Canada as its first production. To create the piece, she interviewed family and community members from her reserve; commissioned original music from Indigenous musicians; developed a story line based on Haudenosaunee understandings of birth, life, and death cycles; incorporated these and other Indigenous ideologies into her movement explorations, vocabulary, and choreographic decisions; and then wrote a thesis for her MA in dance from York University about the process.

Her thesis references the Haldimand Covenant and Treaty, and the history of continuing colonization of Haudensaunee people, and she argues that *Kaha:wi*'s vibrant, insistent focus on life and celebration defiantly responds to this history of loss. But only obliquely. The piece, she explains, was conceived not as a narrative or document of colonization, but as a celebration of Haudenosaunee people and worldviews. 'We know about the history, we know about colonization. The history has been told to me, and I feel it, I feel the loss,' she said. 'But at the same time, the philosophies are maintained. So there's something important to hold on to, to celebrate and express. Yes, our families, our lives, are continuing.'[5]

Kaha:wi, in other words, maps a different landscape from that created by the Haldimand Treaty map, with its small red corner inside a larger outline of loss. The piece's focus is on performing – and thereby reaffirming and communicating – Haudenosaunee understandings of the world. This performance creates another, different kind of document for the museum (here, the National Museum of the American Indian, but in a sense any mainstream representation of American Indian history and culture): one of continuing, ever-changing, engagement. This performance-as-document reframes the Archive, 'The Museum' (that repository of American Indian artifacts) as a site of object collection in a number of ways. For one, it reframes the primacy of the archival object – the masks, documents, baskets, which 'American Indian' museums, including the NMAI, exist in large part in order to house and display – positing alongside them contemporary dance-making as a register of historical and cultural existence. It also reframes the objects, so what one can see is not just the bible in Lakota, but also its intricately beaded cover, that is, not just colonization and assimilation, but, as well, the hours and hours of craftsmanship that went into creating it, the energies inscribed in it (and in many so-called inanimate objects contained in museum cases). In addition, it helps enable museum viewers to shift focus from these objects to the live bodies around them. In enabling these shifts, it reframes the act of (only) collecting archival objects, or (only) focusing on treaties and the maps they inscribe, as locations of resilience and restitution, asking instead that we think of the Archive of Indigenous Culture and History as a constantly changing repertory of tools, engaging with, even as they press against and extend beyond, the maps, treaties, guns, and bibles that demarcate colonization.[6]

Kaha:wi

The theater buzz hushes as the dance opens to Smith curled in a circle of light, slowly writhing. Her mouth opens, and her strong bare legs extend apart, mouth and opened crotch invoking one another as she reaches up from her groin area, sinewy, then comes to squatting, creature-like. It takes a long time, minutes. This is life emerging from the mud and stretching its legs. The recorded voice of someone speaking in Cayuga interweaves with the music: the Thanksgiving Address, recited at the beginning of all Haudenosaunee activities, social gatherings, and ceremonials and at the start of each day, a way in which human beings acknowledge and appreciate their relation to natural, plant, spirit, and animal elements (Smith, 2004: 19).

In the next scene, three men slink and crawl onto center stage: the humans emerging from the earth. Three women join from each side, sinewy and long, dancing in sync with the men. They do shuffle-dance turns, their weight down on the beat, come together in a circle, and arching and bending in rhythm to the music's beat, travel en masse in the four directions. Meanwhile, an Ancestor Spirit can be seen dancing to the same beat behind a tree. The scene shifts to four women, smiling, strong, flipping their hair back with such pleasure in their bodies, weight down on the beat, swooping, releasing and sliding their hands up their sides to their breasts and to the sky. The men rejoin the celebratory scene. As the set darkens to night, some men and women couple up, the men lifting and turning with the women. The narrative of the dance intensifies as one young woman begins a dance of sensual attraction, reaching with her arm and turning a full circle, beckoning, instigating, lightly gasping at the pleasure she finds in her own swoops and stretches. Her hands are on her belly, she reaches out, her legs apart; she cups her hands in front of her thighs and groin, her hair flipping, while the Grandmother, watching from the shadows, dances with her. A young man responds, entering the stage, and they circle each other; he lifts her leg, and lifts her again so she is right against his chest. She jumps into his arms and they roll, ending with her on top. Then laying down she arches, he arches, and then they arch together to gasps in the music. Playful, joyful, and full of pleasure, they curl asleep.

After the love-making, the young woman wakes to a nightmare signaling her mother – the Grandmother's – death. Grandmother dances with the Ancestor Spirit who has come to claim her, arching her back and drawing her breath or spirit out of her mouth. Now she arches way back, free of her body. As he lifts her, she climbs on his back and with their arms outstretched, they turn in a circle. The lovers mourn her, and Mohawk hymns – Amazing Grace, Twill Be Glory By and By (*Ka se neh*) – resound. The music becomes much more energized, and the dancers respond, athletic, full of muscle, while the Ancestor Spirit dances around and through them, invisible to them but present among them.

This story of death does not conclude the piece, but is rather a node along the journey. The birth and naming of the daughter, who is given her grandmother's name, Kaha:wi, follow a Moon Dance in which the Young Woman and four Midwives prepare for the birth, running their hands up their chests. In the birthing dance, the mother's arms swing out evoking her pregnant belly, and then clutch it as another dancer, the baby, crawls through her legs. In this birthing scene, the Grandmother Spirit dances behind while the Ancestor Spirit carries the Child on stage. She crawls out from behind a tree, curling in repetition of the life force that opened the piece. The Mother comes to her, examines her legs and head, rocks and cradles her, back to back laying down, then sitting then turning on the floor. The joyous eroticism of the piece ripples through the Mother and Child's dance together as, hand on belly, legs out, the mother lifts the daughter from behind, holds her hand, then they run and cross the stage, arms encircling, rolling apart, hugging, the mother arching the daughter back, cradling her head, and then come together and touch each others' bellies, as the Grandmother Spirit in the back echoes their movements.

Just before the final scenes of the piece, the daughter, a young woman now, dances with other young women from the community. With hands starting on their hips and abdomens, their strong bare legs kneeling out to the side, they draw a path up the center of their bodies to the sky, powerful, sexual, as the music resonates with a heart-beat sound.

Choreographing the archive

Kaha:wi, as a Haudenosaunee dance presented in a museum theater, uses the tools of dance – movement vocabulary, spatial orientations, narrative, bodies trained and attuned to physical ways of knowing – to shift understandings of what constitutes knowledge production and collection. It presents these dance acts – performing and repeating particular physical movements, moving in particular relations to space, carrying knowledge in ones body and the way it moves – as themselves acts of cultural documentation and historical publication.

Kaha:wi incorporates specific Haudenosaunee ideologies within this documentation. The use of spatial patterns, for example – its choreographic embodiments of circularity – is in keeping with Haudenosaunee cosmology. Smith explains that 'The choreographic phrases of *Kaha:wi* were consciously created to emulate the circle or continuous spiral symbol. Spiraling movement through the torso creates the movement language for the piece. Circular floor patterns of the ensemble work reflect this strong connection to the continuous circle' (2004: 23). The performance genre of dance inscribes this spiral/circularity and its understandings of both continuity and change. Other aspects of the dance movement, Smith explained, also weave together Indigenous and contemporary dance corporeal conventions. For example, the piece incorporates and combines traditional steps such as the *Ehsgna:nye: gae:nase* (New Women's Shuffle Dance), Stomp Dance, Stick Dance and *Gayowaga:yoh* (Old Moccasin Dance) (2004: 39), with newly created movement phrases.[7] Smith explained that the approach she is developing often involves merging Haudenosaunee steps, rhythms, or energies of the lower body with a more 'modern dance' approach to the torso and upper body.[8] 'The shuffle dance stayed pretty much the same in the feet and legs. The arms were different though,' she said. 'What was maintained was the beat and the connection to the ground. We had arms up and reaching out to the side of the body. The lower body is very much grounded, and the upper body should be able to move.' Haudenosaunee understandings, she explained, are rooted in these ways of dancing; 'rooted in the way your body steps onto the ground and rooted through your energy,' she said. Her intention, in her choreography, is 'finding a way to explain things through movement – really trying to be rooted in the story line, in all of the cultural line, and to get it out to the rest of the world.' Through these engagements and articulations, *Kaha:wi* not only communicates Haudenosaunee worldviews back to her community and the larger society as a form of cultural affirmation, but also affirms contemporary dancing and dance-making as a form of Indigenous knowledge, and a site of its articulation.

These dance steps are merged with contemporary dance moves in ways that might make them hard for all audience members to discern as distinctly Haudenosaunee, but Smith explained they are 'very clearly visible and recognizable' to those from her Six Nations community, for whom she performed the piece during its development, as a way of inviting feedback on what she was doing. 'If you're Iroquoian and had any real connection, you could see [the Haudenosaunee dance steps],' she said. 'They were happy to hear some of the music, to see the steps,' she added. 'People are really wanting those positive things. We need to see this positive recognition of culture, because so much of what we see is the opposite, we see the reverse.'

To viewers stepping in off the street with no context for the performance, or glancing at photographs of it, though, *Kaha:wi* might look at first quite a lot like other contemporary stage dance. 'It's modern dance!' shouted out one woman from the audience at a recent research presentation when I showed photographs of the piece, one with five dancers arching, one arm gracefully curved and torso lifting, from an open legged back-bended position. And it is. Yet her comment invoked a desire for separation between 'modern dance' and 'Indigenous dance,' a need for these two traditions to stay in their places, in line with conventional 'world dance' texts and curricula. *Kaha:wi*, on the other hand, interweaves both contemporary dance vocabulary and conventions with distinctly Indigenous dance vocabulary and conventions, and via them Indigenous philosophies, stories, and ideologies. Smith, I suggest, is thus using the tools of contemporary stage dance to articulate Indigenous worldviews. She engages contemporary dance – a genre with (in part) European roots and colonialist/orientalist histories, yes – but also as a performance genre in which bodies carry knowledge. Because its narratives can teach ways of knowing, it is a practice in keeping with Indigenous epistemologies. It articulates these worldviews both inside of colonialist European frameworks (stage dance, treaties, Bibles, museums), and also imbues these frameworks with Haudenosaunee understandings that extend past the borders of those institutions.

Archiving ways of being and knowing

As *Kaha:wi* asserts dance itself as a way of knowing and telling, it narrates ways of relating to what has come before and will come after that differ from the knowledge searched for, accessed, and held in written historical documents. For example, the piece's inclusion of prophetic dreams as valid sources of information inscribes Indigenous ways of accessing knowledge that extend beyond those of, say, books and museums. In the piece, after the young woman calls her lover to her, she dreams the death of her mother (her newly conceived baby's grandmother). The program reads, 'The young woman is awakened by a nightmare. She cries out for guidance and help from Sonkwaiatison (the Creator), foreshadowing the impending death of her mother.' The next scenes play out the truth of this dreamed-knowing: the Grandmother is met by the Ancestor Spirit who escorts her to the Spirit world. Many Haudenosaunee philosophies are embodied in these scenes, including the concept of dreams as knowledge sources.[9] The choreography shows Ancestor spirits and a spirit world not as haunting, frightening ghosts, but as guides and ancestral teachers. Throughout *Kaha:wi*, an Ancestor Spirit – later joined by the Grandmother Spirit – dances in the background, hovering, largely unseen but clearly present, behind the trees, sometimes mirroring/guiding the dancers movements (as when the Grandmother Spirit dances behind the Mother, as she gives birth), sometimes ignoring them.

In establishing this Haudenosaunee view of creation, *Kaha:wi* articulates against the story told by treaties and other documents of continuing encroachment and loss, and by images of Indians as dying out. Smith writes:

> Despite these overwhelming odds, the Indian people survived, as did their cultures and values. Their leadership grew stronger and throughout the 1960s, they began to assert their rights. The Indians, who were not supposed to be around a hundred years after the Confederation, had become a force to be reckoned with. Along with cultural and social change the persistence of ritual and performance

was maintained by the people as an outlet for expression, communication, and cultural identity.

(2004: 11)

What *Kaha:wi* inscribes in its story, and indeed itself enacts in the document of its own production, then, is both a Haudenosaunee creation
story, and also a historical document of the persistence of ritual and
performance that continued despite colonization.

Another Indigenous ideology that *Kaha:wi* engages with emerges in
the way its narrative focuses on recurring life cycles rather than marriage or death as culmination. The Grandmother's death occurs about
midway through the piece, as a cyclical continuation and release to the
universe, what the program calls 'the highest of ceremonies.' *Kaha:wi*'s
circular bodily and choreographic movements suggest alternative ways
of understanding time and history. The very act of 'archiving' and
'collecting' is dependent upon conceptions that see the past as different from the way it is now, and as containable in time and space. By
focusing on cyclicality in its narrative, and by weaving Haudenosaunee
'tradition' as part of its own very contemporary look and feel, *Kaha:wi*
suggests a blurring between what is past and what is present, what is
traditional and what is contemporary. It suggests this contemporary
performance as itself archival, chronicling ways of being and knowing
that might not be recorded in historical documents.

A parallel might be drawn here between the functions of the dance
and of a wampum belt. Temegami philosopher Dale Turner notes how
Haudenosaunee parties participating in negotiations would, when an
agreement was reached, exchange wampum belts, which 'served as the
"text" in the sense that they materialized the agreement itself' (Turner,
2006: 47). 'What made the wampum belts valuable was that each had
a story attached to it that certain people, called wampum keepers, were
responsible for remembering and reciting at various times of the year.
The physical act of giving or receiving the wampum belt established
the moral significance of the agreement' (2006: 47). The wampum belt,
in other words, is a Haudenosaunee-specific way of holding, a kind of
document, that both carries meaning itself as a material object and also
creates meaning as a mnemonic device for the physical act or oral performance. *Kaha:wi*, while not documenting a particular political negotiation as a wampum belt does, nonetheless perform as a document of
the continuing and expanding vibrancy of Haudenosaunee people. It
shows ways that the little red square on the Haldimand map is perhaps
not as contained as the colonizer might like to think, and it insists that

physical acts (dancing, remembering, and reciting) record this vibrant continuity.

Other aspects of Haudenosaunee culture that emerge throughout *Kaha:wi* include the Thanksgiving Address in the opening scene, the naming ceremony, and the use of Mohawk and Cayuga languages. These all inscribe, within this stage dance piece, particular Haudenosaunee ways of negotiating familial and political relationships. *Kaha:wi*'s use of Indigenous languages, in the hymns, songs, and Thanksgiving Address voiceover, bear particular import. As Turner notes, Indigenous philosophies are embedded in Indigenous languages, themselves embedded in the primacy of spoken language (2006: 83). Turner explains in particular that Iroquoian peoples during the period of early Anglo-American invasion and colonization were 'well known for their highly developed rules of diplomacy, which focused on the importance of oratory' – as opposed to the written text, the 'main form of European philosophical discourse' (2006: 47). Smith, by including Mohawk-language Christian hymns in this celebration of Haudenosaunee vibrancy, honors both the import of Indigenous languages, and of speaking. She also reframes the anthropological drive to translate Indigenous peoples as objects of study into terms and languages (i.e., English, writing) for colonizing cultures to follow, and instead reverses the translation. Here, the hymns are disarticulated from the English that most audience members could understand, and engaged with as Mohawk oral and performing traditions: it is the non-Mohawk speaking audience members who are asked to recognize the limits of our understanding. This is how the performance reframes the story told by the Native-language bibles encased in the NMAI as documents of colonization used against Native peoples. *Kaha:wi* animates the Christian hymns with Indigenous language, rhythms, and tones. 'You really feel it – it's in here,' says one of the hymn singers that Smith interviews, hand patting her chest, noting how to her and to those listening, singing in Mohawk feels different from hymns sung in English.[10] For Smith, the Mohawk hymns used in the musical score of *Kaha:wi* reflect 'the social and historical importance of hymns and the idea that the hymns have become a source of Iroquoian identity for many people' (2004: 31). She adds, 'In a sense, the hymns are unique because they express a connection to the Creator in terms of the use of the metaphoric Mohawk language, which changes meaning and intent from that which is expressed through the English language. *Kaha:wi* takes this a step further by incorporating newly composed arrangements of the Mohawk Hymns paired with movement expression' (2004: 38). The Mohawk hymns in *Kaha:wi*, then, infuse notions of Christianity with Indigenous theology – seeing them as performing a 'connection to the Creator' that is experienced bodily, both by the singers and also in dance.[11]

This relationship to Christianity as a tool of the dominant colonial culture – yet one whose songs many Haudenosaunee have deployed for Indigenous purposes – echoes, in some ways, that of the relation to treaties that many Indigenous political councils, such as the Six Nations, are insisting upon. Numerous scholars have addressed what Chadwick Allen calls the 'appropriation and redeployment of treaty discourse' by Indigenous people who *'re-recognize*, rather than deconstruct, the authority of particular colonial discourses, such as treaties, for their own gain' (2002: 18). Of course, the relationship to Christianity engaged with in the Mohawk hymns differs from that of treaty agreements since no one is holding up the hymns as documents that acknowledge Indigenous political rights and recognize tribal sovereignty. Nor are dominant North American cultures attempting to disavow the discourse of Christianity inscribed in the hymns (as they attempt to disavow Indigenous sovereignty recognized in the treaties). At the same time, however, both *Kaha:wi*'s use of hymns and the current approach to the treaties theorize a relationship to colonizing institutions that reinforce colonialist discourse *in order to assert* Indigenous philosophies and forge political inroads. As Allen writes, 'they reinstate and reinvigorate this colonial discourse's original powers of legal enforcement and moral suasion' (2002: 19). The approach is not, in other words, about only deconstructing treaty agreements or hymns (or modern dance vocabularies and conventions), but also, pragmatically, about harnessing them as vehicles for Indigenous political goals.

Turner insists upon the political importance of this kind of tactic. While acknowledging that 'the very ways that we frame the language of rights, sovereignty, and nationalism are also steeped in colonialism' (2006: 95), his work calls for Indigenous 'word warriors' to refashion these discourses (72). He writes, 'Word warriors do the intellectual work of protecting indigenous ways of knowing; at the same time, they empower these understandings within the legal and political practices of the state' (2006: 8). In *Kaha:wi*, I suggest, Smith functions as a kind of 'dance warrior,' using stage dance choreography to insist that Haudenosaunee ways of knowing can be archived within colonizing discourses (like Christianity) and empowered to express Indigenous values even within the discourse of contemporary modern dance.

Re-framing gender

Perhaps the clearest challenge the piece – which Smith describes as an exploration of women's 'feminine strength and fertility' (2004: 13) – offers to histories that chronicle Native culture as loss lies in its fore-grounding of the vibrant sexuality and fertility of Haudenosaunee women. *Kaha:wi*'s erotic engagements with sexuality overtly address the gendered effects of colonization on Haudenosaunee and other Native peoples, and the way colonization has affected traditional understand-ings of gender and gender balance. Smith notes that in Haudenosaunee culture, women are powerful, and celebrated as such. Haudenosaunee culture is matrilineal and matrilocal; traditionally, women owned land, and clan mothers formed a council which, as scholars have recognized, 'selected the males who would hold positions of power on a second council [...]. If at any time, particular male council members adopted positions or undertook policies perceived by the women as being con-trary to the people's interests, their respective clan mothers retained the right to replace them' (Jaimes with Halsey, 1992: 317). Yet, Smith writes, 'In the western-based contemporary society of today women endure on unequal footing comparative to men [...]' (2004: 33). Nonetheless, she adds, 'Even after five hundred years of colonization the power of women within Iroquoian society persists' (32). *Kaha:wi*, then, 'affirms, celebrates and reclaims the female spirit and feminine presence within the universe. *Kaha:wi* acknowledges and shares with audiences women's role in the continuation of Life for the coming generations' (2004: 33).

When I have shown students the DVD of *Kaha:wi*, most do not notice how sensual it is, or even register the coupling scene between the lovers until we start to reflect upon it (at which point they seem almost taken aback by their own failure to remark on it). This might be, in part, because most contemporary modern dance audience members are not trained to acknowledge the sexuality of bodies touching and moving beside one another on stage (acknowledging how sensual dance is has not been part of the modern dance tradition) (Foster, 2001: 147–208). Thus although it clearly depicts heterosexual coupling and procreation, audience members are kept at a distance from it by its stage dance aes-thetics. Even the lovers lying together on the floor, head to foot, each of their torsos arching up, elbows down, head back, mouths open as the music gasps, then gasps again, reads enough like the initiation of a Graham-technique contraction to mask its overt orgasmic referents. In a way, the piece taps into modern dance's Orientalist legacy (for example, Ruth St Denis, presenting herself as a Nautch dancer in order to be erotic on stage in an era when middle-class white women were forbidden from performing desirability), yet harnesses them for Smith's own decolonizing agenda: a celebration of Indigenous women's sexual and erotic power.

Parts of this piece, especially on second viewing and reflection, are very sensual and erotic. Smith explained that claiming women's sexuality as part of *Kaha:wi* was important to her because 'Native women were portrayed in two ways – as the squaw, old ladies, asexual – not human, basically, not having human qualities and not having ownership of their own bodies. Europeans were extremely shocked that [Haudenosaunee] women were so powerful, and that children were regarded as such special beings.' Alternatively, Indigenous women have been portrayed as dark, exotic, and erotically available – especially to white men (who can then, through patriarchal sexual relation to these women, stake a claim to Indigenous territory). Smith navigates this trope of the erotic dark woman with its possibilities for sexualized viewing not only via (sexually obscuring) modern dance conventions and aesthetics, but also through the lack of a narrative entrance point for white viewers. This piece is not about white people getting to watch and fantasize about dark erotic women; it is not the Disney-esque story of Pocahontas, with Native woman as sexually available bride to white man. Non-Haudenosaunee viewers are of course welcomed and expected at *Kaha:wi* performances – the piece toured in major metropolitan locations in the United States and Canada, and Smith notes that her intention, in her choreography, is 'really trying to be rooted in the story line, in all of the cultural line,' and then 'finding a way to explain things through movement,' in part, 'to get it out to the rest of the world.' But the focus of the piece's narrative is the embodiment of Haudenosaunee ways of knowing.

Turner notes, in his pragmatic call for Indigenous intellectual engagement with ongoing colonialist legal and political discourses, that the impetus is not cross-cultural awareness. 'It must be remembered that the need to explain ourselves to the dominant culture arises primarily for political reasons and only secondarily from a desire to attain some kind of rich cross-cultural understanding of indigenous philosophies' (2006: 72). A similar dynamic emerges in *Kaha:wi*. The piece's foregrounding of female eroticism and sexuality are embraced, and staged, not as titillating for viewers, but as integral to bringing into balance what patriarchal colonialism disrupted. They thus challenge sexualized, Orientalist depictions of Native women – like so many women of color – as lasciviously exoticized by the white male gaze, instead claiming the sexual and erotic for the primary benefit of Haudenosaunee family and community members who, as Smith said, 'need to see this positive recognition of culture as traditional.' While it engages with colonizing institutions, in other words, *Kaha:wi* also 'protects indigenous ways of knowing,' as Turner calls on word warriors to do.

Kaha:wi's focus on female naming more directly shifts colonialist and patriarchal impulses, just as it protects Haudenosaunee worldviews. It is, after all, not the name of the father, but the grandmother that the dance celebrates and passes on in its own production. Postcolonial feminist Anne McClintock, drawing on Luce Irigaray, recounts how male insistence on 'the name, the patrimony,' 'the son with the same name as the father,' signals male anxiety over the visibly central role women play in gestation. McClintock then links male insistence on patrimony to the flamboyant imperial 'naming' of new lands (McClintock, 1995: 29).[12] The centrality of 'Kaha:wi' – translated from the Mohawk as 'she carries' (and the name of Smith's dance company, and her own grandmother and daughter) places women's creative, gestational agencies, both artistic and reproductive, at its center. In so doing it refutes both patrimony, and its analogy in imperial conquest, via both Indigenous dance-making and baby-making, and the creative power evidenced in both.

Smith notes that the focus on women as child bearers and the dance piece's narrative celebration of childbirth might not sit well with some today. 'It's now almost not politically correct to say we're here to have children,' she said. Yet from a Haudenosaunee perspective, she notes, this focus is important – both culturally and politically, given the genocidal threats to Indigenous peoples ('for continuation of culture, you have to have sex, there has to be a man and a woman [...] it's a conundrum, if you're going for perpetuation of life'). She notes that her community has always been 'pro-creation.' 'In my family, we celebrate the female, knowing that, yes, women are powerful beings, we were given the gift of creation. People in our community still believe that, that this is a gift we were given.' Her family rejoiced at the birth of her daughter, Smith recounted, because of the gifts that women carry in Haudenosaunee culture and understandings.

Even as *Kaha:wi* celebrates the centrality of women's ability to give birth, its choreography also supports other sites of pleasure, strength and power. It celebrates men's sexual vibrancy (the male dancer in the love-duet is as erotic as the woman), and the physical, loving, and erotic relations between women, whose dancing together on stage forms the bulk of the piece: the midwives who come from the four directions, the mother's relation to the grandmother, the mother's charged and tender curling around the daughter.

Remarking the archive II

In February 2006, a large group of Six Nations protestors occupied territory in Caledonia, on the Haldimand tract, and refused to leave. At issue was how, despite the fact that this tract was part of a land claim filed by the Six Nations in 1987, the province sold this land to an American company, which proceeded to build a residential complex on the site. This was done in violation of Canadian federal legislation that prohibits the sale or leasing of territories cited in land claims. Protests and barricades in spring 2006 led the province to buy out the land developers that June; legal debates around, and discussion of, this issue continue.[13]

These protests, and the bodies resisting this encroachment – and through it, over 200 years of history and transactions – by staging themselves there, provide one model with potentially expansive reverberations for addressing the colonizing history described by the map circulated by the Six Nations council. *Kaha:wi* provides another. This model utilizes stage dance choreography as a tool for asserting the vibrancy and continuing viability of Haudenosaunee ways of knowing and of understanding balance (including gender balance); it harnesses what have been colonialist frameworks (modern dance, proscenium stages, museums) in ways that insist upon Indigenous worldviews, including the importance of oral, performed, embodied ways of telling and learning. The dance thus becomes a simultaneous record and embodiment of a living, vibrant, matrifocal, culture that, as evidenced through the work of this talented dancer and choreographer and the many Haudenosaunee musicians and other Indigenous collaborators on this project, is not curtailed, but expanding in impact. It narrates the continuing persistence of ritual and performance, and of Indigenous worldviews.

Kaha:wi's performance at the National Museum of the American Indian does not so much reframe the institution of that museum as reinforce the ways its design emphasizes Indigenous epistemologies within the context of what has historically been a colonizing site. The NMAI, which opened in 2004, was designed over a ten-year process with the active engagement of Native people (Blue Spruce, 2004: 19). The desire was to create a museum whose architecture evokes Native place, and which focuses on creativity and Indigenous cultural practices, enabling Native peoples to be seen as 'communities and cultures that are very much alive today,' rather than a museum that houses American Indian 'artifacts' and documents colonization (West, in Blue Spruce, 2004: 56). With this in mind, some of the community consultants suggested that 'each visitor should be greeted personally and offered a seat and a cup of coffee, in the way that Indians welcome guests into our homes' (Horse Capture, in Blue Spruce, 2004: 42). While this suggestion was not implemented (at least not while I've been there!). it signals a focus not only on the shape of the museum and the framing of its collections, but also and especially on the ways that people move into and through the museum, and on the ways that bodily actions and interactions – ways of welcoming, directing, seating people who enter into a particular space, what might be called performance or even choreography – constitute part of the museum 'archive.' While numerous museums now include performance spaces, the NMAI's multiple venues for performance – theatres inside and outside the museum, the museum's stunning circular point of entry (the Potomac area), and various classrooms, walkways, and lounges throughout the museum – reinforce how integral live presentations and performance interactions are to this site.

The museum's design, calling attention to the ways bodies move through space, also raises possibilities about the 'object' status of the artifacts the museum holds. 'We are more than a curious medicine bundle on a museum rack,' writes Gerald Vizenor (Vizenor, 1994, in Turner, 2006: 71), but so too, perhaps, are the museumified medicine bundles more than objects on a shelf. *Kaha:wi* shows how Indigenous bodies animate Christian hymns – the way the singer feels it in her chest when she sings in Mohawk, makes it part of her bodily experience. Perhaps the Native-language Bibles, some intricately and beautifully beaded, also contain embodied knowledge inscribed during many hours in which a woman's skilled and knowing hands held and worked the cover, hunched forward, engaged, licking her lips in concentration. The dance animates the archive or, rather, dance performance helps make clearer the animation that is already inscribed.

Dancing's new worlds

Kaha:wi thus intervenes in 'world dance' practices, in part by using modern dance traditions and conventions to present Haudenosaunee ideologies and epistemologies as contemporary, vibrant, effective, and expanding. Dance history's relation to Indigenous dance typically maps a story of shrinkage and loss. Frequently still, if 'American Indian' or

'Native American' dance is included in 'dance history' or 'world dance' text books or syllabi in the United States, it appears either circumscribed in time – the past, exemplified (often) by Southwest ceremonials such as the Hopi Snake Dance or by the so-called 'Ghost Dance,' both usually situated (only) in the late nineteenth century – or if contemporary, limited to Plains-based powwow events. Even these approaches, when included, are usually at the start of the history texts, near the 'origin' story about 'animal' or 'primitive' dances, dozens of pages before chapters on social dance or modern dance or ballet, or photos of Martha Graham, Nijinsky, or Alvin Ailey's *Revelations*.[14] In syllabi, Indigenous dance is covered (if at all) in units maybe two weeks long.[15] Other contemporary Indigenous dance practices – from other communities (like Six Nations), or in forms, like stage dance, not easily recognizable as 'ceremonial' – seem rarely to evoke recognition.[16] Even rarer is discussion of Indigenous choreography or choreographers.[17] *Kaha:wi* thus complicates common discussions of 'traditional' Native dance, and of the stage as (only or simply) a 'Western' tool. Instead, it suggests possibilities for the proscenium stage – like the museum, and the treaty – to be inhabited as a space of connection to (in this case, Haudenosaunee) land, spiritual understanding, and to history.

In a broader sense, Smith's dance, and contemporary Indigenous histories and stories engaged through contemporary dance also intervene in 'worlding dance' practices by deconstructing the archive, both of the conventional museum, and of 'world dance' as containing practice. American Indian museums conventionally 'collect' precious artifacts and materials, holding them in glassed-in collections of contained historical truth, conveniently packaged for viewers to take in as they meander by. The National Museum of the American Indian complicates and refuses this role for museum goers. It is a space where not only what one sees – the objects behind the glass – but also how one moves into the space, acts in it, and experiences relations to others within it, compels a way of understanding the world. The glassed-in documents come to read as only part of the museum's archive, and as themselves perhaps more animate, via the hours of engagement with them Indigenous people have had, than objectified. It also remakes the archive by including contemporary performances as part of its 'collection;' producing dance pieces like *Kaha:wi* is part of its ongoing agenda. The NMAI asks us to engage with the museum, and the objects in it, as we might a performance event, and asserts contemporary performance as archivally valid.

By producing *Kaha:wi* and other contemporary Indigenous performances as part of the archive, the NMAI not only explodes the validity of engaging with museum objects collected behind glass, but also provides a way of questioning the validity of engaging with 'world dance' by cataloguing or collecting it in text books or classrooms, as 'authentic' examples of culture that can be absorbed by interested festival viewers, or students in ten-week classes, seeking a taste of non-Western dance forms they can consume as 'other.' This, instead, calls attention to understanding dance by noticing bodily interweaving in and out of relation to one another – in museum and theatrical and scholarly spaces. This noticing includes students' attention to their historical and political relations to the dancing they study and practice, as well as my own actions as a witness-participant in this dance audience, in the museum, interviewing Santee, bringing her to my campus to perform, writing about her work, helping her get published, serving as a job reference for her, benefiting from the work she has done in my own promotions and publications. This attention to our interweavings does not so much bring an awareness of students', or my, positioning (as if the spotlight were positioned on me), or even on our dialogue (as if it were just the two of us, talking), but rather, attention to our movings into and out of relation with one another, with Indigenous dance history, and with other scholars and dancers and stages.

Kaha:wi's attention to women's embodied experiences of spiritual connection thus strengthens Haudenosaunee culture within engagements with colonizing institutions (like treaties, linear history, Christian hymns, modern dance). By mining what has been seen as Western in music (hymns) and in dance (modern dance) (both of course also deeply embedded with the ideologies and contributions of Indigenous and other non-European peoples) for tools that articulate Indigenous worldviews and further Indigenous political goals, the piece harnesses the force of the archive and of what has been glassed into it, and deploys it to mobilize against colonialism's presumed success in North America.

Notes

1. The Haudenosaunee Confederacy, also known as the Six Nations or (less preferably) the Iroquois Confederacy, is comprised of the Seneca, Cayuga, Onondaga, Oneida, Mohawk, and Tuscarora Nations.
2. The tree references the Haudenosaunee creation story in which the Celestial Tree lit up the sky world, from where Sky Woman fell to earth. Designs on the trees and elsewhere on the set depict Haudenosaunee two-curved lines (Parker, 1912: 608–20).
3. This 64 page booklet is available at http://www.sixnations.ca/LandClaimsUpdate.htm and http://www.sixnations.ca/Nov3ClaimsBooklet.pdf

4. See at http://www.sixnations.ca/FAQS.pdf, p. 1; April 5, 2006 newsletter of the Six Nations Elected Band Council, Land Claims Community Update.

5. Unless otherwise noted, all quotes taken from interview, 26 January 2007, National Museum of the American Indian, Washington DC.

6. For more on the archival possibilities of embodied practice/knowledge, see D. Taylor, 2003. Here I suggest in particular the importance of dance-as-archive for its delineation as an enduring space of creative investigation.

7. Smith writes, 'As the creator for *Kaha:wi* I wanted to capture the essence and the spirit of traditional Iroquoian aesthetics, including the tones of the voices heard, the fall of the foot on the ground and weight of the body in space, the sensory emotions of real life and ultimately the connection to the spiritual dimension' (2004: 40).

8. Smith has not trained extensively in a specific 'modern dance' technique; her dance background is in ballet (she attended the National Ballet School of Canada from 1982–88) and in Indigenous dance (including at the Aboriginal Dance Program at the Banff Centre in Canada from 1997–2001). In noting 'modern dance' approaches to movement in her work, I reference what in Canada would be considered 'contemporary' stage dance elements, developed in part, I suggest, out of modern dance vocabulary and choreographic conventions, and related to its history.

9. In her MA thesis (2004: 22), Smith quotes D. George-Kanentiio (2000: 92–4), who writes: 'The Iroquois would affirm that there is an "afterlife" and those whom we loved are waiting for us on the other side. They would agree that when one dies, there is the experience of being released to a pulsating light. They would say that our spirits are part of a divine whole, imparted to us as individuals but for a short while, that we might experience this planet before moving on to the next reality and finally, back to the centre, to the totality of all things, the conscious Creator.' Smith also described the death of her grandmother, and quotes Leigh Smith (her mother)'s experience of it: 'She had always told us at the end you would have someone to come and take you to the other side [...] you could tell her spirit was lifting away slowly, releasing and slowly going [...] you knew there was nothing you could do but let her go' (2004: 21).

10. See 'CD of major project' produced as companion to Smith's MA thesis, 2004.

11. One subtle but interesting reverberation of this challenge to linear conceptions of time and history lies in the reframing of Christian Ideology it poses. Numerous philosophers and theorists have written compellingly of the Christian conceptualizations undergirding even 'secularized' notions of continuous, linear time that structure modern notions of history. *Kaha:wi*'s engagements with cyclical notions of time do not outright reject Christianity, or the linear notions of time it propels; instead, it interweaves into them alternative rhythms and tones.

12. Thanks to Michelle Raheja for this reference and discussion of it.

13. This is too complicated an issue to address in detail here; my intention is to gesture toward this kind of embodied protest, and the issues it raises, as one model for addressing continuing colonization. For information on it, see: http://www.sixnations.ca/CourtDecisionDec14.pdf

14. This describes, for example, G. Jonas, 1992. See also J. Cass, 1993, which in its third part, on 'Dance in America,' includes one-and-a-half pages on

Native American Dance in its opening pages under 'American Dance up to the 1900s,' referencing Reginald and Gladys Laubin, a 1989 American Indian Dance Theatre's performance of a Hoop Dance (demonstrating that 'Native American dance in its original form has not disappeared entirely'), and the Ghost Dance (210–1), and discussion of Maria Tallchief in its section on ballet (336).

15. These inclusions do provide students with some awareness of the history, and continuing practice, of Indigenous dances in North America – especially when teaching units on powwow are co-ordinated with campus powwow events, where students can actively witness and engage with contemporary Indigenous dance and dancers, watching the dance competitions and also eating and shopping and mingling and talking with their friends. Yet the limits to these approaches are clear. Even as written discussions of 'Snake' and 'Ghost' dances might mention that these 'traditional' dances continue today, inclusion of historic photos and paintings alongside situate them in the past, as exotic and alluring 'primitive' dance rituals captured, museum-like, and held for modern viewers to marvel at. And the focus on powwow, a competitive event involving Plains dances that grew, in part, out of Buffalo Bill's Wild West, and the familiarly 'Indian' regalia of many powwow dance forms (feathers, bustles), reinforces the Wild West show's inscription of Plains Indians as the sole marker of 'authentic' Indian identity, a marker against which those with connection to the hundreds of other diverse Nations, tribes, and bands in North America who do not fit these markers must regularly articulate themselves.

16. A more common assertion among dance scholars and critics is that the proscenium stage 'exists primarily to serve pictorial illusion and crowd control,' and inscribes a process that, when used for performances of 'participatory dances and those that last longer than the two to three hours we normally devote to a performance', 'fundamentally distorts and trivializes everything subjected to it,' as Lewis Segal writes (Segal, 1995: 47, 41). I am suggesting a reconsideration of ways the proscenium stage is seen to function in relation to 'world' or 'multicultural' dance.

17. Notable exceptions include J. Kealiinohumoku, 2001, who addresses this question in the context of Hopi dances; and R. Jones/Daystar, 1992, who directly addresses contemporary Indigenous choreography. Discussions of the American Indian Dance Theatre are also relatively frequent.

3
A 'Material'-ist Reading of the Bharata Natyam Dancing Body: The Possibility of the 'Unruly Spectator'

Priya Srinivasan

This chapter weaves back and forth between reading a stage perform-ance of the Bharata Natyam body, its labor on and off stage, and exam-ining the material accoutrements that invest the body with its symbolic, ritual, cultural, and physical power.[1] A localized materialist reading of the Bharata Natyam body in performance reveals its labor within spe-cific historical, ethnographic, and critical global discourses. As assistant to this analysis, I offer the notion of the 'unruly spectator,' a corporeal being who critically engages with the female dancing body and is able to view its multiple and material performances even while accounting for the seduction of its aesthetics. I turn to feminist ethnography, and par-ticularly to the concerns of third world feminists, in order to envision the unruly spectator as one who works through the seduction of nation-alist, Orientalist, and patriarchal discourses that saturate the Bharata Natyam female dancer on stage and is then able to see beyond them to account for multiple histories of capital flow and domination.[2]

Writings that describe Bharata Natyam dance performance in Euro-American contexts often focus on the material layers that cover the dancing body – be it the sari, jewelry, make up, hair ornamentation, or bells.[3] These items are treated as fetish objects separated from the performance practice as a whole. The Bharata Natyam dancing body is thus overdetermined by its heavy layers of eye-catching and exotic paraphernalia that distract the dance critic or researcher from focus-ing on a 'technique' that forever remains inaccessible. Such readings of the Bharata Natyam body place it in opposition to the modern or postmodern dancing body where the latter emphasizes a lack of costuming and thrives on the 'natural,' where indeed technique can be examined, analyzed, and dissected devoid of other distractions. This focus on the layers of clothing and the fabric that catches the eye contribute to an overdetermined nationalist, Orientalist reading of the Bharata Natyam body. In what follows, the unruly spectator views these layers differently and approaches these bodily encumbrances as actually constituting the Bharata Natyam body, wherein the sari, jewels, objects, technique, body, discourses, cannot be separated in performance.

The seeming binary created between the body and the objects that cover it also serves to hide the labor that goes into the performance. I argue in this chapter that it is important to value and evaluate the labor that produces the dancing body instead of abstracting or veiling it. In the labor of dance, the dancing body as a commodity cannot be separated from its means of production. Yet somehow the objects that construct this body seem to have a fetishized life of their own. I attempt to trace these objects not as fetishes, but as tangibles that have material lives and are embedded in human labor. I am concerned with making visible the class encounters that help construct the classical female Indian Bharata Natyam dancing body.[4] In post-Independence India, Bharata Natyam practice has become dominated by middle-class and upper-caste women. The scholarship on the foremothers of Bharata Natyam in the form of *sadir* as practiced by *devadasis* has proliferated since the 1980s, and helps us to account for caste differences.[5] What is not dealt with very often are the class differences in relation to global capital that currently create and stabilize the practice of the form both in India and the diaspora. For example, there are few critical discussions that analyze the directions of the flow of global capital between India and the United States generated by Bharata Natyam. This chapter highlights some of these issues and offers perspectives on the intersection of labor, capital, objects, individual bodies, and collective bodies that creates the Bharata Natyam performer.

Although typically a solo form, Bharata Natyam deserves consideration as the result of the labor of many bodies, techniques, and material objects that produce the body on stage. The sweat, and sometimes, blood that emerges from the dancer's body in performance imprint onto the sari that frames the body. The sari and the technologies of hand labor that determine the way it is woven,[6] sold, worn, and performed, operate within cultural and economic capital whose discourses imprint themselves back onto the dancing body. The Bharata Natyam body on stage thus cannot be studied in isolation and must be understood contextually in the nation-space and diaspora, as already embedded in both local and global contexts, but very differently in each.

In order to present this argument, I borrow from the structure of the *varnam*, often the central item in a Bharata Natyam recital. The *varnam* transports the dancer and the audience imaginatively to different places, to experience different bodily subjectivities, often through a series of interruptions in the dance structure. It combines abstract rhythmic dance sections interrupted by mimetic textual sections. The dancer begins by executing a complex rhythmic section known as the *jathi*, and then interrupts this by interpreting a line of text sung to music that is repeated numerous times through *abhinaya* (mime, gesture, and expressive emotions). Although the text repeats, the dancer improvises multiple scenarios for understanding the text by taking on different character positions, evoking an emotional quality, or by describing a scene or event. The audience is thus transported to many places in short amounts of time. Once she has explored the single line of text to her satisfaction, she quickly moves into two *jathi* sections. She then returns to another line of text that again shifts the spectator into focusing on her mimetic improvisation. She repeats this pattern another three times and then begins the second half of the piece with a faster rhythm and quicker overall pace. A *varnam* can take over an hour to execute depending on the dancer. To some audience members, the shift from the slow-moving, descriptive *abhinaya* to the fast paced *jathi* can seem abrupt. To others, the movement seems to flow, allowing them to make the voyage from place, scene, or subject in their mind seamlessly. I make a conscious effort through my writing to account for these movements in the actual execution of the dance through the device of interruption and transportation.

I examine the Bharata Natyam body on stage from the position of an unruly spectator who takes pleasure from critically looking at what is not supposed to be seen in an 'ideal' performance. The unruly spectator is also the third world feminist performance ethnographer who doesn't accept an inactive stance and is instead moved to action. Far from the *rasika* (ideal spectator) of Indian theatrical lore who operates from a shared understanding of the dance, its histories, practices, and forms, the ideal spectator in the twenty-first century is a subject whose body is disciplined to be idle and forced to comply with nationalist revisionings of culture, history, and politics. The *rasika* of the twenty-first century operates within the economy of desire for, and consumption of, the Bharata Natyam dancing body, girded by the framework of capital. This twenty-first-century national/global viewer in the geographic nation-state and diaspora consumes the female Indian dancing body on stage, exercising a patriarchal, heterosexual gaze, while 'his' body is rendered inactive, or at least suspended in the state of spectatorship, by these discourses of power. The dancer, on her part, labors actively on the global stage to mask the nationalist rewriting of dance history and makes numerous sacrifices with her own body to achieve this. Simultaneously, she attempts to efface the labor of the multitudes of bodies and their histories that have helped create her performance. The unruly spectator is thus a subject position that demands a call to action. 'She' moves between different positions, discourses, and gazes to revel in, critique, historicize, deconstruct, and participate in the performance. The unruly spectator's movement is not spectacular; rather it is more minimal, sometimes unconscious, at times tactical, but it leaves her with corporeal marks on her body and transforms her.

The sweating sari

When Mallika (a pseudonym) appeared on stage at the Music Academy in Mylapore that *margazhi*[7] night in 2005, it was cold and wet in Chennai. The yearly classical music and dance festival was in full swing, and the large auditorium was packed with over 200 people who, despite the unusually cold weather and rain, had ventured out to see this renowned dancer. I was there to witness her performance in Chennai because I had missed her recent concert tour in the United States, where she had performed in over 20 cities in just under two months. My grandmother kindly accompanied me to the performance that day and let out a loud exclamatory sound of approval when Mallika entered the stage. I had been busy searching for the mosquito repellent and missed her grand entrance till I heard my grandmother say *adaada*.[8] I looked up to see Mallika, who was indeed a striking figure, resplendent in her simple but elegant costume and jewelry. She wore a deep-pink sari with a contrasting purple blouse that matched her *pallu*, the customary temple jewelry adorning her head, ears, neck, and wrists, and of course the five rows of dancing bells around her ankles.

To the beat of the *mridangam* and the sound of the *carnatic* vocalist's *alapana* in the haunting raga of *Bowli*, Mallika walked to the front of the stage positioning herself right in the middle.[9] Raising her arms above her head, she saluted the audience with her palms folded together and began her performance. Mallika began with a piece dedicated to Lord Siva. The precise slapping of her feet in perfect rhythm, beautifully formed *mudras*, clear arm and body lines, as well as the decision to perform only *nritta* to *sahityam*, all made the first piece quite spectacu-lar.[10] Instead of translating the vocalist's text through dramatic expres-sion to describe the various qualities of Lord Siva, she chose instead to depict through *nritta* the temple where this *Siva* was located. At chest level, her right hand formed the *shikhara mudra* depicting the phal-lic *Siva lingam*, with four fingers closed tightly inward like a fist but with the thumb raised up, and her left hand rested beneath in a simple *pataka*, with four fingers stretched outward and the bent thumb tucked neatly on its side. This gesture was not enough of a clue as to the loca-tion of the temple. It was when she depicted the peacock with the *may-ura* gesture, that it became clear that the particular temple space she was referring to was the *Kapaleeswarar* Temple down the road in Mylapore.[11] As an audience we were already transported to the site. Imagining our-selves in the temple, we could see the dancer propitiate herself to the *Siva lingam*.

Hers was a powerful performance full of grace and grandeur. Even the way she held her *mudras*, with something as simple as a *shikhara hasta*, depicted elegant perfection and strength. There was no doubt after the first few minutes that Mallika's choreography had indeed been success-ful. Her clean lines were so impressive that a dance critic wrote about it the next day as '*anga suddham* perfected!' To create *anga suddha*, body purity, a clarity and crispness of limbs, their lines, formations, rhythms, and gestures is required. It is also understood in performance in the aural sense to mean precise beating of feet on the ground, through the maintenance of rhythm. Visually, it can mean an articulateness of tran-sitions of hand *mudras* between rhythms, between beats, between text, and between song. The way a dancer appears visually, dressed neatly in her sari, with hair tied back and with face and body belying the labor of the dance is also a key contributor to *anga suddha*. To that dance critic and to many of us in the audience, Mallika did seem to be an epitome of *anga suddha*. My grandmother and several people around us quite literally and loudly voiced their appreciation, varying between *adaada, cha cha cha, aaaha, ohooo,* and so on.

However, I was a miserable failure as a fan, and after the first five or six minutes of the piece I found my mind wandering. I had allowed her choreography to transport me mentally to the temple site of the deity, but my mind/body did not want to stay there. For quite a few years, I had found myself unable to concentrate in dance concerts, particu-larly in solo Bharata Natyam shows. The thoughts would range widely but this evening I found myself thinking about the sweat marks on Mallika's sari and other things normally unaccounted for when looking at the 'ideal' Bharata Natyam dancer. Perhaps I noticed it because my own body, despite the cold evening, began sweating in odd places. The ceiling fans were not cooling me down and the auditorium was not air-conditioned. I could feel the heat traveling down my body causing small beads of sweat to form, and I was not even moving that much. Mallika, on the other hand, was moving all over the stage, so I was curious about how and where she was sweating. Although Mallika was by no means sweating profusely or even obviously, the tell-tale marks were beginning to show, as dark patches appeared from her underarm skin and imprinted themselves on her blouse. Every time she lifted her arms, there were the patches for all of us to see. Beads of sweat had turned into thin rivulets and began flowing from her neck and back, imprinting dark marks on the silk sari. I am sure other audience members saw it too, but most likely they would ignore it. They had agreed to participate in the ideal audience contract, and so they pretended not to see any of the dancer's bodily labor.

It was a beautiful *kancheevaram* silk probably costing her anywhere between 8000 and 10,000 rupees (~US$160–$200 depending on the daily exchange rate). How would she get the sweat marks off? Would it leave stains? I supposed it was easily dry-cleanable. Yet her dancing body was leaving tell-tale traces of its labor. No amount of dry-cleaning could remove all the bodily juices. What a price to pay! This was obviously a very costly sari and a unique one too. I wondered where she had purchased it. Although it could have been at almost any of the large sari shops in Chennai, I decided it was probably from RASI (Radha Silk Emporium) on North Mada Street, Mylapore. This decision was probably influenced by the fact that I had just been there that morning, shopping for a friend of mine, and perhaps because RASI often carries unique sari pieces that attract the well-to-do dancers.[12]

Saris and their contexts

The bells of the *Kapaleeswarar kovil* on North Mada Street were ringing auspiciously as I arrived via 'auto,' a three-wheeled taxi, landing at the doors of the temple at 10am. The temple formed the base structure of the urban sprawl in that area. The water tank, an ancillary but crucial appendage of the temple, was right next to it, forming the usual square shape. Various bazaars, shops, and homes lined the square. On the other side of the temple was the sari store, RASI.

Although I had requested to be dropped next door at the RASI store, for some inexplicable reason the driver deposited me on the temple doorsteps. Deciding it was fate, or perhaps because RASI was not open as yet, I went to have a brief *darshan* before commencing my shopping. I paid the auto driver handsomely for getting me there in record time and stepped out of the vehicle taking care not to trip over the ends of my deep purple *pochampalli*[13] sari. I quickly bought flowers as offerings for the deity, rushing to pay an old woman Rs.20 (~45 cents US) who was competing with at least a dozen vendors to make the sale. The smell of jasmine and tuberoses made me heady as I made my way into the sanctum just as the priest was performing the last rituals of the morning. The priest sang his ritual chants to Lord *Kapaleeswarar* (*Siva*) here instated in the form of the *lingam* (phallus), and his *raga* haunted and distracted me at once.

I was leaning against one of the pock-marked black stone squares that made up the inner sanctum and found myself searching for the melodies of the voices and bodily traces of the *devadasis* who had danced here for 250 years.[14] These women were dancers, cultural workers, sexual beings, and priestesses. Their roles as wives of the Gods, married to the deities of the temples in which they practiced dance, had specific meanings in pre-colonial India. These meanings were transformed through British colonialism, Indian nationalism, and indigenous patriarchy to remove the *devadasi* from her ritual practices in the temple (Meduri, 1997). This was partly because the contradictions of the woman dancer as a sexual and religious being, and as a subject who controlled capital within a matriarchal system, could not be resolved. In fact, the nationalization of Bharata Natyam is a post-colonial formation that in effect stripped away the ritual *devadasi* workers who performed within specific cultural contexts and replaced them with new, upper-caste bodies. Replication of laboring bodies is the imperative of capital. Capital, colonialism, and subsequently nationalism went hand in hand.

Trying not to think too far back in time, I focused on the early twentieth century, attempting in my mind's eye to locate the *devadasis*, the women dancers who had been consecrated at this temple before they had been removed from their God/husband's home. Had a *devadasi* leaned against this wall much as I was doing right now? I had my palm pressed against the wall to support myself, and I wondered if a *devadasi's* hand had been here too. Could her sweat marks have mingled with mine on the temple wall? I was wondering how a *devadasi's* ritual performances to propitiate her God/husband through music and dance might have differed from that of the male priest standing in front of me.[15] In particular, what struck me about *devadasi* ritual practice was the ways in which the dancing woman used her human, fleshy, and female body to protect her husband/God when he ventured out in the temple procession. The *devadasi* fleshy body was always in between the eye[16] of the devotee and the bronze idol that was traveling in procession around the temple. The *devadasi* woman used her entire body as ritual offering, completely surrendering to her God/husband through dance and movement. She had sacrificed her body many times over for her God/husband. She was a truly consecrated devotee, the special one, marked for her undivided labor to the lord. The male priest here made sure his body was not in between the devotee and the deity. Instead, he stood to one side, making sure we could all see Lord *Kapaleeswarar* clearly. I remembered Kersenboom's detailed account of the intricacies of *devadasi* culture, and yet I still could not help myself from playing with the corporeal possibility of sweat mingling and imprinting itself in this ritual sacred space. The coldness of the stone harked back to the reality that there seemed to be nothing left of any *devadasi* women's bodies, only the spaces they had moved in. The deity Siva *lingam* stood mute as if dumbfounded at the loss of its human wives, even as rivulets of milk, butter, and water flowed over it in propitiation, or perhaps to compensate for the diminished power of the divine phallus.

While waiting for the propitiations of the male priest to end, I spied a small statue of Thirugnana Sambanthar along with many of the other *nayanmars*[17] on one side of the temple and thought to myself that perhaps I should pray to this great Saint to restore the *devadasis* back to life now, the way he had brought a woman back from the dead. I was thus reminded of an important and constitutive legend associated with the temple. Story has it that Thirugnana Sambanthar, a great Saivite saint from the eighth century CE revived a dead woman, the daughter of a devotee of Lord Siva named Sivanesa Chettiar, within the temple grounds. One day the young woman was bitten by a cobra and died. After the cremation of his daughter's body, the Chettiar collected her ashes and kept them in an urn. When Thirugnana Sambanthar visited this temple during his pilgrimage of the area, he asked the Chettiar to bring the urn of his daughter's ashes to him. When the Saint sprinkled some water from the temple tank onto the urn, the daughter came alive and walked into the temple. After her miraculous restoration this young woman volunteered herself into the service of Lord Siva and became a *devadasi* in the temple. What kind of prayers would I have to do to restore the *devadasis*? What sacrifice could I make to bring them back? *Was* there even a sacrifice I could make, and what would it achieve? As I was about to give up my nostalgic, ahistorical, and perhaps Orientalist quest, I was rewarded (maybe because I had propitiated the temple deity appropriately?) by a reminder of the famed Mylapore Gowri Ammal, whose title 'Mylapore' came from her dedication to this temple.

Mylapore Gowri Ammal's claim to dance fame came when Rukmini Devi Arundale sought her out in 1936 to guide her reconstruction of the *sadir* form into Bharata Natyam. Rukmini Devi had come to the *Kapaleeswarar* Temple to ask the great *devadasi* to come with her to Kalakshetra, 15 kilometers away in Besant Nagar, to teach her the finer points of *abhinaya*. What had ensued in the temple? How had Rukmini Devi convinced Gowri Ammal to impart her knowledge? By 1947 Gowri Ammal and other *devadasis* dedicated to temples all over India were declared divorcees or widows, ripped from the temples and their God/ husbands.[18] Yet in Chennai, despite the absence of *devadasi* bodies, the cultural, ritual, and urban spaces they had inhabited were now filled by other bodies. Middle-class or often upper-caste Brahmin women had taken over the forms of the *devadasis*, replacing the local cost-effective silk saris that had draped the *devadasi* bodies with costly urban *kanjeevarams* meted out by silk houses such as RASI, Nalli, and Kumaran.[19] A sari house such as RASI thus thrived right alongside the temple.[20] The priest handed me some *vibhudhi*, *kumkum*, *chandanam*, and jasmine flowers as I was being rushed out with the crowds. I placed the red *kumkum* on my forehead beneath my *bindi*, the white *vibhudhi* ash on top of the *bindi*, rubbed the fragrant yellow sandalwood paste on my neck and placed the jasmine flowers in my hair. The traces of the temple and the gifts from the deity were now ritually marked on my body. Consecrated, 'blessed,' and ready, to make my purchase at the sari store, I made my departure after resting for the prescribed few minutes on the temple doorstep.

Choreographies of the thumb[21]

Walking approximately 30 steps, actually it was 35 steps, because I had to avoid a large pile of shit, I arrived at RASI. I was greeted with a burst of cool air as the air conditioners and fans at RASI were on full blast. Normally this store would provide a wonderful respite from the Chennai heat, but it was cool today and I found the hair on my arms and various other body parts standing on end from the cold. I braved the conditions and took a step forward into the heart of sari-shopping territory. I was greeted warmly by the owner and various salesmen who recognized me from the years of dance shopping I had done. I was given 'special treatment' accorded only to the rich and/or famous. Sipping a cup of hot tea and seated comfortably, I secretly thanked my dance guru who had enabled me this special status because of the collective spending we had done for all the dance students back in Australia. I remember one year we had purchased 75 saris totaling lakhs of rupees and thousands of dollars!

Feeling quite caffeinated and refreshed, I sat near the *kanjeevaram* section. Mani, one of the RASI salesmen, spied me and started laying out saris for me to examine. I had not opened my mouth to make my requests known, and yet he deftly and quickly, with a flip of his wrist and a turn of his thumb, displayed a stunning array of *kanjeevarams* in brilliant aquas and deep oranges, *venkatagiris* in mustard yellows, *ikat* greens and black prints from Orissa, *jamdhani* blues shot through with purple, pink interlaced with blue tie dye *bandhnis* from Gujarat, deep red Mysore silks, *mangalagiri* burgundy laced with cream, black *benaras* with elegant *zardosi* borders, all layered one over the other so I could get the full picture of possibilities. Mani was clearly an expert in displaying saris, and he must have recalled some of my earlier purchasing days and thought he could meet my needs before I said anything. His performance had been superb, and I was dazzled into silence. All I could do for quite a while was touch the saris in awe and experience the thrill of feeling the textures of material.

A half-hour or so later I was forced to emerge from my reverie as I felt the sting of a mosquito on my left calf. My first instinct was to scratch the itch and I was just about to do so when I realized I was holding a beautiful, expensive, blue, *jamdhani* in my hand. It would not look good for me to reach down in an ungainly fashion to scratch my calf. Where was my mosquito repellant when I needed it? Mosquito bites are quite sharp in Chennai, so I stoically composed my face, even smiled, controlled my bodily urge to scratch, and instead went about the task of examining *kanjeevarams* as a good customer should. Eventually, I had to tell Mani that, sadly, I had come to buy one sari, and he was to only show me saris within the Rs.4000 to Rs.6000 range, in the colors that had been requested by the young girl. I explained it was for an NRI[22] *arangetram* and he immediately understood. He smiled wryly and commented about my buying power, or lack thereof, these days. Yet he went to a corner of the display area and brought out some beautiful and unique pieces. Carefully and slowly Mani layered one or two pieces with exquisite characteristics such as unique borders, body designs, or colors. Although his dark hands seemed manicured, his thumbs had long nails growing out of them. I could not tear my gaze from those irregular thumbs. They teased open sari borders, ripped out staples that bound the packaging of the sari, darting in between the elegant silk cloth panels and then out to smooth the material. The thumbs were doing a lot of work at an even rhythmic pace. While it is true that the other fingers helped enhance this performance, they were merely framing devices acting as weights to control the material. The thumbs were the principal performers. In particular the thumbnails played important roles in allowing Mani to gauge the layers and thickness of the sari material, often inserting themselves between the folds to move layers of material apart. A duet would unfold in front of my eyes when Mani would run his right thumb silently but quickly down one yard of the gold *zari* border of the sari to show me the exquisite work that had gone into making the design, and the nail would make a slight rasping noise in accompaniment. The other thumb with the assistance of the forefinger would hold the remaining five yards of the sari. The dark finger would be highlighted, frozen in time against the brilliant hues of blues, greens, and red silk material until the next sari was displayed.

The movement of Mani's thumb as I was viewing it in isolation sharply brought to mind a vision of severed thumbs. I recalled the Indian weavers in the mid-nineteenth century whose thumbs were cut off so that the East India Company could monopolize trade with Indian textile merchants in the region.[23] This violent act, along with the deliberate destruction of native Indian factories, damaged the technology of weavers and was accompanied by the forced trade with cheaper but inferior British textiles that ultimately led to the collapse of the Indian economy and the subsequent colonization of India. This colonization of India, accompanied by an array of complex discourses, led to the destruction of the *devadasi* and her cultural practices. When M. K. Gandhi began his famous 'Quit India Movement' to rid the Indian subcontinent of British colonizers, he encouraged Indians to weave their own cloth by hand and thereby boycott the inferior British cloth imported into India from factories in Birmingham and Manchester. A deeply political and 'materialist' move, this agenda in its heyday had the desired effect and severely impaired the British export infrastructure. After Independence, the Indian flag still sports the symbolic wheel (which can be read in multiple registers) at its center. At Kalakshetra, Rukmini Devi followed Gandhi's grand design and further enhanced it by not only setting up local weaving centers in the confines of the dance center that produced saris and various cloth, but also by emphasizing other local technologies that supported dance performance and production. Thus the histories of cloth, saris, independence, nation, and dance have long been intertwined.

Blood 'memories'

A beautiful deep-pink sari with a purple border caught my attention. It was quite unique, but its memory vanished as I was suddenly interrupted and transported back to Mallika's performance at the music academy. I thought I saw her glancing my way, so I made a pact with myself that I would focus on her dance completely. She had moved on to the main piece of the night. It was not a *varnam* as one usually expected. Rather, it was an unframed piece that seemed to offer a political commentary on global warming and animal rights of sorts. At least that is how I read the encounter between Yudhishtira and the deer he was hunting. Mallika was not performing the hero's perspective, but instead telling the story from the deer's vantage point. Was this a move towards eco-politics in dance or was it simply my desired interpretation?

She had me quite focused for almost six minutes when I became distracted by a small bell that had detached itself from the rows of bells adorning her ankles. I could not help noticing it. Why was no one else concerned about the danger this bell posed to Mallika? It strayed a little from center stage and moved stage right, and lingered tantalizingly on the side. I was sure Mallika had seen it and would avoid it to complete this dance piece. However, springing to and fro as the deer she did not see the stray bell and landed on it with her right foot after one very high jump. Landing on the sharp metal with such weight must surely have been painful and yet Mallika showed no signs of injury on her face. She was after all a very seasoned dancer, adept at creating the 'ideal' performance. Her foot, however, revealed otherwise! A tell tale stream of blood flowed from underneath her foot. The bloodstream followed her movement and she began creating patterns on the floor marked with her own juices. Unlike *devadasi* performers who actually used their feet to create powdered, colored artistic masterpieces of peacocks and palaces,[24] Mallika had just created a Picasso-esque abstract. I thought this unintentional abstract was getting quite interesting, but to my dismay she abruptly stopped and sat down right in the middle of her own blood floor painting to portray the character of Yudhishtira. This destroyed any further interpretation of her artistic creation and furthermore her pink sari now became stained with her own deep-red blood. What would the dry cleaner say? More than that, what could we do about this stray bell that was still firmly ensconced right beside her on stage. Perhaps Mallika's body resisted being weighed down so much with the layers of sari, jewelry, and heavy ankle bells. Maybe her body had willfully and violently attempted to rid itself of the bell. Or as

Avanthi Meduri (1997) suggests, the *devadasi* foremother was haunting the contemporary Bharata Natyam dancer, and in this particular performance the ghost was perhaps exceptionally angry because she had been written out of history. Was the bell the trace of the ghost of the *devadasi*? Or was it that whoever had sewn this belt of bells together had not done a very good job? Maybe it was a combination of all these factors.

Having finished my purchases at RASI, I began walking towards the opposite side of the water tank where Radha Gold jewelers were based. I needed one temple jewelry necklace to complete my list. The street perpendicular to North Mada Street was quite narrow, and I had to walk through this dusty road to get to the other side. As I walked, a number of street vendors caught my eye. In particular, the bell-weavers sparked my interest. The women who wove the bells together into one belt had tough hands. One woman in particular stood out. She was wearing a crème-colored cotton sari with a dark pink border that was fading either due to the sun, or as a result of constant wear. She used the *pallu* to wipe the sweat away from her face, and also as a polishing cloth for the belt and bells she held in her left hand. Her sweat mingled with the metal on her sari cloth. Her dark right hand was wrapped around the white and pink *pallu* because she was engaged in the cleaning and polishing process of one bell, so I could only see her fingers and thumb. Her thumb, forefinger, and middle fingers were her principal performers, engorged with fat and fluid on the inner sides that lightened the color of the skin there. Clearly, they had labored intensely for her over the years. Ironically, she had worked for the middle-class Brahmin woman dancer's performance, but had most likely never even seen the dance. She let go of the sari, and I saw her inner palm for the flash of a second. It was scarred deeply with many wrinkles, but the skin looked tough all the same with all the calluses.

Hers was an arduous performance, very different in quality and flow to both Mallika and Mani's performances. This performance had sweat, strength, and ritual elements to it, and although it was not dazzling, it had depth in terms of corporeal labor. She had to make sure all the bells were tightly woven together. Taking one large needle and very strong string, she battled to thread the string through the tough leather belt and finally string one bell through. She tightened it and knotted it carefully and bit off the remaining thread with her teeth. The process started all over again with the second bell. I was taken aback when she actually looked up at me quizzically, wondering why I was looking at her. Her performance moved me deeply, but I was uncomfortable that she was looking back at me. Our locked gaze was broken when my body jerked rather violently as a result of a bicycle that knocked my elbow and then grazed my ribs. It was enough to throw me sideways, but luckily I jumped and grabbed onto a pole nearby to steady myself. I was breathing heavily and sweating profusely in the heat of the morning, but my mind would not stop racing.

The street was even busier than it had been 15 minutes earlier. Had it been this crowded when Rukmini Devi had arrived here to meet Gowri Ammal? The dance business and industry only took off in the mid to late 1950s, accompanying the popularity and growth of RASI and other sari stores. This street had been filled with bodies that primarily catered to the temple, which was both the physical and spiritual center of Mylapore. The new economy around the water tank was recent and an offshoot of nationalist reconfigurings of the dance practice that had led to its boom by the 1970s. It was Rukmini Devi's inventions at Kalakshetra that set the process in motion. She had prioritized the hand weaving of cotton saris (giving rise to the famous Kalakshetra cotton sari itself), and had carefully selected the costuming and grooming of the 'ideal' Bharata Natyam dancer. For her, it had been about respectability and a set of aesthetics alternative to the *devadasi* women. Hers was an aesthetic that was internationally developed, informed by a global vision of theater and performance. Now, there were numerous vendors working for the dance economy. The division of labor was such that the poor working-class women and men who created the dance accoutrements from the raw material, never encountered the shopkeepers who sold them at marked up prices to middle-class and upper-caste female dancers. I was told there were large factories, too, where these products were being made, but the detailed labor still had to be done, and this was evidenced in the work of the bell weaver.

I heard a thunderous applause since the dance item was over and the audience was cheering wildly. Perhaps the sight of blood had driven the 'natives' wild. They thought Mallika had sacrificed some of her blood on stage for them. The propitiations had been deemed appropriate and so the applause was overwhelming. Mallika clearly had to change out of the sari and wear a new one. The musicians took charge and went into an interlude that lasted a good ten minutes. Would she appear in a green, blue, mustard, or black number? I could sense the women in the audience waiting with bated breath to see what her choice would be. My grandmother said loudly to her neighbor that she was sure Mallika would come back with a blue number. I, too, was intrigued [...]

Intermission

It was a peacock-blue sari with a deep-burgundy border. On the edge connecting the sari to its *zari* border were embroidered peacocks that intensified the peacock-blue color and the richness of the sari. The dancer's tall stature and slim, yet shapely form was enhanced even further by the beauty of this sari, but unfortunately it could not improve her dancing. It was not the sari I had bought for her. She had already worn that one in the first half of the performance for the *varnam*. This sari would have to last the entire second half of the performance, including the speeches and the *mangalam*. I was not sure I had the patience to sit through to the end. It had been hard enough watching the first half of this performance, and now there were still four or five items left, not to mention the tiresome speeches. My body was aching already from sitting in the auditorium for two hours, and I knew there was still an hour and a half to go. I was also jetlagged and exhausted from the flight. I found my eyes closing on more than one occasion and was fighting to keep myself from literally falling off my chair. I had only arrived from India yesterday and had not adjusted to Pacific Standard Time. But I had no choice. I had to be here today. After all I had brought one of the saris for her *arangetram*, along with a pair of bells and some jewelry. My suitcase was heavy and my back was aching from lifting it on and off the baggage claim and carts. My right thumb was particularly sore from dragging the suitcase. It didn't help that I was not allowed to go through the green channel even though I said I had nothing to declare. I had been fingerprinted and made to wait. My baggage was thoroughly searched, and I was made to explain to three separate officers that the pickles my grandmother had sent were drug free daily edibles, and that the jewelry was fake and not worth more than a $100. Finally, without any help from any of the officers, I had to clean up the mess they had made, repack the suitcase, and hoist it back onto the baggage cart. I think that is when my right thumb folded itself between the metal of the baggage cart and the hard fabric of the suitcase. My thumb could not move after that. It was silenced.

These *arangetrams* were getting tedious. But I had respect for the girl's guru and knew her parents. It would be difficult to leave early unless I timed it well. I told myself I should be more patient. After all, this was Madhavi Manoranjam's first solo full performance on stage, and the *arangetram* was a special event for her and her family. It was the culmination of a decade of dedication to dance practice. The audience cheered wildly when she appeared in the new sari. Hooting, whistling, and roaring, the primarily South Asian audience, with a smattering of mainstream Americans who were friends and local dignitaries, was cheering Madhavi on. For the South Asian audience, Madhavi was transporting them back to an India over 3000 miles away in distance and a hundred or a thousand years back in time. The exact date didn't matter because the India that Madhavi's body conjured up was timeless. Madhavi's body was the vehicle for the immigrant diaspora community's imagination of a pre-colonial, authentic India. Her sari, costume, and jewels clothed the perfect and iconic Indian woman's body. Time and space could stand still, and the immigrant community could feel free to project their nostalgic desires of home and an 'ideal woman' onto her. I was feeling nostalgic, too, thinking of the delicious food that had been served during the intermission. The *samosas* and *chana batura* had left an indelible impression, not to mention the warm tea afterwards. It couldn't have been a more perfect combination as the precursor for an afternoon nap. But that was not meant to be.

Ironically, although it was her first solo debut in the United States, it would most likely also be Madhavi's last. She would leave for Princeton shortly to begin a career in the sciences, engineering, or computing, and her dance practice would end, unlike the *devadasis*, for whom the *arangetram* signaled so many new beginnings. Madhavi could sever herself from dancing completely in ways that the *devadasi* women never could. In this first piece following the intermission, Madhavi was describing a *nayika* playing the *veena*, a stringed instrument. The *nayika* in this instance, was an imaginary character/heroine loosely based on the life of an actual *devadasi*. Madhavi began the piece center stage in a spotlight. She was balancing with only some slight wobbling on her right leg with the left ankle placed over the right knee. Madhavi was gesturing towards holding the *veena* on an angle with the heavy part resting on her left ankle. She made a pretty picture especially once she got her balance. I saw some photographers capturing the still image of her quickly and quietly. This pose deserved a photo frame in her dorm room! It was perhaps the glitter of the large gold anklet she wore above the bells that got me thinking. It seemed like it was about to slip off. I was worried for the girl. It might cause her some serious injury if it fell off in the middle of her dancing. I was taken back to another image of Madhavi, a *devadasi* who emerges from a Tamil literary text.

Madhavi, the 13-year-old *devadasi* presented herself to the Chola,[25] King Karikalan, performing on 'stage' with her *veena* and other instruments for the very first time in front of the King, his Queen, artists, scholars, learned men, connoisseurs, and courtiers. The grand Tamil literary marvel of *Cilapattikaram* in which Madhavi is featured is dated around the fifth century CE.[26] Credited to Prince Ilango Adigal, the brother of the Cheran King, Senkuttuvan, it is said that the story was based on an existing legend of a Goddess Woman named Kannagi. The *Cilapattikaram* text, though fictional, contains within it one of the earliest and most detailed accounts of *devadasi* performance practices. It is this text, among others, that has been used to secure an uninterrupted history for the contemporary performance of Bharata Natyam, devoid of colonial contact.[27] Ilango Adigal's fictional account of Madhavi is believed to be indicative of his contemporary experiences with *devadasis* during the fifth century CE.

I felt goosebumps on my arm and the back of my neck and a current of energy travel through my body and into the top of my head. It was the *raga Huseini* enveloping my body. Even before I saw the vocalist, I heard and felt the notes of the *raga* emerging from his full-throated singing. I started to hum the *raga* quietly, sometimes pre-empting where the vocalist would take his *alapana* improvisation and elaborations. I felt my eyes well up with tears at the emotion this *raga* carried with it. It shook me back into Madhavi Manoranjam's performance of the *padam*, *Netrandhil Neyrathiley*. She was by a body of water and saw her lover in an embrace with another woman. Madhavi as the main character, the *nayika*, was confused. Hadn't her lover promised he was faithful only to her? And yet, here he was behind the bushes with this other woman. Perhaps she was mistaken. Maybe it was the other woman who had propositioned him, and he had nothing to do with it. He was perhaps helpless in the face of this woman's bold advances. She would give him a chance to explain himself. I wondered why the mythical *devadasi* was so important to contemporary Bharata Natyam performances? The mythical *devadasi* who pre-dates the colonial encounter is indeed a beautiful, unsullied, and desired creature. She could be imagined as each dancer chose, through the interpretation of the *padam* text, where the *devadasi* was fictitiously housed. The *padam* text being a poetic text written by the male poet in his encounter with actual *devadasis* of the sixteenth century, who represented them as heroines, *nayikas*, who had erotic encounters with their lovers who were sometimes Gods. The contemporary dancer has the ability to encounter these fictitious but accessible *devadasis*, in the form of archetypal heroines and then embody the textualized heroines through her own body using her interpretation. *Padams* were perhaps the only structure in the Bharata Natyam recital that had the ability to hold my interest. I was curious about how each dancer would perform a known text with her own interpretations, and these were not even her own interpretations. Although the item was choreographed by her guru, her performance held the possibility for seeing Madhavi's ideas in the dance.

I had to admit Madhavi Manoranjam was doing a nice job of this *padam*. She was also sweating a lot less than she had done in the first half of the *arangetram*. Perhaps because the *padams* did not involve much aerobic activity and focused instead on the dancer's facial and bodily expression. The male vocalist was singing the first line of the poem repeatedly. In the Tamil language: *Netrandhil neyrathiley neer-aadum karaidhanile neringi ummai jaadai kati azhaithaval yaro swami?* Roughly translated it reads: 'Yesterday at dusk time by the bathing *ghat*, there was a woman who approached you, making overt signs and calling to you, who was she?' Madhavi interpreted the line angrily the first time, asking through facial, hand, and bodily gesture. She went on to create multiple interpretations of the line of text. I was surprised that Madhavi held my attention throughout the *padam* performance. Although she was a young dancer, she seemed to have really gotten into this *nayika's* role. What was it about the *nayika* in this *padam* that captivated Madhavi and resonated with her? Why did the *padam* format allow her to project her own emotions into the text? Or was it so easy to imagine this *nayika* because she was such an ahistorical and mythical figure that it allowed Madhavi to unproblematically portray her? Were those the very reasons I was able to focus on Madhavi's performance without distraction or was it simply the music itself that held me in thrall?

I reached down into my handbag to take out my book so I could take some quick notes in the dark, when suddenly the house lights came on. I realized Madhavi had to do her obligatory thank you speech that has become part and parcel of diaspora *arangetrams*. It was sometimes jarring to see the silent dancing girl come on stage with a microphone and break out in a thick American accent, but there it was. Her voice was loud and her posture garish. She had her feet spread out and her back was hunched, but she seemed confident. She began by thanking 'aunty,' meaning her guru who was sitting on stage right with the musicians, explaining that it was 'aunty' who had taught her about Indian culture and tradition. Now that she knew the ancient history of the dance she practiced, she would cherish it forever. She knew she was dancing for the Gods and that this was a divine form she had been given. Like dancers of 2000 years ago in India, she was continuing to practice Hinduism in her own small way. Madhavi had made many sacrifices along the way to get to today, and yet she was thankful and would not have it any other way.

I was struck by the fact that unlike other *arangetrams* speeches, this girl was calling on the fictive history of the Bharata Natyam form with such conviction. The religious reference was a common one – but drawing on the history of the *devadasis*, that was interesting. What was the investment in this fictive authenticity, of drawing a particular history from the nation into the diaspora? It disturbed me to think of this constant pull of authenticity, whether it was the need for 'authentic' objects such as the sari from India or 'authentic' discourses that falsified histories that seem to plague the Bharata Natyam practice. I was also besieged by waves of jetlag shooting through my body, and my thumb ached from the pain of traveling between India and the United States. I asked myself why, along with so many other girls having done their *arangetram*, I too participated in the myth of the *devadasi*. Why was no one thinking about the actual *devadasis*, *nachwalis*, and dancing girls who had arrived in the United States in the nineteenth century?[28] Why was nobody performing these early dancers' stories? I reminded myself wryly that this was perhaps because few people knew anything about these early dancers, and I was asking too much. Anyway, most Indians had collective amnesia about things happening in the United States before 1965, since that was the year the National Origins Immigration Act was instituted to enable a large number of Asians and Indians to emigrate there. Before this time there had been many racist anti-Asian immigration policies that prevented Indians from consolidating in any great numbers. It was only after 1965 that droves of different Indian dancing women started landing on American shores. Madhavi's guru had arrived in California in 1981 with her husband, who came as a professional in search of a job.

Madhavi's guru was thanking the audience for coming to the *arangetram* and telling them there would be one more piece left for the dancer to perform. Madhavi bowed to her guru who was sitting on stage right next to the musicians. She gave the musicians and her guru a bouquet of flowers. She then turned to the audience and made a deep bow with hands folded to their cheerful applause. She looked up grinning at the audience. The sweat stains under her arms had dried up temporarily during the speech. This was not the dainty *nayika* she had performed earlier, it was Madhavi in all her bodily form. The full-toothed grin said it all. She was rather proud of herself and so was the audience. She had fulfilled their nostalgic desire. But did the audience see the many performances that were undertaken to make this one solo performance happen? Madhavi's body and all the objects and discourses that constituted her Bharata Natyam dancing body including the jewels, bells, sari, and the various histories of transnational labor were performing also. Mallika, Mani, the bell weaver, unnamable imaginary and real *devadasis*, her own guru, her guru's guru, were performing alongside Madhavi. They were all laboring. The transnational bodily labor that is unaccounted for in watching Bharata Natyam dancing in the United States is performing itself through Madhavi's body. These many performances are happening simultaneously and we do not know how many of them are being seen. Many sacrifices were undertaken to enable this performance to happen. The biggest sacrifice comes from the audience who pretends to not see these many sacrifices laid bare before them. What would it take for these sacrifices to be acknowledged?

In a global economy, the labor plain in sight and yet not always visible is that of various classed Indian bodies in India. In viewing performances of middle-class dancers in Chennai, the labor 'down the road', needed for cultural nationalism, is just as unacknowledged as the 'off-shore' labor needed for Indian American diasporic production in California. A materialist analysis brings to light the sweat stains, the falling bell, the blood, and the dangling flowers as some of the telltale signs of bodily labor that point to 'other stories' of global capital's contradictions, excesses, and ruptures.

Madhavi's sari fan was flying behind her as she rushed off stage. She disappeared into the wings and was getting ready for the *thillana*. I thought this would be a good time for me to leave in the dark before I got caught. I sprang out of my seat just as I spied a bell that had rolled off Madhavi's ankle and was sitting on the stage where she would enter. Would she step on it? I could not stay to find out the next series of performances that would unfold. I made it outside the door just as the music began for the *thillana*.

Notes

1. In the last few decades, however, the work of scholars such as Avanthi Meduri (1997), Ananya Chatterjea (2004), Janet O'Shea (2007), and Pallabi Chakravorty (2008), to mention a few, have transformed the previous scholarship on Indian dance. Still there is a dearth of critical dance ethnographies of Indian dance. Perhaps this is because ethnography under the discipline of anthropology has primarily been viewed as a colonial and Western methodology often used by Euro-American anthropologists, dance ethnographers, and ethnomusicologists to study 'other' non-Western cultures. The more recent developments in South Asian 'indigenous' or 'halfie' (Lila Abu-Lughod, 1993) ethnography where the 'natives' have written back and complicated anthropology itself is demonstrated in the work of

Arjun Appadurai and Kamala Visweswaran, but there are few comparisons in dance ethnography.

2. In attempting to represent the ethnographic experience, I write from a feminist, post-colonial perspective that also incorporates stylistic approaches of Tamil women poets and writers from the third, sixth, and eighth century CE who combine thick description, metaphors, history, myth, and parables to convey their multiple messages. I am also influenced by the writing of historical ethnographers such as John and Jean Comaroff (1991), and third world feminist ethnographers Lila Abu-Lughod (1993), Chandra Mohanty and colleagues (1991), Kamala Visweswaran (1994), Piya Chatterjee (2001), and Assia Djebar (1997) to mention a few. Although very different in approaches, these authors deftly combine elements of ethnography, auto-ethnography, and history to account for the imperatives of capital and its intersection with women's bodies.

3. I refer here in particular to the standard Euro-American dance critics' responses to live performances. See June Vail (1995) for more details.

4. I am informed by the work of third world feminist scholars such as Chandra Mohanty (1991), Margo Okazawa-Rey (2004), Piya Chatterjee (2001), and others who argue there can be no feminist analysis without a critique of Capital.

5. I refer in particular to the work of Saskia Kersenboom (1987), and Amrit Srinivasan (1983), which instigated debates and discussion of the *devadasi* question in dance circles in India and abroad.

6. Saris have a complex history of production. Some are hand woven, others are produced in textile mills and factories, while many others are created through a combination of hand-woven and industrial technologies (Lynton, 2002; Bhachu, 2003).

7. In the Tamil calendar, the month of *margazhi* begins in the middle of December and ends in the middle of January.

8. *Adaada* is a Tamil term lacking direct translation. It is a term of approval, marvel, and astonishment all at once.

9. *Mridangam* is a double-headed barrel drum, part of the music ensemble along with the vocalist and instrumentalist comprising the orchestra for dance. The *alapana* is a melodic improvisation devoid of text, focused primarily on finding key phrases that highlight the *raga*, its melodic scale. *Bowli* is one of many thousands of *ragas*.

10. Usually the abstract and rhythmical dance element of *nritta* is performed to complementary abstracted formations in the music. However, in this piece, the vocalist was singing *sahityam*, a text-based piece that would normally be interpreted through dramatic expression, *natya* or *abhinaya*, and thus the dancer's interpretation through *nritta* was unusual.

11. Legend has it that Parvati, Siva's wife, was transformed into a peacock (*mayil*) and born on earth. She waited at the site where the *Kapaleeswar* Temple was built, and was rejoined with Siva in her female human form after performing penances for many years. The temple has a peacock gazing up from one of its turrets and is unique in this aspect. Hence it can be identified in performance through the depiction of the peacock. It is also said that the neighborhood became known as 'the peacock town' and was subsequently translated into English by the British as Mylapore.

12. My friend is a Bharata Natyam dance guru in Southern California and one of her teenage students was having her *arangetram* shortly. Apparently the girl needed a few extra things to complete her trousseau for the gala evening event. I offered to help complete this trousseau.

13. *Pochampalli* saris are famous for their durability, vibrant colors, and comfortable cotton material. The name also refers to a small town in the state of Andhra Pradesh where the saris are woven. In general, sari names reflect the town in which they were traditionally woven.

14. My great-grandfather C. S. Srinivasachari (1939), a renowned Indian historian, has argued persuasively that the history of the *Kapaleeswarar* Temple in Chennai goes back to the Pallava Empire in the seventh century CE. However, he argues that archaeological evidence suggests that the history of this temple is not what it seems, suggesting that Portugese traders destroyed the temple in the sixteenth century and built a Cathedral over it in its original location by the seashore in Santhome (a suburb of Chennai). Although there are artifacts within the temple that date back to the seventh century, the present temple foundations were built as recently as 300 years ago. It is believed that remnants from the first temple were moved from its original location and rebuilt in Mylapore.

15. Saskia Kersenboom (1987) in her excellent anthropology of the *devadasi* practice in Thiruvaroor has elaborated on the various temple rituals of *devadasis* in numerous ways.

16. South Indian Hindu beliefs in the *evil eye* extend from protecting human beings to temple deities from harm. While, in the case of a human, a small lamp is used in a circular pattern, three times clockwise and three times in the anti-clockwise direction; for the deity, *devadasis* would wave large pot-lamps in front of the deity as the procession circumambulated the temple.

17. *Nayanmars* are the 64 men and women saints celebrated in South Indian Hindu history as great devotees of Lord Siva. These men and women sang and wrote praises of Siva, many of whose texts remain inscribed in the walls of temples today.

18. Dancing women, and in particular saris became an important symbol in the struggle for national independence. According to Chatterjee (1986), Indian nationalists attempted to resolve the stigma of colonization and the woman question by demarcating the public sphere as a male agenda and relegating women's practices to the private sphere. Women were therefore expected to maintain pure Indian culture by performing the agendas of a fixed notion of 'tradition' that valued the icon of the 'ideal woman,' understood as Brahmin and upper class/upper caste. The sari became the symbol of 'tradition' and therefore of the 'inner' Indian sphere that had to be guarded, and thus functioned as a metaphor for womanhood and nation.

19. Kersenboom's (1987) monograph details the kinds of saris worn by *devadasis*. Additionally, photographs of *devadasis* from the late nineteenth century and early twentieth century reveal that they wore saris that were from the local region where they were based. These saris were often cheaper than *Kanjeevaram* silks, which are the trend now among Bharata Natyam dancers.

20. This sari house had its beginnings in the 1930s when K. Thiruvengadam Chettiar opened shop. It grew in popularity along with nationalist independence struggles, but it really began flourishing in 1959 when it

opened a large modern showroom and created unique designs through highly specialized weavers.

21. I am interested in examining more closely the technologies of the hand related to Bharata Natyam *mudra* formation. In Bharata Natyam practice the articulation of the hand and particular fingers are extremely important in laboring to create symbolic meaning. In this section, I explore the ways in which a reading of finger movement in sari display as performance can reveal alternate forms of labor that provide a materialist understanding of dance practice.

22. NRI is an acronym for Non-Resident Indian, often used as a derogatory comment to refer to Indians from the diaspora, particularly from the United States. What this scenario demonstrates is the outsourcing of labor that happens in the Bharata Natyam practice in diaspora. The objects that construct the Bharata Natyam performance cannot be easily obtained in the United States. and so the journey to India has to be undertaken to buy the various 'authentic' accoutrements, including the sari, the dancing bell, the jewelry, and flowers. Recently, however, an online store has begun advertisements offering some of these products to dancers in the United States so that they do not need to travel to India for their objects.

23. By the mid-nineteenth century, the export, import, and manufacture of goods moved from the hands of independent Indian merchants to intermediaries hired by the British East India Company. Often this required force. Sepoys of the East India Company were sent to destroy the factories owned by Indian rivals to the East India Company. Independent weavers who refused to work for the pitiful wages that the East India Company offered had their thumbs cut off. In a matter of three decades, the East India Company achieved a virtual stranglehold on the economic and political life of Eastern India (Sinha, 1962).

24. Kersenboom (1987) notes that *devadasi* performers had many kinds of dance items in their repertoire. Here I refer to the kollam dance where *devadasis* used their feet to manipulate different colored powders to create an artistic powder painting while dancing.

25. Three separate regions existed in the South of India around the fifth century CE. The three regions known as Chola, Chera, and Pandya formed the Tamil Kingdom.

26. There is controversy surrounding the date of the literary text. The renowned Indian historian, Nilakanta Sastri dates it to the ninth century, while many others date it to the fifth and second centuries.

27. Nirmala Ramachandran's (1966) essay 'Bharata Natyam – Culture and Dance of the Ancient Tamils' is a classic example of a Nationalist and Orientalist revisioning of Tamil history wherein the contemporary frameworks of the dance form from Sanskrit dramatic treatises are collapsed with Ilango Adigal's description of Madhavi's dances.

28. I have discussed the presence and contribution of these early Indian dancers elsewhere in greater details. See Srinivasan (2003, 2007, 2009) for further details.

4
Race-ing Choreographic Copyright[1]

Anthea Kraut

Introduction, Part 1

In 2002, a Federal District Court in New York awarded the copyrights to most of white modern dance legend Martha Graham's choreographic works to the Martha Graham Center of Contemporary Dance, rather than to Graham's heir, Ronald Protas. The case and the ruling set off a flurry of debate and discussion in the modern dance community about the ownership of choreographic works. Some celebrated the decision for enabling the Graham Company to continue performing works from the Graham repertory after a hiatus of several years. Others in the modern dance world, however, greeted the decision with grave concern. For this camp, the court's finding that Graham was an employee of the non-profit corporation she set up in 1948, and therefore not in a position to bequeath the rights to her choreography to Protas, set off alarms. How could the most towering figure in American modern dance, widely considered an artistic 'genius,' *not* own her own choreography (Van Camp, 2007)?

Also in 2002, the Indian-born yoga guru Bikram Choudhury copyrighted a sequence of 26 yoga poses and two breathing exercises – performed in a specific order in sauna-like heat – and threatened lawsuits against yoga studios offering classes that followed his model. (Though yoga and dance are by no means equivalent, Bikram's lawyer compared his yoga series to ballet choreography as justification for his intellectual property claims.) While a federal judge ruled in 2005 that Bikram's copyrights were valid, his actions, self-described as 'the American way,' helped spur a counter-response from India. Historians and scientists there have initiated a project that will catalog hundreds of yoga poses, along with ayurvedic remedies and other 'traditional knowledge,' to protect them from being copyrighted by anyone else

(Fetterman, 2006; Mehta, 2007: A21).[2] Meanwhile, the United States has started using 'free trade' agreements to pressure countries like South Korea, Peru, and Colombia to bring their intellectual property laws into compliance with US and European Union standards – measures that ensure greater protection and profits for Western conglomerates (Surowiecki, 2007: 52).

Although property laws are specific to nations, it is clear that they also serve as key instruments of globalization, with American definitions of copyright being imposed, exploited, and resisted within and across national borders.[3] Yet the example of the Graham case suggests that even within the United States, notions about authorship and ownership of embodied forms of expression, and about the relationship between the individual and the collective, are still being worked out. Because American copyright law has become a hotly contested global issue, it seems all the more important to understand the local and national politics that have shaped it. Toward that end, this chapter approaches the institution of choreographic copyright as a valuable site for teasing out some of the contradictions that inhere in intellectual property law. As I hope to show, the emergence of copyright protection for choreography within the United States depended in part on the same racial ideology that has underwritten the formation of something called 'world dance.' In other words, choreographic copyright has itself been an operation of 'worlding.'[4] Let me explain.

Introduction, Part 2

In the logic that sustains the category 'world dance,' non-Western cultures, regarded as unified wholes, possess dance traditions worthy of study and documentation by Westerners. As conventionally conceived, these dance traditions are created and maintained by communities of anonymous producers. In contrast, this line of thinking goes, Western traditions like ballet and modern dance are made up of discrete works with individual, identifiable authors, whose innovations propel their art forms forward.[5] Over 30 years ago, scholar Joann Kealiinohomoku argued that such divisions between Western and non-Western dance forms are the product of myth. As she pleaded in her 1969 essay 'An Anthropologist Looks at Ballet as a Form of Ethnic Dance': 'Let it be noted, once and for all, that within the various "ethnologic" dance worlds there are also patrons, dancing masters, choreographers, and performers with names woven into a very real historical fabric' (2001: 35). Despite her efforts, the constructed opposition between the solitary, creative genius of the West and the collectively created dance cultures of the Rest continues to hold sway.

A similar dichotomy between the individual and the communal obtains in the legal arena. In *The Cultural Life of Intellectual Properties*, legal scholar and anthropologist Rosemary Coombe identifies two areas of law that govern expressive output: one covering intellectual property, the other cultural property. This bifurcated schema, Coombe explains, 'reflect[s] and secure[s]' a colonialist logic that divides the realm of Art from the realm of culture.' Citing James Clifford's mapping of an 'art-culture system' that assigns different value to artistic masterpieces and cultural artifacts, Coombe describes how 'authors with intellect are distinguished from cultures with property' (Coombe, 1998a: 243; see also Clifford, 1988). For example, while copyright laws 'were developed to protect the expressive works of authors and artists – increasingly perceived in Romantic terms of individual genius and transcendent creativity – in the service of promoting universal progress in the arts and sciences,' laws protecting the cultural property of nations or groups 'enable proprietary claims to be made only to original objects or authentic artifacts.' As a result, 'Those who have intellect are entitled to speak on behalf of universal principles of reason, whereas those who have culture speak only on behalf of a cultural tradition that must be unified and homogeneous before we will accord it any respect' (Coombe, 1998a: 219, 225, 243).

The twin logics that animate our dance categories and our legal categories converge in the development of copyright protection for choreography in the United States. The distinctions between art and culture, and the notions of authorship that govern each, have shaped the property status of dance in meaningful ways. Under the Federal Copyright Act of 1976, choreographic works are eligible for copyright so long as they are 'original work[s] of authorship' and 'fixed in any tangible medium of expression,' that is, film, videotape, or any of several notational systems. The statute declined to define 'choreographic work' explicitly, maintaining that the term is one of several with 'fairly settled meanings.' Nonetheless, reports issued by both the House and the Senate deemed that it was not 'necessary to specify that "choreographic works" do not include social dance steps and simple routines' (Van Camp, 1994: 61). The flat exclusion of participatory dance forms not designed for presentation on the proscenium stage mirrors and inscribes into law the hierarchies between different modes of dance that have long characterized the field.[6] Even within the United States, then, the art–culture divide continues to operate, determining what counts as choreography and what merits legal protection as intellectual property.

Although the 1976 law marked the first time choreographic works were expressly identified as a subject of copyright, some dance compositions were copyrighted before then under the category of dramatic and dramatico-musical works. In 1952, the German-born modern dancer Hanya Holm copyrighted the dances she choreographed for the 1948 Broadway production *Kiss Me, Kate* and reportedly 'made history' as the first to secure a copyright for a choreographic composition. Because Holm's choreography was not technically 'dramatic' in the sense of telling a story, the dance community heralded her copyright registration as a triumphant circumvention of the law's failure to offer protection for choreography as such. In subsequent years, the Copyright Office seemed to relax its restrictions against copyright protection for 'abstract' works of choreography, and additional choreographers, such as Ruth Page, George Balanchine, and Agnes DeMille, followed Holm in obtaining copyrights for individual dances as dramatic works (Arcomano, 1980: 58–9). Under intense lobbying from several prominent dance figures, including Holm, DeMille, ballet impresario Lincoln Kirstein, and dance critics John Martin and Anatole Chujoy, Congress finally revised the Copyright Law in 1976 to give choreography its own separate classification, rendering it 'no longer a mere stepchild of drama' (Singer, 1984: 288).

Holm was not the first to attempt to obtain copyright protection for choreography.[7] Over a half-century earlier, in 1892, Loie Fuller famously brought an infringement suit against a dancer whom she accused of performing an unauthorized copy of 'The Serpentine Dance,' a description of which Fuller had filed with the US Copyright Office. In the precedent-setting Fuller v. Bemis, the New York Circuit Court denied her request for an injunction, determining that 'a stage dance illustrating the poetry of motion by a series of graceful movements combined with an attractive arrangement of drapery, lights, and shadows, but telling no story, portraying no character and depicting no emotion, is not a "dramatic composition" within the meaning of the Copyright Act' (qtd in Arcomano, 1980: 59).[8]

While the Fuller v. Bemis case looms large in accounts of the history of copyright and choreography, another reported early attempt to copyright dance has been entirely overlooked by dance and legal scholars. According to several sources, in 1926 the African American blues singer Alberta Hunter copyrighted the Black Bottom, a black vernacular dance that was popularized on the US theatrical stage and became a national and international craze. Although the accuracy of this claim is uncertain, the contention itself is noteworthy on several counts. As a social dance with no single author, the Black Bottom seems precisely the kind of dance the law has consistently barred from copyright protection. The allegation that Hunter obtained a copyright for the dance thus presents a challenge to the logic on which both dance and legal arbiters depend to draw distinctions between modes of dance. It also raises questions about the racialized nature of that logic.

The remainder of this chapter considers Alberta Hunter's rumored copyright claim alongside Hanya Holm's more celebrated 1952 claim in order to take a closer look at what one dance scholar has termed the 'arduous process' of winning copyright protection for choreography in the United States (Doughty, 1982: 35). As Mark Rose writes in *Authors and Owners: The Invention of Copyright*, 'All forms of property are socially constructed and, like copyright, bear in their lineaments the traces of the struggles in which were fabricated' (1993: 8). The cases of Hunter and Holm provide an opportunity to probe key aspects of the struggles that led up to the 1976 law granting copyright protection for choreographic works in their own right. An examination of the conditions surrounding each case sheds light on the stakes involved in copyrighting dance, as well as its messy cultural politics. In particular, this chapter will demonstrate, the construction of dance as a form of intellectual property depended on and concealed a set of racialized power relations. By pairing these two historical examples, I hope to problematize notions of authorship that have supported distinctions between art and culture and that have in part justified the existence of a separate genre called 'world dance.' By implication, I also aim to expose the American stage as a site of the 'worlding' of dance and, concomitantly, to destabilize the construct of 'world dance' by showing how its operations and categorizations have played out at home.

The Black Bottom and battles over the 'little ewe lamb of originality'

There is no consensus on the origins of the Black Bottom as a social dance or stage dance. In 1919, the African American musician and songwriter Perry Bradford published a dance-song called 'The Original Black Bottom Dance.' He maintained that it was a version of a much earlier dance popular in Jacksonville, Florida, updated with new lyrics and a new name. Others claimed that the 'Black Bottom' referred to a black section in Atlanta – or to an area of Nashville or Detroit – and still others that the dance originated along the banks of the Suwanee River, or, alternately, in the Louisiana swamps (Lee, 1927: 289; Stearns, 1968: 110–11).[9] According to Marshall and Jean Stearns, African Americans had been performing variations of the Black Bottom dance in tent shows and vaudeville for years prior to Bradford's publication, and the dance may have first reached New York in Irvin C. Miller's 1924 revue *Dinah* at the Lafayette Theatre (Stearns, 1968: 110–11). Whatever its genesis, the white dancer Ann Pennington's rendition of the Black Bottom in the 1926 version of George White's annual Broadway revue *Scandals* introduced the dance to a much broader audience, and it quickly came to rival the Charleston as the latest rage. The Black Bottom spread across the country and jumped the Atlantic, appearing on theatrical stages, in dance halls, and, in 'refined' form, in ballrooms. Performed to the same syncopated music of the Charleston, the Black Bottom required moving on the off-beat and involved some combination of hopping forward and back, stomping, swaying the knees, and, in some versions, slapping one's own backside.

Two chronicles of American theatre state that Alberta Hunter copyrighted the Black Bottom. In their history *Show Biz: From Vaude to Video*, published in 1951, *Variety* reporters Abel Green and Joe Laurie, Jr. assert that Hunter was 'the first woman to present the dance' and 'had it copyrighted' (227). And in the 1970 edition of the *New Complete Book of the American Musical Theater*, David Ewen writes that the Black Bottom was, in the opinion of some, 'invented by Alberta Hunter, who copyrighted it in 1926' (175).[10] Frank Taylor's 1987 biography of Hunter refers to Green and Laurie's claim but does not corroborate it. Instead, Taylor explains, 'Alberta was embarrassed by the suggestion that she had much to do with a dance that was heavy bump and grind. When asked to describe it, she said, "Oh, it was just a certain, tricky kind of step"' (Taylor and Cook, 1987: 74).

A search of records conducted by the Library of Congress's Copyright Office turned up no documentation of Hunter's registration of the dance.[11] It is possible that her claim was rejected by the Office on the grounds that the Black Bottom was not a dramatic composition. It is equally possible that Hunter's claim was only ever rhetorical, meant to deter others from usurping credit for the dance. But if Hunter later distanced herself from the Black Bottom, and if the allegation that she copyrighted the dance cannot be substantiated, it is no less significant. The assertion that this black blues singer secured legal protection for a dance with African American roots just as it was capturing the fascination of the white mainstream has much to tell us about the history and nature of debates over authorship and ownership in dance.

Though Hunter (1895–1984) is known primarily as a singer and song-writer, she also headed up a vaudeville act that toured the Keith circuit for several years in the mid-1920s, performing a combination of song, dance, and comedy (Taylor and Cook, 1987: 68–86). And if she believed she was among the first to introduce a stage version of the Black Bottom, she had good reason to seek copyright protection. When *George White's Scandals* began its 424-performance run at the Apollo Theatre on Broadway in June 1926, its chief claim to fame was the originality of the Black Bottom dance it featured. As the display advertisement that ran in the *New York Times* announced, 'The Dance Black Bottom was invented and staged by George White and the Black Bottom can be seen only at George White's Scandals' (1926: 29). An article in the *Times* reiterated and elaborated on the claim, stating that White hoped to 'make it clear that he, and he alone, was the originator of those grotesque gyrations to which the name Black Bottom has been applied' ('Concerning George White,' 1926: X4). Though White was a hoofer before he became a producer, there is little question that his claims were, at best, exaggerated hype.[12]

Indeed, challenges to White's claims were immediate. In a letter to the editor written in response to the *Times* article, famed African American composer Will Marion Cook took exception to the contention that White was the creator of the Charleston and Black Bottom:

> I have the greatest respect for Mr. White, his genius as an organizer and producer of reviews; but why do an injustice to the black folk of America by taking from them the credit of creating new and characteristic dances?
>
> From 'Old Jim Crow' to 'Black Bottom,' the negro dances came from the Cotton Belt, the levee, the Mississippi River, and are African in inspiration. The American negro, in search of outlet for emotional expression, recreates and broadens these dances. Either in their crude state, or revised form, in St. Louis, Chicago or New York the dance is discovered (?) by white theatrical producers and sold to the public as an original creation….
>
> [F]or many years, the 'Black Bottom' has been evolving in the South. Irvin Miller first produced the dance about three years ago in New York at Lafayette theatre. Two years ago Louis Douglass [sic], famous in Europe, thrilled all Paris as he and Josephine Baker 'Black Bottomed' at the Champs-Elysée Theatre.
>
> Messrs. White et al. are great men and great producers. Why, with their immense flocks of dramatic and musical sheep, should they wish to reach out and grab our little ewe lamb of originality?
>
> (Cook, 1926: X8)

Though couched in deferential language, Cook's indignation is plain. Accusing White of depriving 'the black folk of America' rightful credit for the products of their creativity and labor, Cook implies that the 'little ewe lamb' of originality is African Americans' one source of capital in a cultural marketplace dominated by 'flocks' of white wealth and resources.

For Cook, the mis-credited authors of the Black Bottom are African Americans as a group, not Alberta Hunter. Still, claims that she secured a copyright for the Black Bottom may have been motivated by precisely the sentiments he articulates. For Hunter, that is, copyright may have functioned largely as a 'defense mechanism' against what Andrew Ross, writing about the American musical arena, has termed a 'racist history of exploitation exclusively weighted to dominant white interests' (1989: 68). Whereas Cook counters George White's professions of originality by alerting newspaper readers to the African American progenitors of the Black Bottom, Hunter's copyright claim (real or rumored) raises the stakes by declaring the Black Bottom a work of individual black authorship deserving of intellectual property rights.

Certainly, Hunter had first-hand experience with exploitation in show business. As a solo singer at the Dreamland Café in Chicago, Hunter attracted notice from a number of white entertainers, including Al Jolson, Sophie Tucker, and Eddie Cantor, who attended her performances, studied her style, and put it to their own use (Harrison, 1988: 203–4, 210; Taylor and Cook, 1987: 38–9). Without question, emulation and borrowing were par for the course in the realm of cabarets, nightclubs, and vaudeville. But under a racist power structure, white performers received top billing and greater remuneration.[13] Record executives, meanwhile, routinely cheated black talent out of royalties. Always interested in securing credit and compensation for her musical compositions, Hunter received her first copyright in 1922 for 'Down Hearted Blues,' her most successful song, co-authored with Lovie Austin. Yet for years, as biographer Taylor writes, 'she got no royalty payments for most of the songs she recorded, much less for the songs she wrote that other people recorded' (1987: 65). Part of the problem was that the black manager of Paramount's 'race' record series, Mayo Williams, regularly added names to the list of authors of Hunter's compositions, and then withheld their cut of the royalties.[14] Hunter's experiences made her vigilant. As she once told an interviewer, 'I never hum a song for anybody until I have it copyrighted' ('OnStage': 118).

Though Hunter fought hard all her life to receive due credit and payment for her work, white control over the means of production made for an unequal playing field that put African American performers at a serious disadvantage. By way of comparison, as a singer in the touring production of the musical revue *How Come?*, one of her most financially successful gigs in the early 1920s, Hunter made around $125 a week. This was no paltry sum relative to the average annual salary for an American worker, around $1400 (Harrison, 1988: 207).[15] But by 1920, the white dancer Ann Pennington, who began her career earning $40 a week in 1916 as a Ziegfeld Follies chorus girl, was making $1000 a week (Freeman, 1971: 46). And the weekly box-office receipts of George White's 1926 edition of *Scandals*, in which Pennington danced her version of the Black Bottom, topped $40,000 ('News and Gossip,' 1926: X1). Economic disparities aside, the productions in which Alberta Hunter appeared could hardly compete for audiences with a white-produced musical revue with white stars and a long run on Broadway. Her ability to garner recognition for her staging of the Black Bottom was thus severely compromised. Without the stamp of copyright to authorize Hunter's version as an original, George White's claim to be the inventor and exclusive exhibitor of the Black Bottom was capable of steamrolling evidence to the contrary. Asserting collective authorship in this climate was not enough; a work had to be individually authored to qualify as intellectual property. Even unsubstantiated, Hunter's copyright claim should thus be seen as a weapon against and check on white hegemony in the theatrical marketplace.

Approached in this light, the assertion that Hunter copyrighted the Black Bottom, coupled as it usually is with references to George White and Ann Pennington, may hint at an alternative interpretation of copyright: as an individual claim made partly on behalf of a disenfranchised group. As Hunter told the *Daily Worker* in 1939: 'For every Negro who reaches the top in the face of all the rank discrimination in the commercial theatre [...] thousands of other gifted Negroes never have a chance. Their folk songs [...] eventually die without ever being recorded, and if they are recorded, then some song promoter gets the credit for composing them and the cash for selling them' (Randall: 1939). I am not suggesting that Hunter was somehow uninterested in her own personal advancement. But given her relative commercial success, it is certainly possible that her claim on the Black Bottom was made in recognition – rather than in contradiction – of communal African American authorship of the dance.[16] The fact that reports of Hunter's copyright persisted in several channels is proof of its effectiveness as a discourse of power. At least some in the theatre world believed that, however many African Americans contributed to the creation of the Black Bottom, it met the criteria for copyright protection when transformed into a stage routine – and that, as such, Hunter was entitled to credit.

Hanya Holm and *Kiss Me, Kate*: high-brow meets 'low-down'

On 30 December 1948, *Kiss Me, Kate*, the backstage musical about a group of performers in a Baltimore production of Shakespeare's *The Taming of the Shrew*, opened at the New Century Theatre on Broadway. Written by Bella and Samuel Spewack, with music and lyrics by Cole Porter, the show ran for a staggering 1077 performances, becoming 'one of the outstanding successes of the American theater' (Ewen, 1970: 277). The musical's choreographer was the German émigré Hanya Holm (1893–1992), considered one of the 'Big Four' pioneers of American modern dance, along with Martha Graham, Doris Humphrey, and Charles Weidman. A disciple of German expressionist dancer Mary Wigman, Holm moved to the United States in 1931 and directed the New York branch of the Wigman School, renamed the Hanya Holm school in 1936. From 1934 to 1939, she also taught at the Bennington School of Dance in Vermont, the precursor to the American Dance Festival. In 1937, she premiered her celebrated dance work *Trend* and began touring the country with her own dance company. Forced by financial pressures to disband her troupe in 1947, Holm went on to choreograph dances for several Broadway musicals in addition to *Kiss Me, Kate*, including *My Fair Lady* (1956) and *Camelot* (1960).

In the dance community, the popular success of *Kiss Me, Kate* was less notable than the copyright registration Holm obtained for its choreography in March 1952. During rehearsals for a London production of *Kiss Me, Kate* in the fall of 1950, Holm enlisted the help of Ann Hutchinson to notate the musical's dances using Labanotation, a system of symbols used to record movement based on the ideas of Rudolf Laban ('Copyright by Hanya Holm,' 1965: 44). It was this Labanotated score (actually a microfilmed version of it) that Holm submitted to the Copyright Office in Washington DC. Though the score was registered as a dramatico-musical composition since there was still no separate classification for choreographic works, the dance press celebrated the news as a momentous first and a major step forward for the entire dance field. As the *Dance Observer*'s Lucy Wilder proclaimed, 'Thus the battle of choreographers for legal recognition and protection passed into history. From now on, dance works are to be considered artistic property and must be protected as such' (1952: 69). In *Dance Magazine*, Nelson Lansdale wrote that the 'creation of dance has at last been legally accepted in the same way, and on the same level, as creation in other fields. Protected by a copyright, the choreographer has the same rights as the author, the composer, and the playright' [sic] (1952: 21). John Martin of the *New York Times* explained that the development not only gave 'official recognition to the dance creator' but also demonstrated the 'practicability of dance notation' and laid the ground for establishing 'an available literature of dance compositions [...] for future generations to study and consult' (1952a: X10). Or, as he later summarized, 'technological progress, property rights and the tangibility of artistic creation are all served' (Martin, 1952b: X2).

However much the copyright achievement signaled the growing currency of Labanotation as a method of 'fixing' movement, it is the elevation of the choreographer and the choreographic work afforded by Labanotation that most interests me here. If, as Lucy Wilder maintained, 'Th[e] seemingly simple procedure [of Holm submitting her Labanotated score to the Copyright Office] has changed overnight the status of choreographers and their works,' what kind of conceptual redefinition of the choreographer accompanied her new legal standing, and what can this tell us about shifting constructions of authorship in dance (1952: 69)? In particular, I want to explore some of the implications – and contradictions – of bestowing property rights on a renowned modern dance choreographer for dances enacted on the Broadway stage. A review of the conditions of production and reception for *Kiss Me, Kate*'s choreography reveals the tangled racial and artistic politics that needed to be covered over in order for the choreographer to emerge as a protected author of an original work.

The choreography for the 'relentlessly danced' *Kiss Me, Kate* ran the gamut of dance styles, including, as Walter Terry wrote in the *New York Herald Tribune*, 'classic ballet, modern dance, jitterbugging, softshoe, acrobatics, court dance, folk dance and episodes which might be described as rhythmic playfulness' (Mordden, 1999: 256; Terry, n.d., n.p.). The musical's show-within-a show framework lent itself to this variety, with the Shakespearean segments facilitating a pavane court dance, for example, and the backstage scenes calling for jazzier, more contemporary dance numbers.

This was not exactly the kind of material that Holm was known for. Her lecture-demonstrations and choreographic compositions from the 1930s and 1940s melded German expressionist and emerging American modern dance styles and were comprised of ballet-inflected lyrical movements, repetitive exercises, and methodical explorations of space. Though Holm made her Broadway debut earlier in 1948 in *Ballet Ballads*, a suite of three one-act dances to which she contributed a number called 'The Eccentricities of Davey Crockett,' *Kiss Me, Kate* was seen

as a departure for her, and critics took note. As John Martin gushed in
the *Times*:

> Nobody could have stepped more gracefully into a new field than
> Hanya Holm has done in her transition from the concert dance to
> show business. The dances she has created for 'Kiss Me, Kate' are her
> first for a Broadway musical, but they have about them the ease and
> finish of a veteran. What is equally noteworthy, they have retained
> the taste, formal integrity and the respect for the movement of the
> human body which belong to the concert dance, without in the least
> disturbing the equanimity of the paying customers.
>
> The surface of Miss Holm's dances, ranging as it does frequently
> into the hot and the blue and the jittery, is so remote from what she
> has done in the past that there is a temptation to be startled, even to
> feel a momentary doubt that she could have had anything to do with
> it. But one who knows his Holm soon realizes that, paradoxically
> enough, the very atypicalness of it all makes it typical [...].
>
> It is highly unorthodox to think of a Broadway musical as having
> style, though all of them do, whether by design or misfortune. 'Kiss
> Me, Kate' has a definite style – two of them, as a matter of fact, which
> are inclined either to supplement each other or undo each other,
> depending on your point of view. It is, on the one hand, smart, witty,
> intellectually fresh and charming, as when it deals with a pair of
> actors playing their own marital give-and-take against a background
> of 'The Taming of the Shrew'; on the other hand, chiefly in a series
> of fairly irrelevant interludes, it goes in for a style that can perhaps
> be described as a kind of chichi low-down.
>
> Miss Holm indulges both of them to the top of their bent. The
> choreography is at all times completely of the texture of the show.
> Nowhere, from the rise of the first curtain to the fall of the last, is
> there a characteristic Holm movement; she has apparently not been
> tempted in the least to superimpose herself upon the production, but
> has given her attention wholly to bringing out and pointing up what
> is inherent in it.
>
> (1949b: X6)

Martin's praise is telling for its apparent paradoxes. He seems to bend
over backwards to applaud Holm for bringing her concert dance sens-
ibility ('taste, formal integrity, and [...] respect for the movement of the
human body') to Broadway and for simultaneously effacing herself,
so much so that he briefly questions whether she choreographed the

musical's dancing at all. Here, then, the 'original' stamp of the choreographer is significant in – and precisely for – its absence. For Martin, it is the ability of this 'highest-browed of modern dance creators' to produce 'a set of completely un-highbrow dances' that merits commendation (1949a: SM18).

The class dimensions of Martin's appraisal are barely veiled. Though Holm hails from the high art realm of concert dance, she refuses to 'look down her nose at the Broadway medium.' Rather, she delivers dance numbers 'rich in invention and in formal design' to 'paying customers' who are 'not aware that they care about such things' (Martin, 1951: X8). The effect of his comments is only to reify the art versus entertainment divide.

Yet the shock of Holm's engagement with the 'chichi low-down' also betrays a more subtle racial dynamic at work. Martin's reference to 'the hot and the blue and the jittery,' I want to suggest, is code for the presence of African American dance styles in Holm's choreography. While noting his preference for the 'elegan[t] dances of the Shakespeare scenes,' Martin also admires Holm's efforts in two of the backstage numbers: 'Another Op'nin', Another Show,' in which Holm's 'compositional skills [...] give distinction to what might otherwise be just an ordinary jazz routine,' and 'Too Darn Hot,' 'one of the show's more popular but less memorable items,' for which she provides 'a background and a continuity' (1949b: X6).

In contrast to Martin, most critics favored these two numbers, described by Holm as 'intrinsically American jazz dancing' (1951: n.p.). 'Another Op'nin',' which launched the first act, was sung by Hattie the maid, one of a handful of black parts in the almost exclusively white musical, played in the original production by Annabelle Hill. The dancing, however, featured an all-white ensemble – six men and six women – who performed in a 'lyric jazz' style that was essentially an amalgamation of jazz and ballet (Labanotated score, Todd, 1949: 28–9, *Kiss Me, Kate* Dance Clippings File).

'Too Darn Hot,' meanwhile, which opened the second act, displayed a 'different style of jazziness' that was no doubt attributable to its black performers (Guest, 1993: 363). Set in a back-stage alley where cast members played dice and smoked cigarettes, the number was sung by Lorenzo Fuller, who played the black valet Paul, and featured the 'lusty Harlem hoofing' of a pair of 'Specialty Dancers': the African Americans Fred Davis and Eddie Sledge, who were eventually joined by the white soloist Harold Lang ('Theater Dance,' 1949). Notwithstanding Martin's quibble, 'Too Darn Hot' was a show-stopper.

Holm's contributions to 'Too Darn Hot' were limited to creating 'some non-intruding but atmospherically effective jitterbug passages' for the Dancing Ensemble, who supported Fuller, Davis, Sledge, and Lang (Terry). The Labanotated score for 'Too Darn Hot' records only this background dancing, with the explanation that 'The exact arrangement varied according to what the negros [sic] could do' and that a stage reconstruction would require 'fresh choreography' (*Kiss Me, Kate* Labanotated Score). Indeed, it evidently became custom to employ an African American dance duo in this slot. As reported by the Stearns, the comedy-dance team of Charles Cook and Ernest Brown appeared briefly in *Kiss Me, Kate* while it was still on Broadway (it ran until July 1951) (Stearns, 1968: 245). And in 1953, Honi Coles and Cholly Atkins performed in a summer stock production of the musical in Texas (Atkins and Malone, 2001: 97).

This format of inserting African American 'specialty' dancers into a Broadway musical was hardly new.[17] Yet even if Davis and Sledge's tap dancing was not included in the Labanotated score submitted to the Copyright Office and struck some as 'rather alien to the rest of the choreography,' the recognition Holm received as choreographer of *Kiss Me, Kate*, including her copyright victory and a New York Drama Critics' Award, raises key questions about white ownership of black choreographic labor (Todd, 1949: 28–9). The experience of Coles and Atkins in another Broadway musical proves instructive. In 1949, the pair joined the cast of *Gentlemen Prefer Blondes*, choreographed by Agnes DeMille, and were featured in a second-act number called 'Mamie is Mimi.' Recounting the episode in *Jazz Dance*, Cholly Atkins offers a window onto the choreographic process:

'During rehearsals Agnes de Mille didn't know what to do with us,' says Coles, 'so finally Julie Styne, who hired us, took us aside and said, "Look, why don't you fellows work up something, and I'll get her to look at it." ' They located arranger Benny Payne, who knew how to write for tap-dance acts, and the three of them worked out a routine. 'One afternoon, Miss de Mille took time off to look at it,' says Atkins. 'She liked it and told us to keep it in.'

On went the show with the Coles-Atkins-Payne routine a hit, and Agnes de Mille listed as choreographer in the program. 'Later on we had to get her permission to use our routine on Jack Haley's *Ford Hour*,' says Coles. 'She was very nice about it.' In her autobiography Miss de Mille writes that the 'Mamie Is Mimi' number, along with several others, was devised 'in a single short rehearsal,' presumably by Miss de Mille. This was the standard practice.

(Stearns, 1968: 309)

Though it would be specious to treat the cases of Coles and Atkins in *Gentlemen Prefer Blondes* and Davis and Sledge in *Kiss Me, Kate* as interchangeable, it seems safe to assume that 'Too Darn Hot' was put together in a somewhat analogous way. There was, of course, a long history in the American theatre of white artists and producers taking credit for dancing created by African American performers, as George White's claims to have invented the Black Bottom attest. And much as White's economic capital trumped (or tried to trump) black artists' claims of originality with respect to that dance routine, Holm's cultural capital – as the 'highest-browed of modern dance creators' – eclipsed the labor of the African American dancers on whose creativity her choreographic success partly depended.

To be sure, Holm's legally sanctioned status as sole choreographer of *Kiss Me, Kate* masked the labor of additional dancers as well. As others have noted, Holm characteristically relied on improvisation as a compositional method in both her classes and her choreography. Modern dancer and choreographer Alwin Nikolais, for example, recalled that 'when Hanya was working on a particular subject she would frequently ask the dancers to improvise on the subject and she would spot the interesting aspects the individual dancer might come up with. Once recognizing these aspects, she would hold onto them, remake them, or develop them from that point into her choreography' (qtd Sorrell, 1969: 165). Holm biographer Walter Sorell emphasizes the importance of this method for choreographing solo dances in musicals, describing how 'Hanya watches the particular attributes of a soloist and then tries to find a range of movement to suit that particular body' (1969: 165).

Interviews with dancers from the original *Kiss Me, Kate* production, recorded on the 1988 video *Hanya: Portrait of a Pioneer*, make clear the extent to which she imported this modern compositional technique into the Broadway milieu. Glen Tetley, who both danced in and worked as Holm's assistant on *Kiss Me, Kate*, explained that 'this was an unheard of way of working in the speeded-up atmosphere of a Broadway stage, and when Hanya [...] set up the structure of an improvisation class, say for the first day of a show like *Kiss Me, Kate*, there were a lot of blank looks [...].' Some, like Harold Lang, one of the musical's leads, were openly hostile to Holm's improvisational methods. A principal at the American Ballet Theatre, Lang initially protested, declaring, 'I will do anything you want but you are going to have to show me. I am not going to make up steps.' Eventually relenting, he 'threw in a few steps of *Swan Lake'* and started to 'blend what she was giving me with the techniques that I had learned in performing musical comedy and ballet' (*Hanya: Portrait of a Pioneer,* 1988). Like Lang, Shirley Eckl, another lead dancer in the musical, was a renowned member of the American Ballet Theatre, so it is likely that her classical technique also left its mark on *Kiss Me, Kate*.[18] It would seem, then, that what critic John Martin identified as the musical's stylistic split between the more 'elegant' Shakespearean dancing and the jazzier interludes was in part a manifestation of the different corporeal dispositions and choreographic contributions of the dancers with whom Holm worked. That is not to say that Holm was undeserving of the credit she received for the dances in *Kiss Me, Kate*, nor that her own choreographic labor was any less than that of the cast. It is to point out, rather, that the choreography that became her intellectual property did not originate solely or directly from her.[19]

If Holm's use of improvisation to generate movement seemed 'out of this world' to the ballet-trained Lang, it was a compositional strategy that was far from alien to those trained in African American dance traditions (*Hanya: Portrait of a Pioneer,* 1988). Scholar Jacqui Malone names improvisation as 'one of the key elements in the creation of vernacular dance,' and both Brenda Dixon Gottschild and Susan Leigh Foster have pointed to the Africanist influences on white modern and postmodern choreographers' turn to improvisation (Dixon Gottschild, 1996: 49; Foster, 2002: 24–34; Malone, 1996: 33). Though Holm's improvisational practice traced back to her training with Mary Wigman, the copresence of European 'high art' and Africanist 'low art' choreographic approaches in the making of *Kiss Me, Kate* suggests how constructed the opposition between the two is. At the very least, there is irony in the fact that a white modern dance artist 'made history' by winning copyright protection – and thereby elevating the figure of the choreographer – using a compositional technique long embraced by African American artists, whose expressive output has so often been dismissed as custom-bound and derivative rather than experimental and innovative.

Instead of calling into question notions of the choreographer as the autonomous creator, however, Holm's working methods in the mixed-race and mixed-genre venue of Broadway seem to have had precisely the converse effect. As John Martin's comments evidence, perceptions of a stark contrast between the high-browed Holm and the low-browed (or middle-browed) arena of musical theatre served to make Holm's choreographic expertise more conspicuous, not less.[20] The distinction that Holm gained through her association with racialized forms and styles, I would argue, may well have played a role in the Copyright Office's decision to award her a copyright for her *Kiss Me, Kate* choreography. In other words, it was not just Labanotation that was gaining acceptance in official halls of power, but also the pre-eminence of the white choreographer.

While Holm's bid for copyright protection traded on and bolstered her cultural and racial capital, it was also motivated by economic considerations. In addition to granting her sole choreographic credit in 'theatre programs, billboard posters and newspaper advertisements,' Holm's *Kiss Me, Kate* contract earned her a salary of $4500, plus one-quarter of one percent of weekly box-office grosses for try-out engagements and touring performances.[21] Though she was given the option to oversee subsequent stagings by Arnold St Subber's production team (an option she exercised for the 1951 London production of the musical), this apparently did little to prevent others from pilfering her movement material for their own productions. In a 1985 interview, Holm maintained that she sought the copyright 'because there was an awful lot of lifting going on' (*Eye on Dance*, 1985). And as she told reporters at the time of the registration, 'Some people have wonderful photographic memory [...]. The creative goods are used without proper credit and justice to the originator. They even do their own stuff and use your name on it' (qtd Beckley, 1952). Critics viewed Holm's copyright achievement as a solution to this problem of piracy. 'When Broadway musicals are released for stock,' John Martin spelled out, 'it is not infrequent for a summer theatre to engage as choreographer some member of the original dance company to restage the dances after the manner of the original production. For this, the original choreographer receives neither credit nor royalties' (1952a: X10). Nelson Lansdale of *Dance Magazine* saw appropriation abroad as a more insidious threat than summer stock, citing duplications of Broadway musicals in London, Norway, Sweden, Denmark, and Australia, with no recompense or credit for the shows' original choreographers (1952: 41). With the Copyright Office's acceptance of Holm's *Kiss Me, Kate* score, the *Dance Observer* stated, 'piracy in the dance will not only be a matter of ethics; it will be a matter of law' (Wilder, 1952: 69). Like Alberta Hunter's alleged copyright claim on the Black Bottom, Holm's copyright was propelled in some measure by reproductions that cashed in on her labor without due reward (or, in the other case Holm suggests, that cashed in on her name while misrepresenting her labor). The circumstances surrounding Holm's copyright for the choreography in *Kiss Me, Kate* thus demonstrate the impossibility of disentangling economic, cultural, and racial capital.

In point of fact, it is uncertain how much and what kind of legal protection Holm's registration of the Labanotated choreographic score of *Kiss Me, Kate* actually afforded. In a 1950 letter to Ann Hutchinson, Richard MacCarteney, the Library of Congress official, admitted, 'I do not know that a court of law would necessarily hold that copyrighting a dance notation score thereby resulted in the dance itself being copyrighted. The Certificate of Registration may or may not be of great value.'[22] Absent an infringement lawsuit to test its validity, Holm's copyright may have held more symbolic than substantive legal weight.

The importance of this symbolic weight, however, should not be underestimated. Like rumors of Hunter's Black Bottom copyright, reports of Holm's copyright registration rippled through the concert dance community, augmenting Holm's authority in the process. For those who championed the cause of modern and ballet as 'serious' forms of artistic expression, Holm's copyright achievement represented a proxy victory for the figure of the choreographer at large, now officially recognized as an author in her own right. No doubt, too, the *Kiss Me, Kate* case helped garner momentum for the 1976 Copyright Act, which explicitly gave choreography protected intellectual property status. Yet granting the choreographer property rights necessitated papering over the non-autonomous and non-original aspects of the choreographic process: its collaborations, borrowings, appropriations, and vitally, its dependence on the labor of racialized others.

Conclusion

What can we draw from this comparison of the cases of Alberta Hunter and Hanya Holm? To begin with, the conditions that engendered Hunter's and Holm's copyright claims support Rosemary Coombe's assertion that 'Authorship as a social and legal institution historically originated and was shaped by encounters with others' (1998a: 257). Whether it was in Hunter's case, the clash between black and white dancers over the Black Bottom, or in Holm's, the brush between a European modern dancer and African American tap dancers, interracial entanglements lay at the root of both attempts to establish choreographic authorship. It is not insignificant that these encounters occurred within US borders. The fact that Holm's copyright victory depended on a racialized logic that granted single-author property rights to a white woman while withholding those rights from African Americans makes plain that the 'worlding' of dance has not been exclusively a transnational phenomenon. The same classification schemes and operations of power through which the West has defined itself against the Rest, that is to say, have been equally at work at home, no less within that most American of institutions, Broadway.

At the same time, these examples suggest that the racialized categories of authorship on which choreographic copyright has depended in the United States cannot be sustained. Even as the logic of copyright inscribes a division between individual artistry and collective culture, the cases of Hunter and Holm put the lie to this dichotomy. Reports of Hunter's copyright of the Black Bottom demonstrate that vernacular dances, however multiple and complex their origins, are hardly immune from individual claims of authorship and contests over attribution. The choreography that resulted in Holm's copyright milestone, meanwhile, fell far short of the Romantic model of the solitary genius creating in a void. If the distinctions between art as single-authored choreography and culture as anonymously-produced dancing cannot be upheld, and if those same distinctions have supported the existence of a separate category called 'world dance,' it seems only appropriate to ask: Can something called 'world dance' continue to exist?

Yet finally, the foregoing analysis reveals just how complicated the power dynamics of copyright can be. As evidenced by the privileging of fixed, 'original' creations over improvisatory, participatory forms, and by the success of Holm's claim relative to Hunter's, copyright has unmistakably favored majority white interests. But it is also clear that there has been no monopoly on turning to copyright for protection. Hunter's association with copyright is a compelling illustration of how invocations of property rights could be mobilized in a bid to redistribute the power held by white producers and dancers in the theatrical marketplace. Crucially, then, copyright has been a tool for both consolidating and contesting power. As copyright debates heat up around the globe in the twenty-first century, it is worth bearing this duality in mind. Rather than rushing to condemn copyright claims as greed-motivated power grabs that squelch the 'free' exchange of ideas, or championing copyright as the best safeguard of artists' livelihood and integrity, we need to scrutinize the specific contexts in which copyright claims arise and play out. Above all, we need to remain alert to the particularized relations of power that inhere in contests for credit and ownership.

Notes

1. This chapter has benefited enormously from the incisive feedback of the fellow authors represented in this volume. My sincere gratitude to all of them.

2. Mehta's op ed piece points compellingly to the interrelationship between India's pre-emptive cataloging of yoga poses, the widespread Western profiting from Indian knowledge and resources, and regulations enacted under pressure from the World Trade Organization that make the copying of Western drugs illegal in India. On the issues of copyrighting yoga see Machan, 2004; Susman, 2004/05.

3. In the late twentieth century, the United States became a party to multilateral intellectual property law treaties like the Berne Convention and the World Intellectual Property Organization. In 1994, the Agreement on Trade Related Aspects of Intellectual Property Rights, administered by the World Trade Organization, set uniform standards for intellectual property protection between nations. For more on property rights in an international context, see Goldstein, 2001.

4. On the notion of 'worlding,' the process by which 'the third world' is constructed as a foreign, untapped resource, see post-colonial feminist scholar Gayatri Spivak's essay, 'Three Women's Texts and a Critique of Imperialism' (1986). Spivak cites Martin Heidegger as an influence on her development of the concept.

5. See Susan Leigh Foster, Chapter 5 in this volume for a discussion of how the early twentieth-century emergence of the term 'choreography' in the United States functioned to authorize modern dance's individual creator and exclude racialized bodies and practitioners of 'world' forms.

6. As legal scholar Melanie Cook writes, the restriction against copyrighting 'social dance steps' and 'simple routines' is 'tantamount to a legally imposed standard of artistic merit' (1977: 1299). In fact, shared thinking on the matter of art versus culture in the arenas of dance and law is no accident, for a number of legal writers have relied on Curt Sachs's *World History of the Dance* in assessing the state of copyright for dance. In a study on copyright submitted to the US Senate in 1961, Borge Varmer cites Sachs for his assessment that 'The dance is one of the oldest forms of human expression. Originally, perhaps, the bodily movements of a dance were a spontaneous expression of the dancer's emotions for his own satisfaction. Group dances following an established pattern, as in a ritual dance or a community folk dance, became a means of expressing the feelings of the group of dancers. Ultimately, the dance was developed into an art form, a work of choreography for theatrical presentation, by which bodily movements to be performed by dancers are devised to convey thought or feeling to an audience' (93). The continued authority of Sachs's book decades after its publication suggests both the far-reaching influence 'official' dance history accounts can have and the general currency of the views Sachs espoused.

7. In the years leading up to Holm's copyright victory, both Balanchine and Eugene Loring tried and failed to secure registration for their ballets. In the early 1940s, the Copyright Office apparently rejected Loring's choreography for *Billy the Kid* on the basis that the method in which it was recorded – Laban notation – was 'not yet recognized as a set system for recording movement' (in Lansdale, 1952: 21). Balanchine's *Symphony in C*, meanwhile, also submitted as a Labanotated score just a year or two prior to Holm's *Kiss Me, Kate*, failed to meet the 'dramatic' requirement (Arcomano, 1980: 59).

8. See also Doughty, 1982.

9. Other songs devoted to the Black Bottom followed Bradford's. In 1927, Jelly Roll Morton recorded the 'Black Bottom Stomp,' and in 1928, Ma Rainey recorded 'Ma Rainey's Black Bottom,' whose lyrics touted her skill at performing the popular dance (Lieb, 1981: 142–5).

10. Ewen's entry on George White's *Scandals* in an earlier edition of the volume contains no reference to Alberta Hunter or her purported copyright of the Black Bottom (1958). Although neither volume contains a bibliography or footnotes, one possible source for these texts is a 1926 newspaper article written by Lester Walton, which states, 'Alberta Hunter, a well-known Negro singer of the blues, claims the distinction of having done the [Black Bottom] before the first white audience at one of the New York vaudeville houses in 1925. She says she had it copyrighted' (6). Walton also points to an earlier source for the Black Bottom, explaining: 'So far as known, the first time the Black Bottom was put on at a New York theatre was in 1923, by Ethel Ridley in a colored musical comedy at the Lafayette Theatre in Harlem.'

11. The search was conducted by the Copyright Office in January 2006.

12. Perry Bradford was convinced that White first saw the Black Bottom in the Harlem show *Dinah* and subsequently enlisted *Scandals*'s three white composers, Buddy de Sylva, Lew Brown, and Ray Henderson, to compose a song for it (Stearns, 1968: 110–11).

13. See Brenda Dixon Gottschild (2000) for numerous examples of the exploitation of black performers in the white-controlled entertainment industry.

14. Once Hunter caught on to Williams's scheme, she arranged for artists like Ethel Waters and Fletcher Henderson to write letters to the record company avowing that they had nothing to do with songs Hunter had written (Taylor and Cook, 1987: 65).

15. According to a survey of wages conducted in the 1920s, the average annual earnings of an American worker in 1926 was $1473 (Zieger and Gall, 2002: 45). Brenda Dixon Gottschild reports that the average musician who toured the black vaudeville circuit in the 1920s received a weekly salary of $35, plus a $5 meal ticket (2000: 93).

16. This would accord with Rosemary Coombe's reminder that the use of 'the idiom of property' by indigenous peoples may be a call for 'a preliminary recognition of proprietary claims – not as exclusivity of possession but as bundles of multiple rights and relationships [...]' (Coombe, 1998b: 208).

17. For example, Lew Leslie hired Bill Robinson as an 'Extra Attraction' in the *Blackbirds of 1928*, Bill Bailey appeared as a 'Specialty Dancer' in *Swingin' the Dream* (1939), and the Nicholas Brothers performed in *Babes in Arms* (1937) and *St. Louis Woman* (1946).

18. Ann Hutchinson Guest's discussion of the musical corroborates the recollections of the original cast members. 'The nature of the dances in *Kate*,' she writes, 'allowed for specific contributions to be made by the performers' (Guest, 1993: 364–5).

19. Evidently, Holm also relied on the work of dance collectors like Curt Sachs in deriving the folk choreography for *Kiss Me, Kate*. Her notes for the production contain descriptions of the Fandango and the Tarantella transcribed directly from Sachs's *World History of the Dance* (Hanya Holm Papers). Holm's turn to Sachs is another indication of how pervasive his influence was.

20. See Levine, 1988, on the racial roots of the terms 'high-brow' and 'low-brow,' which derived from the nineteenth-century pseudo-science of phrenology.
21. Contract between Hanya Holm and Arnold St Subber, The Salem Company, 30 September 1948 (Hanya Holm Papers). It is not known how much the dancers were paid, although a later contract indicates that $2500 of Holm's salary was deducted to pay for her assistant, Ray Harrison. Contract between St Subber, Salem Company and Hanya Holm, 5 October 1948 (Hanya Holm Papers).
22. Letter from Richard S. MacCarteney to Ann Hutchinson, 4 August 1950 (Hanya Holm Papers).

5
Choreographies and Choreographers

Susan Leigh Foster

The *Oxford English Dictionary* offers two definitions for the word 'choreography': the first, a beguilingly simple assertion, informs us that choreography is 'the art of dancing'; and the second, marked as an obsolete usage, refers to choreography as 'the art of writing dances on paper.' The first definition identifies all aspects of dance as choreographic, whether the process of teaching someone how to dance, the act of learning to dance, the event of performing a dance, or the labor of creating a dance. The second definition, used perhaps for the last time by Rudolf Laban in his *Choreutics* (1966), specifies choreographers as those who endeavor to notate through the use of abstract symbols the spatial and rhythmic properties of movement. Neither definition, it seems to me, conveys its current usage as the act of arranging patterns of movement. Within the last year, for example, the *Los Angeles Times* has utilized the term to describe troop movements in Iraq, the management of discussion at board meetings, the co-ordination of traffic lights for commuter flow, the motions of dog whisperer Cesar Millan, and the art of making a dance. This variety of usages suggests that choreography has come to refer to a plan or orchestration of bodies in motion. And in this refined definition, the plan is distinguished from its implementation and from the skills necessary for its execution.

At the same time that the term is being implemented in a wide variety of contexts, it is also being ignored or suppressed in others. Two recent and highly popular TV shows that feature dance, *So You Think You Can Dance* and *Dancing With the Stars*, consistently refrain from addressing the creative process of selecting and sequencing the movement that is performed. The young artists who audition for *So You Think You Can Dance* have devised their own original dance; however, once they are accepted onto the show, they are placed in technique classes for weeks and judged, not on the basis of their compositional skills, but instead on their abilities to take the dance class – that is, to faithfully copy what another body is doing and then perform that movement fully. They are never given a course in dance composition or taught anything about how to invent or sequence movement. Similarly, the 'trainer-partners' on *Dancing With the Stars*, who make up the routines that make the stars look good in performance, are only credited with being excellent dancers and partners. Why ignore or suppress this labor? Is it the lure of a pure or natural performance, achieved by hard work at disciplining the body but not at crafting its motions? Is it a reluctance to imagine that one's identity can be and is shaped through the moves one makes? Or perhaps it is a function of the hierarchical distinctions between art and social or popular dance forms.

What is at stake in partitioning 'the art of dancing' into the acts of making, performing, and learning to dance? And how has the categorization of dance into traditional or contemporary, social or artistic, effected the interpretation of the processes by which it comes into existence? This chapter excavates two distinctive meanings of the term choreography in order to assess how they have impacted our understanding of dances and dance-making worldwide. By 'our understanding' I refer particularly to US dance scholarship and its connection to dance curricula located within university settings. The integration of dance as a discipline into universities across the United States was accomplished through an emphasis on the individual creative process that early twentieth-century modern dance espoused. Courses in learning to dance and making original dances, inflected with universalist assumptions about the nature of movement and expression that I will outline below, formed the core of the curriculum. These were followed by courses in other techniques such as ballet, jazz, and European folk forms, occasional social dance forms, courses in history or anthropology of dance, and eventually, courses in dances from around the world, most often South and East Asia, Indonesia, and West Africa. Positioned within programs that valued single-authored, non-improvised, experimental works of art and techniques based on 'universal' principles of movement, these folk and non-Western forms were often seen as unchanging, culturally specific traditions that preserved an older and perhaps vanishing way of life.

In her ground-breaking essay 'An Anthropologist Looks at Ballet as a Form of Ethnic Dance,' Joann Kealiinohumoku addressed the marginalized status these forms have endured in US universities by proposing to look at the unmarked form of ballet as an ethnic form. In addition, she alluded to the typical association of choreography with individual innovation by observing that among the Hopi Indians of Northern Arizona, there is no practice of naming a choreographer. Nevertheless they definitely know who, within a Kiva group or a society, made certain innovations and why (1983: 36). Here Kealiinohumoku, questions the tendency to envision 'traditional' dances as unchanging. And she prompts us to consider whether the concept of choreography can include a consideration of dances that are authorless, improvised, and collaborative.

This chapter follows on Kealiinohumoku's inquiry by examining historical uses of the term 'choreography.' In the same way that Anthea Kraut's essay in this volume interrogates the influence of copyright on dances and dancers, I evaluate the ideological legacy of 'choreography,' paying special attention to how it has been used to consolidate and regularize dance practices, and to instantiate typologies of dance with distinctive artistic and social merit. By examining the cultural work it has performed at different moments in history, I hope to offer a perspective on its meanings today and their impact on the ways we teach and conceptualize dance around the world.

Choreography as notating

The term 'choreography' was neologized by French dancing master Raoul Auger Feuillet with the publication of his collection of notated dances in 1700. Feuillet's *Chorégraphie, ou l'art d'écrire la danse* consolidated work that had been done by principal Dancing Master Pierre Beauchamps in response to Louis XIV's mandate to 'discover the means of making the art of dance comprehensible on paper' (qtd Harris-Warrick and Marsh, 1994: 84). According to Beauchamps, he set about 'shaping and disposing characters and notes in the form of tablature in order to represent the steps of the dances and ballets' in such a way that they could be learned 'without need of personal instruction' (qtd Harris-Warrick and Marsh, 1994: 84). Although at least three other distinctive notation systems emerged in response to Louis' mandate, Feuillet's version of Beauchamps' system predominated, becoming so popular that new collections were distributed annually for the next 30 years.

Edmund Fairfax (2003) rightfully admonishes scholars to take into account the small range of dance practices that were actually notated with Feuillet's system. They do not adequately represent dancing on any of the various stages, whether the elite, licensed productions of the

Opera or the experiments with pantomime at the fair theaters. Nor do they document the kind of aesthetic traffic in styles and vocabularies proliferated by itinerant companies of dancers who traveled back and forth across the continent and to England. Instead, these collections documented a small number of stage dances, mostly solos, as well as a variety of dances to be taught and then performed at balls and other social gatherings. They provided teachers with new material with which to instruct their students and alerted practitioners to some of the latest fashions in the art of dancing.

Nonetheless, this regularization of dances so that they might travel and be reproduced 'without the aid of personal instruction' profoundly influenced both the conceptualization of dancing and the categorization of diverse dances. Using a single classificatory rubric, the notation subjected dancing to laws that all movements appeared to share. Symbols on either side of a continuous line, tracing the dancer's pathway, indicated the exact positions and motions of the feet. As Feuillet observes, dancing is composed of 'Positions, Steps, Sinkings, Risings, Springings, Capers, Fallings, Slidings, Turnings of the Body, Cadence or Time, Figures, etc' (Weaver, 1706: 2). Sinking, rising, and springing were measured in terms of the body's vertical positioning, whereas slidings and turning marked its horizontal progress through space. Through notation, the body's motions were thereby removed from their locale and cast into the space of pure geometry.

Implementing these geometric laws of movement, the cultural specificities of particular dances were smoothed out or erased. As literary historian Jean-Noel Laurenti explains:

> The French dancing masters had to unify a vocabulary of steps with diverse origins, from the provinces or from abroad: to discover what this vast repertoire had in common, it was necessary to first distinguish all the constituent parts. This would permit the use of the same signs (in different sequence of course) to note down a minuet or passepied, originally from the west of France, as well as a gavot or a rigadoon, imported from the southeast, or a 'Spanish-style' sarabande or chaconne.
>
> (1994: 87)

Such a system allowed instructors to master various regional styles and assimilate them into a single repertoire. What had been a region's indigenous production was transformed into stylistic features of a single repertoire that set one dance apart from another.

Prior systems for documenting dances typically listed the sequence of steps with occasional references to spatial path and facings for each dancer. For example, Fabritio Caroso's explanation of the Laura Suave (Gentle Lady) in 1581 includes this description:

> the gentleman does a symmetrical variation [...of] two limping hops with the left foot raised and the right limping, two fast half Reverences [...] two falling jumps, one foot under with the left and a cadence with the left forward; repeat beginning with the right. The lady does two doubles in French style [...] two double scurrying sequences together, turning first to the left and then to the right in the shape of an S; and approaching each other, they take customary hands.
>
> (1986: 162)

The 'reverences,' 'falling jumps,' and 'doubles' referred to here were standard steps in the sixteenth-century court dance repertoire. A major innovation of Dancing Master Thoinot Arbeau, who first made the effort to notate these dances in 1589, consisted in substituting abbreviations for the names of the steps.

Feuillet's system differed markedly from these earlier attempts to record dances because it broke steps down into constituent parts, posited as universal actions. As Laurenti explains:

> Thus the notation of an apparently quite simple and very dynamic contretemps balonné [...] requires no less than eight indications: a step forward with the free leg, a sink, a spring, a foot in the air, a second sink and a spring on a half-position sign; the two groups of signs, corresponding to the two movements, are joined by a trait within the frame of the measure.
>
> (1994: 87)

Whereas the 'reverance' or 'double' in Caroso's description named a step that could be sequenced in different orders or performed at different speeds, the 'sinking,' 'rising,' and 'springing' actions in Feuillet denoted properties or characteristics of a given step. Because these characteristics were imbued with universal status as actions occurring within vertical or horizontal dimensions of space, they served as tools for analyzing any and all dances.

Although Feuillet seemingly offered the potential to evaluate the specificities of any dance, the advantages of the system seemed to lie not only in its capacity to collect and store diverse dances, but also in its portability. It enabled the dissemination of the latest and most fashionable Parisian innovations. Especially valuable for provincial instructors, these collections established a basic rubric for the teaching of dance – a set of fundamental positions and steps for the student to practice. They also offered a gradated curriculum, moving from simpler to more complex steps and phrases. And, like books of fashion plates depicting the latest sartorial innovations, they celebrated the most recent vogue in dancing. This motion from the urban centers to the periphery helped to consolidate recent efforts across the continent to build the nation-state. Securing the dominance of urban over rural aesthetics, it reinforced class-based hierarchies while at the same time transforming regional distinctiveness into genre or style.

The notation also hinted at another kind of motion, the colonial expansion from Europe and England into the rest of the world. The fact that dance's ephemerality had been conquered by notation intimated success in all kinds of colonizing projects, as this excerpt from Soame Jenyns's poem 'The Art of Dancing,' written in 1729, suggests:

> Long was the *Dancing Art* unfix'd and free;
> Hence lost in Error and Uncertainty:
> No Precepts did it mind, or Rules obey,
> But ev'ry Master taught a diff'rent Way:
> Hence, e're each new-born Dance was fully try'd,
> The lovely Product, ev'n in blooming, dy'd:
> Thro' various Hands in wild Confusion toss'd,
> Its Steps were alter'd, and its Beauties lost:
> Till *Fuillet* [sic] at length, Great Name! arose,
> And did the Dance in Characters compose:
> Each lovely Grace by certain Marks he taught,
> And ev'ry Step in lasting Volumes wrote.
> Hence o'er the World this pleasing Art shall spread,
> And ev'ry Dance in ev'ry Clime be read:
> By *distant Masters* shall each Step be seen,
> Tho' Mountains rise, and Oceans roar between.
> Hence with her Sister-Arts shall *Dancing* claim
> An equal Right to Universal Fame,
> And *Isaac's Rigadoon* shall last as long
> As *Raphael's Painting*, or as *Virgil's Song*.

(1978: 31)

In Jenyns's estimations, seventeenth-century dance had been saturated with uncertainty and confusion because it lacked rules or precepts, and hence, each teacher could interpret it differently. The transformation in form resulting from the person-to-person transmission of dances compromised or even contaminated their original beauty. Only the invention of Feuillet notation at the beginning of the eighteenth century imbued dance with a composed permanence and newfound clarity, creating a parity with dance's sister-arts of painting and poetry, and also the opportunity for dances to travel around the world.

In Jenyns's ambitious vision, the fact that dances can now travel to every climate of the world confirms the triumph of rules and order over undisciplined variation. It can likewise introduce the world's dancers to the finest accomplishments of a colonial power, or at least maintain a crucial aesthetic continuity between those living at home and those living in colonies. Perhaps this kind of transportability assuaged anxiety over profuse varieties of cultural difference being encountered and the impact that such difference might have on British culture. Perhaps this system for mastering movement even intimated standards for evaluating the civilized and the savage. Whether or not it fortified a colonizing orientation toward the world, choreography, like the taxonomic project of botany, invited its practitioners to envision the world's dances as subject to placement within a single classificatory framework.

Despite its promise, as pedagogical tool, fashion template, or portable collection of dances, the Feuillet system never enjoyed widespread use.[1] However, its conceptualization of the body helped lay the groundwork for the subsequent development of dance technique. In her comparison of mid-and late-century dance manuals, Sandra Noll Hammond shows the consistencies in their cultivation of the basic principles of movement that Feuillet had identified (Hammond, 2005). Students practiced each position and the accompanying posture necessary to perfect its presentation, and then they practiced the pliés and relevés, formerly sinkings and risings, that enabled the body to execute more complex steps and sequences.

Analogous in many respects to the musical exercises practiced by students acquiring expertise at instrument playing, these sequences confirmed the suggestion, implicit in the notation itself, that music and dance were separate yet related art forms. In Arbeau's analysis of dancing, the musical meters and rhythms were discussed first, and the movements presented as a translation or emanation of musical structure in steps. Feuillet notation, in contrast, presented a catalogue of possible types of steps, without making any mention of musical types or rhythmic structures that would necessarily correspond to these steps. The several collections of dances that used Feuillet notation likewise detached dance from music, placing the musical notation at the top of the page and the notated dance below. Dance movement thus began to acquire a materiality, one that suggested an egalitarian relationship, rather than a fusion, with music.

When the Feuillet system was devised, the acts of composing a dance, learning a dance, and learning to dance were conceptualized as over-lapping, if not identical projects. The Dancing Master, as he was called, performed professionally, and also taught students to dance by teaching them dances. He introduced new dances in order to maintain his reputation on stage and in the salon. The first choreographers, Dancing Masters themselves, typically documented dances created by others, implementing a system designed to assist in composing and transport-ing dances, one that would celebrate individual authorship by record-ing the composer's name on the page.[2]

Yet the analysis of dance movement that the notation offered implied a new status for dance in which these three functions, composing, per-forming, and practicing would, over time, become distinct practices. Notation's transmissibility and its ability to authenticate a composer imparted an objecthood for dancing as a pursuit separate from music or theater. This identity was further confirmed through the analytical framework established in the notation that broke dance down into its constituent parts. Not only were movements broken down into their most basic units, but each movement was also imbued with and located within absolute temporal and spatial matrices that delineated a meter as well as horizontal and vertical positionings of the body. Students of dance who mastered the vocabulary of positions and steps thereby mas-tered the universal laws of movement.[3]

Choreography as composing

The term choreography generally fell out of use during the nineteenth century in both French and English languages. When it was utilized in newspaper reviews or journals, it named indiscriminately the acts of dancing, learning to dance, or making a dance.[4] Only in the late 1920s and early 1930s does the term 'choreography' start to come into widespread and new usage, especially in the United States. In 1927, all three major New York City newspapers hired dance critics, and they implemented the term in all their reviews of dance concerts (Connor, 1997: 1). Reviewers began to refer not only to the choreographer as the author of a dance but to choreography as a staged presentation of movement resulting from the creative process of originating a dance. Programs for concerts also often labeled the choreographer, the composer, and the lighting and costume designers, especially when there were multiple artists contributing pieces to a single evening's presentation. And significantly, the term was introduced in the curriculum of the Bennington Summer Dance Festival, a course of study attended by many of the dance educators who went on to found university departments of dance around the country.

Beginning in 1935, Bennington offered a General Workshop that included courses in dance composition, music analysis, history and criticism, and stagecraft. It also offered a Workshop Program that consisted of a Technique course taught by Graham and a Choreography course in which she created and rehearsed her new work *Panorama*.[5] For the next several years, the workshop program was directed by different artists; Doris Humphrey and Charles Weidman in 1936, and Hanya Holm in 1937.[6] The distinction made at Bennington between composition and choreography seems to imply that students should first learn compositional principles that primarily impart an ability to analyze movement in terms of space, time, and weight.[7] In such a course students might create short studies that demonstrated their understanding of the possibilities for shaping the body as a three-dimensional object in space, and for sequencing those shapes according to various musical structures, but they did not focus on the development of a vision or argument in dance form. Only in the Choreography Workshop could these students witness and assist in the birth of a dance, one whose thematics depended upon the inspiration and genius of the artist. When, in 1936 Bennington added a new Program in Choreography, a course in 'independent composition for advanced students,' who each 'completed and presented two full-length compositions,' it reaffirmed this elite conception of choreography by identifying an exceptional few students as eligible for its study.[8]

The choreography, as the outcome of the creative process, was the property of an individual artist, not an arrangement of steps that are shared amongst a community of practitioners, as in Feuillet's time, but rather a creation of both the movement and its development through time. Furthermore, the term relied upon an even more pronounced separation of dance into the pedagogical process of learning to dance, and the creative process of making a dance. By the 1930s one trained to become a dancer using a regime of exercises, often devised by the choreographer, that, on the one hand, exemplified the choreographer's aesthetic vision and, on the other, embodied universal principles of motion. At Bennington, for example, Martha Graham, Doris Humphrey, and Hanya Holm each taught their own versions of modern dance technique, proposing distinctive sets of principles as the underlying foundation for dance movement. Students enrolled in two-week courses with two of these four choreographers, and they also studied continuously with Martha Hill in a course entitled 'Principles of Movements.'

Hill's Principles of Movements, like her approach to composition, implemented universal conceptions of space, time, and weight. Whereas Feuillet notation located the body spatially in relation to horizontal and vertical axes, and temporally in relation to a metricized progression across space, Hill envisioned space as a void into which the body projected various shapes and energies, and time as a measure of the quickness or slowness of motion. Rather than positioning the body at the calm center of an embroidering periphery, as Feuillet indicated, Hill activated a momentum-filled relationship between central and peripheral body. Both systems imagined that they could accomplish an analysis of all dance movement, but Feuillet assumed that this was possible because all bodies share the same mechanics – the ability to rise, sink, turn, and so on – whereas Hill, borrowing from Laban and Dalcroze, assumed that all movement shares the same fundamental properties of shape, rhythm, and force.

Hill had studied with dance educator Margaret H'Doubler in the summer of 1925, the same year that H'Doubler's book on dance pedagogy, *The Dance*, was published. In it H'Doubler implements the ideology of modernism, arguing that dance is the translation of emotional experience into external form. Yet in order to accomplish this transference, the body's responsiveness as a physical mechanism must be mastered. H'Doubler advocated for a kinesiological understanding of the body's movement capabilities. Often working blindfolded, students were asked individually to explore the range of motion at each joint, based on their study of the skeleton. Abhorring any pedagogical approach based on imitation of movement routines, H'Doubler believed that her lesson plans, incorporating long periods of improvised exploration, offered students the opportunity for real creative work.[9]

Where Feuillet's legacy inculcated an awareness of the relationship between bodily structure and horizontal and vertical grids, H'Doubler's approach focused on the connection between impulse and its kinesiological realization. For H'Doubler, mastery over the body entailed an understanding of the 'intelligent appreciation for, and application of, force and effort' (H'Doubler, 1932: 1). This awareness would enable the student to overcome inhibitions and obstacles to his freedom of control. Unlike Feuillet notation, which implied standards of execution to which the body could be trained to adhere, H'Doubler envisioned her pedagogy as undoing obstacles to the desired performance. Eventually, this training would enable students to produce art, defined by H'Doubler as the free translation of internal emotional experience into external bodily form (H'Doubler, 1925: 11).

Thus, to her scientific exploration of bodily capacity, H'Doubler added sessions in which students would collaborate, under the teacher's guidance, on the making of a dance. For their first experiments in learning composition, she argued, students could work on devising movement sequences for a select piece of music. She explains:

> When the phrasing is understood, have the class skip to the right for one phrase [...] Then ask the class what to do next. Some will suggest going on in the same direction for another phrase; others will recommend going back to the left. Try both. The class will discover that skipping back for a phrase gives balance. Now ask the class if they have a satisfying sense of completion, or if they feel the need of repeating what has been done. Of course, some will want to repeat. So this should be done. They will soon realize that in this case repetition makes for monotony.
>
> (1925: 172)

H'Doubler's own aesthetic preferences, masked beneath the experimental rubric of trying out different options, cultivated students' ability to craft phrasing, floor path, and ensemble shapes. Having assimilated these basic compositional precepts, students could then audition to enroll in Orchesis, a group of advanced dancers who collectively devised an evening of dances for presentation to the public.

H'Doubler's classes imparted an entirely new comfort and exhilaration with the body to her female students, who, otherwise, could count on few options for connecting their bodies to their selves. Focusing as she did on educating the human being through the study of dance, she never developed the study of choreography more fully than to support the student club. Nor did she advocate for the training of professional dancers. When she lectured at Bennington in 1934 and throughout her career as a dance educator, H'Doubler championed the individual's exploration of the bodily capacity to move. Choreography, as on offshoot of this vital physical inquiry, remained an opaque process, one driven by brilliant vision and a need to express the human experience.

Choreography as the art of writing dances had resulted, in part, from the impulse to depersonalize dancing, to lessen its dependence on personal instruction. H'Doubler's and the Bennington teachers' approach, in contrast, suggested a hyper-personalized process so that the individual became origin of the movement, host to the creative process, and craftsperson of the dance's development. In this process, the body functioned as instrument of the expressive subject and not as a medium for collective or individual expression. Where in Feuillet's time, learning to dance entailed a mastering of the standard repertoire of steps, H'Doubler and the Bennington artists investigated a range of possible ways of moving. H'Doubler based this investigation on the body's kinesiological capacity to move in any and all of the ways afforded by its structural organization. Graham, Humphrey, and Holm organized their inquiries around the distinctive aesthetic inclinations they each discovered in their efforts to formulate an original danced vision.

Choreographic exclusions

Reflecting back on the burgeoning of what she calls 'choreographic theory' in the 1930s, Humphrey speculated that the social upheaval provoked by World War I prompted dancers to re-evaluate their mission as artists. 'In the United States and in Germany, dancers asked themselves some serious questions. "What am I dancing about?" "Is it worthy in the light of the kind of person I am and the kind of world I live in?" "But if not, what other kind of dance shall there be, and how should it be organized?"' (Humphrey, 1959: 18). For Humphrey, the new modern choreographers were galvanized by a social conscience that aspired to redress injustices and provide new visions of the potential for human society.

Yet, as Susan Manning has shown in her pioneering study *Modern Dance, Negro Dance*, the new conceptualization of choreography also functioned in an exclusionary capacity because of the prejudicial aesthetic criteria applied to artists of color. Black artists, in particular, were expected to produce 'natural' and 'spontaneous' movement, and this assumption either barred them from dance-making or else discredited their compositional labor. Thus, John Martin, who taught criticism at Bennington, frequently rated African American choreographers who followed the modern dance approach to choreography as 'derivative' rather than 'original' artists; whereas, when they foregrounded Africanist elements, he, along with other critics, considered them 'natural performers' rather than 'creative artists' (Manning, 2004: 1–55).

At the same time, artists such as Graham and Helen Tamiris felt empowered to represent all the world's bodies in their dances, casting their own white bodies in the performance of Negro Spirituals, Native American dances, and Cakewalks. Because the choreographer was an artist who could tap the universal fundaments that all movement shares, they could dance out the concerns and values of all peoples of the world. Even after World War II, when an increasing number of African American and Asian American artists appeared on concert stages, their works were required to display the values and issues associated with their specific communities, while white artists could continue to 'experiment' with an unmarked radical newness in form and meaning.

Louis Horst, who taught 'Primitive Forms' as part of choreography at Bennington, shows clearly how this process of universalizing could work. He asked students to conduct investigations of various styles, and in orienting them towards one variety of 'primitive' aesthetic, the 'air primitive,' he explained:

> The Air Primitive has to do with uncanny airy things; with birds, feathers, witches, fire and fire magic, with omens, apparitions, and enchantments, and with the sun and the wind. The Southwest Indians begin their dance prayers with aspirants such as 'hey-ah.' Their gods are the Great Spirit (Great Breath) and air-borne divinities such as fire gods, the Thunderbird, the Plumed Serpent [...] all of Europe, except Spain, is earth-minded, while the aboriginal cultures of the Americas (Spanish and Indian) are air-minded.
>
> (1987: 63)

Here, Horst equates the physical, the psychological, and the social through identifying a disposition common to each. Horst uses it to rationalize the appropriation of Native American forms by white choreographers who used Native aesthetics as a source of movement and inspiration.

Graham could borrow from Appalachia or from a more generalized notion of primitive rituals material for her dances, and Humphrey could represent the religious community known as the Shakers, but when Katherine Dunham used 'primitive' forms as the raw material for her modernist dances, she was criticized for being too sexual and therefore too commercial. As Gay Morris has documented, the white choreographic practice of modern dance ensured its elite status by working to exclude both social dance and forms of dance that purveyed entertainment (Morris, 2006: 114–46). The choreographer, an inspired individual artist, took on a new luster in comparison with the roles of social dance teachers and arrangers of dances, such as those who were setting pieces for revues, night club entertainments, or other Broadway attractions.

This new conception of choreography accomplished one further exclusion: it secured a special place for dances authored by a single artist as distinct from forms of dance practiced worldwide that could not be traced to a single creator. Implementing the opposition also practiced in anthropology between tradition and innovation, modern choreographers claimed that the movement vocabularies they devised were entirely new. Although they borrowed extensively from Native American, Asian, and 'Negro' forms, they distanced themselves from these 'unchanging' and 'deeply embedded' forms even as they were becoming more familiar. Thus, alongside the modern dance artists who experimented with 'new' forms of movement, the 'ethnological dancer' emerged as one who studied and mastered various enduring world forms.

Russell Meriwether Hughes, known as La Meri, claims to have invented the terms 'ethnic dance' and 'ethnological dancer' as ways to distinguish dances that 'reflect the unchanging mores of the people of all classes [...] of a particular land or race' from ballet, the product of an international elite, and modern dance, the reflections of a genial individual (La Meri, 1977: 1–2). Unlike St Denis, who traveled extensively and 'made up' dances based on her brief contact with peoples of different cultural traditions, La Meri took it upon herself to study and learn various dances in more detail. At the same time, she necessarily invented a theory of how all these dances had been spawned by a universal dance of life, a more fundamental and generative energy than those that produced either ballet or modern dance forms. Her classificatory framework thus reinforced stereotypical prejudices about world dance forms as unchanging and more primitive than either ballet or modern dance.

La Meri studied Flamenco, Barata Natyam, Javanese dances, and several European folk forms, but then arranged her own versions of dances which she performed to great acclaim from audiences around the world. These staged versions, not unlike Feuillet's notation of various regional dances, removed them from their original locations, reframing them within the space of the proscenium. Collecting the dances for the stage, La Meri's concerts subtly de-historicized them. Her presentations obfuscated any indigenous attributions of artistic contributions that might have been made over the years by various masters of the forms. They also eliminated any opportunities for improvisation, especially in the exchange between dancer and musician, by transcribing and notating all the distinctive musical forms for a soloist or small group that accompanied her dancing.

Although she distinguished between ethnic, ballet, and modern forms, La Meri did not intend to exclude the world's dances from the domain of choreographic practice. Her 1965 publication, *Dance Composition*, is intended for students versed in any form of dance. Blending together Delsarte's analysis of the meanings inherent in areas of the body and types of motion, the dramatic analysis of narrative, and a semiotics of the stage space, La Meri puts forward the universalism of the modernist aesthetic: a dance should be about the eternal elements of the human condition; the principles of movement – its dynamics, design, and development – are universally recognizable. As illustration, she includes discussion of various forms, 'Chinese,' 'Japanese,' 'Javanese,' 'Bharata Natyam,' or 'Flamenco,' that exemplify most vividly these principles. 'Many Flamenco dances as well as Kathak and Barata Natyam items,' for example, embody an ascending peak form of dramatic design in which the dancer attains climaxes of increasing intensity over the course of the dance. Alternatively, the ability to present contrasting dynamics within a single body is achieved in 'flamenco, with his slow-moving sensuous arms set above the staccato jab of heels. Another example is the steady, slow-motion dynamics of the Javanese dance, with the wrist suddenly moving with staccato force to send the scarf ballooning in a soft curve. Or, again, in Burmese dance, the smooth curves of the arms and upper torso contrasting to the bright, rhythmic bounce in the knees' (La Meri, 1965: 65).

Like Horst and Humphrey, La Meri emphasizes the choice of a subject or theme for the dance and the methods of developing movement material. Music, a crucial partner, should be studied for its structure and the impulses to move that it inspires, but the choice of music for a given dance should occur only after the theme has been determined. Costuming, props, and lighting, although they make a critical contribution to the impact of the dance, are all treated as effects that are added after the fact to the basic 'stuff' of the dance – its movement.

Even as she endeavors to embrace the world's dances within a single conception of choreography, La Meri also upholds fundamental differences between Western and Eastern forms. Offering her readers a list of some of the most essential contrasts, La Meri observes that occidental dances are built on broad lines that harmonize the entire body, whereas oriental dances manifest infinite shadings wherein each part of the body has a life, a line, and a rhythm of its own (La Meri, 1965: 142). Occidental dances are eccentric and emotionally expressive whereas oriental dances are concentric and compressive (142). The two traditions also differ in their overall dramatic shape, with occidental dances striving to excite by building to a brilliant and exciting climax, and oriental dances working to sooth by maintaining an emotional level that increases only in intensity (142). La Meri's comparison extends to include contrasts in conceptions of art itself – occidental dances are motivated by courtship whereas oriental dances were born in the temple; occidental dances prize novelty and originality whereas oriental dances adhere to ancient rules; and occidental dances point to their own accomplishments so that their physical difficulty is appreciated whereas oriental dances mask their mastery of the form (1965: 143).

Although La Meri's comparison claims essential differences between East and West, it utilizes the tenants of modernist aesthetics to make its argument. Space, conceptualized as a universal medium, and movement work together to signify the journey of the psyche as the dancer's motion either expands, radiating away from the body, or contracts, compressing in towards its center. Movement itself is a tangible and observable substance through which the dance presents a representation of self and world. La Meri's approach to dance composition thus installs modernist assumptions at the core of the creative process, embracing all forms of dance while at the same time establishing itself as the metapractice through which all forms can be evaluated.

Choreography's influence

What is the legacy of these two contrasting meanings of the term 'choreography,' as notation and as individual expression? How do they exercise influence over the ways that dances of the world have been integrated into dance departments across the United States? Both versions of the term impart a permanence to the dance that it may or may not have, since many dances include extensive opportunities to improvise in performance, and even those dances that have been 'set' can and are altered markedly by each performance of them. Both versions also imbue movement with a materiality that dancers might or might not experience. For Feuillet, dance movements take up a certain space and occur in a given amount of time, and these co-ordinates help to solidify any given step and also the 'fact' of moving. Each step thus exemplifies its designated shape and specified timing, and all movement evidences

sufficient substance that it can be translated, via notation's categories, onto the written page. For modernist theories, such as Humphrey's and La Meri's, movement becomes the physical manifestation of the psyche, taking on the material properties of the physical world such as shape, rhythm, and texture. Moreover, its substantiality enables it to be elaborated and varied – expanded or contracted, inverted or interwoven with other contrasting movement. Even though its motionality indicates the peregrinations of the emotions, it maintains an objecthood through which it makes its message felt. It alone makes and conveys the dance's argument.

This objectivity for dance as a movement practice, evident in each definition of the term 'choreography,' also creates a distinct identity for dance as separate from the other arts, especially music and theater. In Feuillet the music notation written above the dance notation reinforces the status of dance as a form parallel to that of music. In modernism, movement, as the medium within which dance develops its vision, relies on music for guidance but at the same time stands separate from it as a physical practice with a distinctive force, what philosopher Suzanne Langer called its 'virtual power'.[10] Arguments in favor of establishing dance as an academic pursuit, separate from music, theater, or physical education, have often been based on this distinctive function and capacity of dance.

This objective status for dance movement, buttressed by dance's appeal as a unique and individual way of knowing the world, launched a large number of programs and departments in universities across the United States. Although she did not teach regularly within the university context, La Meri's categorization of ballet, modern, and ethnic dance implies a division of labor that informed the development of their curricula. As these departments took shape, modern dance, focused on enhancing the creative exploration of the individual, served as the central subject, generating a series of courses in technique, composition, and repertoire – where visiting artists remounted classic works or, like the Bennington choreographers, developed new pieces on the students. These courses were complemented by instruction in music for dance and dance production. Ballet, as it was introduced into these curricula, served to fortify a student's technical competence. Only rarely did it function as a form in which to compose new dances. When they began to be introduced in the 1960s and 1970s, ethnic dances typically provided the pretext for an examination and celebration of different cultures. In such classes, one learned traditional dances as a window onto the cultural and aesthetic values of a given people. Analyzed not as choreography but as the embodiment of a belief system, these world dances were uprooted from their locale and projected into the blank, white cube of the modern dance studio. There, students' expectations inevitably focused on learning the movement first, acquiring technical proficiency, and then dancing a dance. Yet curricular and financial constraints inhibited them from acquiring substantive proficiency. As a result, pedagogy reinforced the image of these dances as unchanging, since students never learned how to improvise within the forms, how to collaborate with musicians, or how to arrange and rearrange material to meet the specific demands of a given performance.

For example, Alma Hawkins, who had studied with H'Doubler and who developed a dance curriculum at UCLA renowned for its inclusion of dance from around the world, remembers: 'I wanted to put the art back in, so students could go where they wanted when they left, to perform or to teach. We were also interested in developing the ethnic forms and ballet' (Ross, 2000: 205). She brought forward H'Doubler's commitment to the creative process as the centerpiece of the curriculum when she began teaching at UCLA in 1953. Yet she was also concerned to professionalize the discipline by ensuring that students received sufficient training in various dance forms, especially modern dance and ballet, that they could enter the marketplace as performers and teachers of dance. In addition, Hawkins determined to expand the curriculum into world dance, then called 'ethnic dance,' by adding courses in forms such as Barata Natyam, Balinese classical dance, and Middle Eastern dance. In 1984 these courses were regrouped under the heading Dancing in Selected Cultures, while various levels of modern dance and ballet persevered with an unmarked status. In 2001 the faculty again overhauled the curriculum and, following Kealiinohumoku's mandate, classified all instruction in dancing under the general heading World Arts Practices, with specific tracks in West African, South Asian, modern, ballet, and postmodern forms, and so on. Yet the division of the West from the rest endures in the naming of some courses according to the country in which the dance originates while others are identified by tradition or genre. These courses, now called 'practice courses,' rather than technique courses, nonetheless stand apart from the choreography courses that are identified as a separate pursuit. Thus the separation of making from learning instigated by Feuillet's system continues to inform the curriculum. And this same legacy influences many of the scholarly investigations of dance in cross-cultural perspective, as the discussion of Sachs's legacy in the Introduction to this volume makes clear.

Wrestling with these very issues at UCLA, the faculty first established a course in the choreography sequence entitled 'Intercultural Composition,' and subsequently redesigned all four composition courses to include examples of dances by artists working in diverse traditions worldwide. Although we no longer imagine that we can teach composition based on Hill's fundamentals of space, time, and dynamics or Horst's notions of affiliations between cultures and types of moving, we continue to privilege artists who have assimilated the modernist model of single-authored creations.[11] Nonetheless, we are grappling with the various ways that the term 'choreography' might be taken to mean in distinctive dance contexts: when and how are the making and doing separate endeavors? how is tradition preserved through innovation? how might the art of making dances become a very different process in contexts where dance is improvised? how do we assess collective as well as individual amendments to a dance? And we hope to keep asking these questions as the term migrates in usage to the *Los Angeles Times* and far beyond.

Notes

1. Collections of notated dances stopped appearing in the 1730s, and even though Louis de Cahusac featured the system in his essay for the *Encyclopedie* in 1755, it had long fallen out of use. Noverre, especially, railed against Feuillet as obsolete and incapable of capturing stage action, particularly facial expressions and groupings of bodies (Noverre, 1966: 133–9).
2. Yet the system's unwieldiness inhibited its use, and Dancing Masters necessarily turned to other methods, most notably the ballet scenario, for recording their innovations. Although the scenario, a description of the plot, established ownership by printing the Dancing Master's name, it neglected entirely to document the dance's movement, and Dancing Masters continued to complain about theft of their innovations. Only Rudolf Laban's radical innovations in the early twentieth century offered a more widespread opportunity to record dance movement, resulting in the first copyrighting of dances in the early 1940s as Anthea Kraut's chapter in this volume explains.
3. This mastery was manifest in the large number of ballets from around the world that began to appear on the early nineteenth-century stage. Rather than a parade of different types, held together by a single narrative proposition, ballets began to be staged in exotic locales around the world. Gypsy, Native American, Caribbean as well as Scottish, Hungarian, Italian, and Russian dances, all assimilated into the vocabulary and style of classical ballet, imbued each ballet with local color while simultaneously displaying the ballet's mastery over all forms. Where the eighteenth-century representations of foreignness typically borrowed a stereotypic gesture or piece of attire to signal the culture, nineteenth-century ballets balleticized actual phrases of movement. What had begun as a rubric for collecting dances evolved into a system for assimilating them into the dancing body.

4. For example, Theophile Gautier rarely uses the term at all, but when he does it references multiple functions. Writing in 1858, he refers to 'Taglioni, Elssler, Cerrito, and Carlotta Grisi, not to mention their own ballerinas, [as] a young choreographic army graduate from their ballet school, one of the best run in the world, agile, supple, marvelously disciplined, and with talents already fully formed that lack only stage experience, which will come with time' (Gautier, 1986: 293). In the same review, he describes Mme Petipa as 'delicate, pretty, light, and worthy to be admitted to that family of distinguished choreographers' (1986: 294). Both these uses of the term choreography seem to emphasize the ability to dance more than prowess at making dances. Yet, earlier in the same review he states, 'the author of a ballet scenario is almost a stranger to his work, the credit belonging entirely to the choreographer, the composer and the designer' (1986: 281) Gautier also frequently refers to the act of composing dance as 'writing for the legs.'

In 1878 the anonymous reviewer for the *New York Times* uses the term ambiguously to refer either to the teaching of dance or the ability to compose dances when he describes the French as 'a nation of dancing-masters, but whatever their capacities for instruction in choreography, they are fearful and wonderful as performers' ('A Dull Season in Paris': 6). Four years later, a reviewer uses the term to refer to the teaching of dancing: 'M. Perrin is a Professor of choreography, who, aided and supplemented by his son Charles, makes something like 100,000f. annually by teaching young people how to trip properly the light fantastic' ('Scenes from Paris Life': 7).

Another review from 1882, uses choreography ambiguously in describing the performance as one that provides viewers 'an opportunity of judging for themselves that symphonic music is not adapted to choreography' ('Gay Parisian Topics': 3). And still another review from the same year refers to the dancers as 'choreographists' ('A Play to Run Six Months': 5). And in 1914, Troy Kinney is described as a 'student of choreography', explaining that 'choreography, or the art of dancing' is enjoying a renaissance with the 'modern dance craze' ('Modern Dances Held to Mean a Modern Renaissance': SM5).

However, in 1913, Nijinsky is identified as responsible for the choreography of *Sacre du Printemps* ('New Ballet Puzzles': 4), and in 1916 Fokine is likewise identified as the choreographer whose 'sources of choreography are three. The interpreters use the ballet steps and movements that have been universally known and practiced for generations, as in *Papillons* and *Les Sylphides*; they introduce the barbaric, startling native dances of their steppes as in *Prince Igor*, and they freely empoly [sic] the oriental and classical, as in *Scheherazade, Cleopatre* and *L'Apres-midi d'un Faune*' (Moore, 1916: III1). (I will refrain from analyzing this characterization of choreography, tempting though it is.) Subsequent performances of Fokine's work throughout the early 1920s are always advertised as 'Choreography by Fokine.' And even musicals, such as *The Jeweled Tree*, premiering in 1926, begin to include mention of the choreographer, in this case, Chester Hale (Display Ad 112, X3).

Prompted in part by Fokine's contributions to ballet, the term may have taken on its new meaning in the early 1920s. Even Martha Graham reminisces about her earliest training, from 1914 to 1923 with Ruth St. Denis and Ted Shawn: 'I had never heard the word choreographer used to describe a maker of dances until I left Denishawn. There you didn't choreograph, you made up dances' (Graham, 1991: 236).

5. Students enrolled in this course were also required to enroll in Composition in Dance Forms and Dance History and Criticism (taught by John Martin). Composer and music educator Louis Horst also taught a course entitled 'Composition in Dance Forms,' which broke down into two parts: Pre-Classic Forms and Modern Forms.

6. In 1936 Charles Weidman led a Men's Workshop where he developed *Quest*, and Doris Humphrey presided over a Women's Workshop where she created *With My Red Fires*. And in 1937 Hanya Holm, a student of Mary Wigman's, developed *Trend*.

7. For example, the description for the course in Dance Composition taught by Martha Hill with Bessie Schonberg as the assistant read as follows: 'A study of dance composition from the standpoint of sequential form and group design in space; a single compositional factor or a combination of factors such as direction, level, tempo, dynamics, and the like; dance content, theme, or idea' (Kriegsman, 1981: 232). Also assisted by Schonberg, Hill taught a course entitled 'Fundamental Techniques' – 'A basic study of fundamental techniques of movement for the dance analyzed into its force, space, and time aspects; the elements of form and meaning in movement for the dance' (1981: 232).

8. This program was co-directed by Hill and Horst (Kreigsman, 1981: 236–7).

9. She writes: 'In the old schools of dancing the instructor had the children memorize the dances as the arithmetic master had them memorize their multiplication tables. Under such a system dancing became a mere routine of imitation. It gave the dancer plenty of chance to display his skill in the reproduction of steps which somebody else had devised, but of opportunity for real creative work, it afforded almost none' (H'Doubler, 1925: 163–4).

10. See, especially, *Feeling and Form*, where Langer considers each art as offering a distinctive kind of aesthetic experience based on the kind of symbolic transformation it undertakes.

11. The fact that artists in Taiwan, India, Indonesia, Senegal, Argentina, and the list goes on, are now choreographing dances for the proscenium stage signals yet a further evolution in the term.

6
Red-Stained Feet: Probing the Ground on which Women Dance in Contemporary Bengal

Ananya Chatterjea

The red lining your/my/their feet: Is it alta or blood?[1]

Ruminations about histories

Charged with rethinking the construct of World Histories of Dance, I wonder about the possibility of constructing histories of dancing bodies across wide terrains of time and space, histories that can only be charted through trace – stilled images in sculptures, paintings, photographs; descriptions in texts; memories; and only recently, the late nineteenth century onwards, through recordings – always, a necessarily selective project. What indeed are the possibilities for creating a 'historical' narrative from tracing those shifts within dancing bodies, marking changes in forums, alterations in costumes, and swings in context? For whom might these histories be important? And what inequities rise in the necessarily selective recordings of 'world' dance histories, as the inevitable consequence of the uneven concentration of capital and resources in particular geopolitical locations?

These questions are vital as I think about how Indian dance has been written about and taught in the broad sweep of 'World Dance' courses, and also curated in dance festivals. More attention has gone into fitting the evidence we have into certain categories that have dominated the organizing of History, and less into thinking about what these bodies might offer to theorizings about the cultural economy or social context of their time.[2] Specifically, what kinds of histories can dancing bodies illuminate if we can extricate historical narratology from the domain of the classical-folk dichotomy that has dominated understandings of

Indian dance? Might we arrive at alternative structurings of historical narratives if we thematize information from dancing bodies along different lines of inquiry? What if the inquiry is about the bodies that dance – bodies gendered, classed, sexualized, and marked in specific ways – and the absences and elisions they embody? My questions are deeply influenced by my own creative research, my search for an idiom that allows for feminist articulation, and my attempt to understand alternative movement aesthetics in a context dominated by what I call the North–South classical bind, where the multiplicity of forms are swallowed up under the Bharatnatyam (from the South) or Kathak (from the North) model.

My previous research on the struggles of Odissi to establish itself as a classical dance form and my current project investigating the possibility of a 'different' historiography of dance practices in Bengal have developed in me a weary wariness about the demands of the classical label.[3] The category produces an overdetermined identity-trap, where guidelines harden into rules and unshakeable expectations. It also generates its own desire so that exclusion from the classical has, at least in the Indian context, signaled less status and privilege, less resources and opportunities, with advocates for several forms demanding classification at least as semi-classical. Without rehearsing arguments laid out elsewhere by Mandakranta Bose, Alessandra Lopez y Royo, and myself among others, let me quote Lopez y Royo to summarize the argument here: 'Thus the adoption of the term "classical" in the Indian context was a political act [...] The adoption of the term [... is ...] motivated by the desire to give recognizable national and international status to the dance that was being reconstituted' (2003: p. 5).

The other side of this trap is of course the classification of 'folk', following a misleading translation of the genres of *margi* and *desi*, a category that generally signifies somewhat less status, prestige, and resources, but fulfills vital functions for the state. The current website of the Sangeet Natak Akademi (SNA), for instance, where the awards given out this year are listed, bears testimony to this, The SNA is the cultural wing of the Indian Government and was inaugurated in 1953 as an institution dedicated to preserving the cultural traditions of the country. Awards are bestowed in each artistic discipline, but in Dance, one award is given in each of the classical forms and one in innovative or contemporary choreography. Folk dance, meanwhile, is folded into the category of 'Traditional/ Folk/ Tribal' and shares that category with music, theater, and puppetry. Further, the classical dance forms, represented through solo forms primarily, are pursued by artists who can claim to have dedicated themselves to the pursuit of refining classicism. These forms, symbolizing tradition and heritage, gesture towards categories of 'high art.' Meanwhile, the enormous range of folk dance forms, primarily represented as group forms, several of which can often be programmed together in an evening's cultural showcase, stand in for the Indian government's policy of 'unity in diversity.'[4]

Given the way these forms are *generally* practiced (solo classical performer vs. groups, longer pieces with elaborate rhythmic and/or emotional development vs. shorter pieces with either no narrative or more direct narrative flow), and the different roles they are made to play in mapping cultural production in the country, a categorical differentiation could occasionally be useful. But they are enmeshed in politics of naming and claiming, the implicit and inevitable marking of tribal and rural organization as inferior to a more urban one, and the ultimate adherence to a categorization drawn from a European model. All of these factors intersect to create a problematic nexus that blurs the particular and unique conditions that determined the formation of these cultural practices and the resulting inequities.

It is in the context of these misdirections, that I started to read the histories of dance in Bengal. Admittedly, I began this project in 'rescue' mode: I wanted to trace a genealogy of dance in Bengal and argue for a particularity of bodily performance and regional heterogeneity, and challenge the dominance of Bharatnatyam and Kathak in contemporary choreography.[5] Indeed, while Bengal has never had a particular classical dance form of its own, dance has been a continuous and vital part of social and cultural life in this context. The literature about dance in Bengal, written primarily in Bengali, is primarily about *loknritya* or folk dance forms, or about individual visionaries like Rabindranath Tagore and Uday Shankar, who re-energized the field of dance here with their innovations. However, my memory of growing up in Kolkata as a dancer during the 1970s and 1980s is that dance was continuously and vibrantly present in our lives, across a plethora of forums and forms, and often as part of our elementary education, little of which is written about or continues today. While all cultural practices change with altered conditions, contexts, and resources, I believe some particular flattenings and simplifications are happening across India generally, and specifically in Bengal, where multiple phenomena of globalization have produced hastily wrought translocal conversations and uniform production of simulacra that read powerfully as results of cultural neo-colonialism. I had intended, in this chapter, to mark the richness of dance practices that I remembered and my perceptions of the growing singularity of choices in aesthetic and forum, while the number of dancers and dance institutions are clearly on the rise.

My 'rescue mission' was also largely instigated by my frustration with the emerging field of contemporary choreography, where there is currently an unarticulated expectation that most innovative and experimental work draws on the usual sources of Bharatanatyam, Kalarippayattu, Kathak, and yoga, which sets up a hierarchy of forms and aesthetics. I have also to admit to the mingling of nostalgia and desire here: Indeed I found the aesthetic of the 'cotton sari–silver earrings–jasmine flowers in hair emphasis on flow and grace in movement' markers of the typically Bengali urban aesthetic in performances of *Rabindra nritya* (Tagore dance) or *Srijanshil nritya* (creative dance) very beautiful. These dances provided rich material to deconstruct and rearticulate in the creation of a contemporary feminist aesthetic. Common enough in my childhood days, this aesthetic has all but disappeared now from most performance spaces, replaced by the silks, stone-studded jewelry, and crisper movement styles of the dominant North and South Indian classical forms.

This aesthetic also finds no place whatsoever in urban popular culture, on the multiple song-and-dance shows on the many television channels that viewers can avail themselves of now. In this domain, where television plays an important role in bringing cultural shows to a wide range of people, current cultural programming swings between being Bollywood-influenced, sparkly, or Bengali rock bands-influenced, still very flashy, leaving little space for less 'sexy' articulations of the kind of Bengali aesthetic I described. These former are dominated by competitiveness (as in some version of American Idol), and often constitute sites where pre-pubescent bodies are necessarily pushed into sexualized performances, clearly illustrative of the cultural colonialism brokered by globalization processes. What bodies are lost between the lure of the classical and the glitter of H/Bollywood?

> *Ebay: 'Drawing alta Red Dye' (read 'exotic natural deco'), priced at $6.50.*

One's research questions have an uncanny knack for tumbling one down a humbling trajectory of realizations. My initial proposal for a historiographic study became more and more jeopardized as I continued my research, specifically during a trip to the Purulia region of West Bengal. This area, although particularly unfertile for crops, is rich in performance traditions. Here I witnessed both the amazing hydro-electricity project constructed by the government by cutting through the hills of the Ayodhya Pahad, and installing huge electricity towers for the transmission of power generated by harnessing mountain streams, and the wonderfully smooth roads governing the access ways of the project. These 'developments' contrasted starkly with the tremendous poverty of the tribal and village communities in that area, whose lives are still untouched by the electricity that was promised them by the government at the time the project was initiated in 2000. I heard again and again from witnesses that so many talented artists in the area have perished because of lack of nutrition and medical care. I realized that a historiographic project of the kind I wanted to undertake must necessarily engage in a concomitant tracing of bodies that have slipped through the cracks of promised 'development' and of how cultural policy is often deployed to try to make up for economic and social injustices. In a country where globalization has deepened the divide between the urban/corporate/elite and the rural/working class, the agenda of 'development' – fueling pipe dreams of electricity and clean water, education and acceptable life and work conditions, for those who have yearned for these minimal gestures from the government for years – is clearly an electoral issue and ultimately a definitive factor in much cultural policy. Given the context, I determined to make my project a feminist one, particularly slanted towards asking questions about women's voices and agency.

This is how I arrived at a necessary reimagining of my initial project. Instead of constructing some kind of historical account, I can, at best, arrive at a series of questions about women dancers who have been able to steer through the multiple threats of appropriation and elimination and still embody some notion of culturally specific performance. Might it be productive to ask about notions of professionalism among women dancers such as *baijis* in Bengal at a time when Kolkata was the center of colonial power? What about Gauhar Jaan, one of the first professional singer-dancers from Kolkata in the late nineteenth/early twentieth century, whose voice is the first recorded voice from Indian music (EMI records, 1902)? What of Protima Devi, Rabindranath Tagore's daughter-in-law, the first woman from a 'respectable' middle-class family to perform publicly, in his dance-dramas, in Santiniketan (1925)? How then do we examine the dances of contemporary choreographer Manjusri Chaki-Sircar, whose work of deconstructing available classical dance idioms to create a different movement vocabulary consciously seeks to give voice to feminist articulations beginning in the 1980s? How can I understand the complex interlocking of forces that has created the phenomenon of women from middle-class families today, home-makers and untrained dancers, who often 'dance' on reality television shows, a completely new trend in this socio-cultural context?

What have been the possibilities that these different women have found within dance? Alternatively, how has it been strategic for them to work with dance in eking out some space for exploring their sexuality, their romantic expectations, while at the same time marking some small but meaningful economic gains? What sort of history do we arrive at in tracing these journeys through a series of questions? I know already that I will not be able to consider these questions in depth, but I note them here to move this chapter towards the kinds of shifts in the historiographic process that Uma Chakravarti calls for when she insists that gender-sensitive historicizing engage with a complex analysis of the 'multiple forms of patriarchies' instead of a narrow focus on 'culture' (2005: 216).

It is difficult to work outside a uni-directional chronology, yet that is indeed my goal here. The thematization that is necessary for that kind of linearity disallows the posing of a constellation of questions which might then impinge upon one another so as to open up some intersections and/or illuminate veerings away, all of which together suggest the complexity of the cultural landscape. Moreover, I want to continuously distance my ruminations from the typical model followed by the reconstruction projects in post-Independence India. These latter sought to establish a continuous link with a deep past, ironing out inconsistencies and inconvenient facts, though I recognize that these narrativizations were strategic negotiations, responding to the needs of the nation-building project. Even the meta-historical thinking I am engaging in here asks for constant alertness in order to differentiate it from some current gestures towards cultural preservation (particularly to save 'Indian culture' from Western influences), enmeshed as they are in callings for power and the accrual of affective, and ultimately material, capital.

So, if I can only separate myself slightly from my own epistemologically induced expectations and agree to work through broken and incomplete lines, and primarily through a series of juxtapositions, might I be able to trace a trajectory through unevenly staged dancing bodies? Perhaps a spatialized history, a collage of several different kinds of forms and genres understood through shifting contexts, might illuminate the range of dance practices and bodily imaginings that constitute the layered cultural fabric, like the constellation of many motifs and patterns that suggest the 'whole picture' in a *kantha*? The *kantha* is a homemade quilt, typically sewn together from bits of old saris with close stitches.[6]

That a unique aesthetic has emerged from this functional need for strength and durability, a necessity for household use, is testament to Bengali rural women's commitment to beauty. Like the *kantha*-stitcher, I will patch together reflections and questions about cultural practices from different sites in Bengal, all of which reflect on one another but none of which are necessarily related causally. Rhizome-like, my mapping will work through multiple points of connection and heterogeneity to emphasize the multiplicity that is inherent in this material.[7]

This messy attempt at focusing in on some specific practices is also a way to evade the necessarily broad-stroke approach evident in scholarship and production circuits as the World Dance survey course and the World Dance festival. Such courses and festivals have gained currency through technology that weaves the magical mantra of shrinking the world, when deterritorialized bodies of migrant laborers and very strategically located multinational company-owning tycoons mark the bookends of a 'global' economy. Indeed, the Internet insists we can access information about virtually any phenomena nameable, and artists have to vie with each other in a cultural market increasingly dominated by the march of global capital. What gains attention in the field of 'World Dance' determines resources in local contexts, effecting different kinds of flattenings, often choking the life energy out of regionally specific forms. I intend to mark the management and erosion of difference without falling into a lamenting for the passing of 'traditions,' even as I glance at huge posters advertising 'Western-style dance classes' alongside classes in the now ubiquitous Bollywood dance style (what style that might be one may indeed wonder), lining the busy streets of Kolkata. Viewed in this way, and remarking on the overarching power of validation from the West, indeed it seems the colonial tool of management through a predetermined set of classifications has continued through time, variously challenged and critiqued, but ultimately unassailable.[8]

Classical lust: the claims of *Gaudiya Nritya*

Even as I argue for aesthetic specificities here, I urgently distance my project from that of Kolkata-based scholar, Mahua Mukherjee. Interpreting evidence assembled from disparate visual art sources and textual references, Muhkherjee has, in the last two decades, argued for a classical dance of old Bengal, *Gaur*, a form of great antiquity that, she claims, 'has its origin in the Natyashastra' and 'vanished from the scene because of lack of patronage and political disturbances,' attributing the latter to 'Western influence in Bengal.' (cited at http://www.artindia. net/mahua/).

Her assertion is backed up by substantial research as is evident from the volume *Gaudiya Dance*, a compilation of papers presented at a seminar on the subject on 9 and 10 February 2002 in Kolkata.[9] Mukherjee's claim shares the fundamental argument with which I began this chapter, about the multiplicity of forms and dance practices that have existed in Bengal from ancient times, and their regional specificity. It is with her attempt to then reduce this multiplicity, which rides across categorizations formulated later, into a single coherent classical form, which is made to conform with the codifications of the *Natyashastra*, and with her modernist anxieties around origin (arguing, for instance, that some dance practices in Bengal predated similar practices in Tamil Nadu), that I take issue.[10] It is not hard to believe that the aggressive colonial regime generated forces that caused the disappearance of dance forms. But the lack of reflexivity around her project which repeats, in a different way, similar moves is deeply troubling. I argue that her project co-opts multiple community-held movement practices through compulsory categorization and classicization, in order to make for a respectable state-sanctioned concert form. Hers is also a project that is favored heavily by the Bengal State Government, who can demand greater resources for their cultural wing from the central government, as well as access to more prestigious venues, based on their own classical dance form.

Bishnupur: in search of the Bengali aesthetic

My search took me back to the terracotta-red Bishnupur temples in 2006, where I witnessed again the intricately carved friezes on all sides, with plentiful images of dancers, men and women.[11] A popular theme is that of the *ras-mandala*, a foundational story in Vaishnavism, where choreography is circular and the gaze circulates as much among the community, as in the mutually held look of the lovers dancing in couples. At the center of this circle seem to be the divine lovers, Radha and Krishna, and in circles arranged as expanding ripples around them are images of the gopinis with Krishna, who has multiplied himself into many so that each adoring woman/devotee, can imagine herself in an intimate dance with Krishna/their lord, a wondrous dance-play, the *ras lila*.[12]

While the original *ras* is a metaphor typical to this spiritual practice, performances of the *ras* happened in the temples, alongside the *kirtan*, the devotional singing highlighting the love and longing of Radha and the gopis for Krishna. The *ras* was danced in the natmandap or the rasman-cha, the performance spaces, of the Vaishnava temples. Indeed, it seems that all through Gaudiya Vaishnavism, there is a practice of dancing and singing in ecstasy and as spiritual expression, and that Chaitanya deva himself would dance wildly, roll on the ground, in his moments of intense spiritual connectivity. There are also many legends about the famous fourteenth-century Vaishnava poet Chandidas and his lover, the talented singer Rami, for whom dancing and singing in praise of divine love, referred to as *nritya-sankeertan*, was customary practice.

Particularly in oral literature from this time on, there are also scattered references to Hindu widows or women who left their homes to join Vaishnavite societies or akhadas, and who chose their male partners through the loose acknowledgement of the *kanthi-badal* ceremony where the couple exchanged a string of beads, and performed as *kirtan* singers and dancers during evening worship or other Vaishnava ceremonies. Some of these Vaishnava women became professionals, performers who inhabited the border zones of rural and urban Bengal from medieval times, definitely living by a 'different' set of rules than were prescribed for women who participated in the accepted familial roles, but increasingly shunned by mainstream Hindu *bhadralok* society, which was embarrassed by the frank celebration of sensuality and physical love in their music and dance.

The Bishnupur temples also give evidence of the extensive presence of *devadasis*[13]: there are images of single or several dancers carved on the walls, their raised heels and flowing sari ends clearly indicative of bodies in motion. Unlike the *devadasis* in temples of Tamil Nadu and the *maharis* in temples of Orissa, there is only sporadic information about the dance practices of the *devadasis* of Bengal. However, this is a system that existed prior to the Malla dynasty, certainly during the rule of the Pala dynasty (eighth–twelfth century) and the Sena dynasty (eleventh–twelfth century) in Bengal. The system seems to have worked as elsewhere, where *devadasis* attached to the temple were granted land and subsistence through royal patronage. The guide who took me through the temples in 2006 mentioned Jogidashi, Bhairabidasi, Kumuddasi, Lakshmidasi, and Padmadasi as some of the well-known *devadasis* of yore. Apparently the last *devadasi*, Usharani, donated Rs. 20,000 for maintenance work done on the Bashantidebi temple – clearly she had the financial wherewithal to make that donation. Did this gift earn her prestige in a society where, no doubt, she was marginalized? The guide did not know, but deflected the question, suggesting her devotion to the goddess.

Who are the foremothers of these women? Might there be a relationship to Behula, the popular central heroine of the *Manasa Mangal*,
one of the *mangal kavya*s, the long poems written in medieval Bengal
between the thirteenth and eighteenth century, usually narrating how
a particular local goddess came to be established as such in the popular imaginary? Behula is the daughter-in-law of the famous merchant
Chand Sadagar, who dances in the court of Indra, the king of the gods,
to bring life back to her dead husband, retrieve the fortunes of her
husband's family, and, through a long chain of events, ultimately to
ensure that Manasa, the local goddess of snakes is assured her status as
a reputable goddess among people. Behula's dance, from all accounts in
jhumur and other poetic traditions, was full of sparkle, enough to get
the attention of the divine court, accustomed to celestial dancers.[14] Yet
Behula was a home-maker, a daughter-in-law and wife (even a widow at
that point), and her status was never endangered by her skills in dance.
From all existing accounts, however, it seems that *devadasis* of Bengal,
like their counterparts elsewhere, ultimately came to be cast as *rajadasis*,
their bodies often at the command of the male leadership of the state. Is
Behula's story only possible in myth?

Who's doing the *loknritya*?

A vital part of my dancing experience in the 1980s and 1990s was performing with some 'folk dance' troupes. Encouraged by the Indian government's cultural policies, these troupes were a typical feature of most
metropolises, and worked within the rule of simplification and bite-sized
culture pills. We would learn folk dances, one from each state, from spe-
cialist teachers who had 'collected' these dance forms from around the
country, and present short pieces representative of each state's unique
cultural fabric. All this without necessarily learning much about the specific context in which they originated and continued to be performed,
or without pausing to reflect on the kind of appropriation that was happening as we, dancers from generally middle-class families, took on the
task of educating the Indian public about the diverse cultural traditions
of the 'folk' of our country. Although not entirely different from some
of the 'World Dance' survey courses I have critiqued, there was some
kind of recognition among the dancers, that the folk dances, immediately associated with the 'people,' presented one way to learn about
the typical lifestyle and practices of folks who were 'Indian' like us,
but very different culturally, linguistically, and otherwise. In contrast,
however, there is currently much government initiative to present the

'dance of the people' danced by 'the people' through several folk dance and drama festivals across India.

I also remember that when I danced for the West Bengal Government's Cultural Exchange Program, which toured to other states presenting a composite program of songs and dances of Bengal, I tired of dancing the pieces performed typically by the women. Although I loved the women's dance from the Santhal tribe of Birbhum, a remarkable exercise in ensemble synchronicity and soft rhythmic flow, I found myself much more interested in the different vigor of the martial dances, such as the Raibeshey (danced with bamboo sticks), Kathi naach (dance with sticks), Dhali naach (dance with shields), Dhaki naach (dance with drums), and certainly the Chhau of Purulia, mostly performed by men. I am still excited by the robustness of the dancing, its highly acrobatic quality, the pronounced use of breath, all of which run contrary to the general impressions about dance in Bengal as comprising rounded and soft, even wimpy, dance forms. Somehow this long-standing stereotype about the Bengali elite as an effete people, popularized largely by the British, came to stand in for all of the Bengali population, and remains in the popular imaginary even today.[15]

It is clear from comments by literary and social leaders such as Bankimchandra Chatterjee, Swami Vivekanda, Sarala Devi Chaudhurani and others that by the nineteenth century, members of the Bengali elite, many of them products of the English education system, took on this self-deprecating stance, often equating the decline of the older traditions of physical culture with the current lack of nationalist fervor. John Rosselli has written about the consequent growing interest in a physical culture and the renewed popularity of sports such as lathi-khela (sparring with sticks) and other practices in akhadas (local gymnasiums) in late nineteenth- and early twentieth-century Bengal.[16]

At any rate, it is these kinds of robust folk dances that Gurusaday Datta capitalized on when he launched the Bratachari movement in 1932, aimed at raising self-esteem and national awareness through a comprehensive pedagogic approach. Elementary school students, girls and boys, learned these dances even in the 1970s and 1980s, as part of physical education. Danced to simple rhythmic poems, these dances celebrated a specific work culture, pertaining primarily to an agricultural way of life. Datta's belief was that these songs and dances would create healthy and strong bodies and minds and instill in students a sense of pride in their cultural heritage and love for the nation and for the world generally.[17] To this purpose, he collected folk songs and dances from across the then undivided Bengal, and also choreographed some dances to existing rhythmic patterns to create the Bratachari system.

Watching young men and women from across the state of Bengal and from Bangladesh practicing several of these dances at a training camp held in December 2007 at the Bratachari Village established by Datta in 1940 in Kolkata, I noticed that the women, mostly from working- to lower middle-class families, were learning some of the more athletic dances (such as the dhali dance), and were quite adept at this kind of physicality. Yet, some of the more complex gymnastic and virtuosic dance-movement forms were still reserved for the men. Even though Datta's manifesto for Bratachari practice, a compilation of songs and rhythmic articulations to accompany the dances, seems to charge men and women equally with the values of serving the nation and upholding a pride in Bengali identity (as in the song *Amra Bangali*, for instance).[18]

Clearly marked by a zeal for 'unity,' many of the songs such as *Kodal Chalai* (lets work the spade) suggest men and women must labor side by side and take pride in physical work. But there are also songs specifically urging the education of girls and women's freedom, though of course, this freedom is so that they can be good mothers. Still, why did this rhetoric of freedom not translate to a bodily transformation for women? When will the young women participants in the training camps demand it? I was told by Naresh Banerjee, faculty at the camp and curator of the Museum, that my desire to learn the Raibeshey was indeed echoed by several women professional dancers from Kolkata, who had trained on an individual basis with him.

Scrub, scrub!!: I want to wash off the alta, that marker of femininity!

I know the individually articulated desires of women who have the wherewithal to cross these tacitly accepted gendered restrictions have much wider stakeholdership. When will they take collective voice in a polyrhythmic dance of different notions of femininity?

Women professionals, sleazy

In a documentary film about Odissi, my guru Sanjukta Panigrahi, talking about her own struggles on the way to becoming the famous classical dancer she then was, quotes from a popular Oriya saying about dancers: 'oti beheya nachiya jaaye' (those who are totally shameless become dancers).[19] Many women who are professional performers, across time and different socio-cultural and economic contexts, have come to understand the disrepute that often attaches to their work. In the post-colonial period, the embracing of dance, particularly by women from the middle- and upper-classes in India, seems to have changed much of this popular perception. Many of us from the Bengali urban middle classes fancied that we were especially immune to the slurs of 'loose women.' We rested on the respectability wrested out for this profession by pioneers like Rabindranath Tagore, whose own daughter-in-law, Protima Debi, was encouraged to dance, and who, along with Guru Nabakumar Singh, choreographed Tagore's first produced dance drama *Natir Pujo* in Santiniketan in 1926. The second production of the same dance drama was staged in Jorasanko, in Kolkata, in 1927, and included several young women who were students at Tagore's Santiniketan school. Reporter Profulla Kumar Sarkar, writing in the widely circulated Bengali daily *Ananda Bazar Patrika*, congratulated the performer, Srimati Gauri, on her performance as the central character.[20] Women dancers in Bengal could also look to Uday Shankar, whose dance company featured several women dancers, including his long-time French partner Simkie, his wife Amala Shankar, and dancer Zohra Sehgal, for instance.

However, I know now beyond doubt that women dancers, even from urban middle classes, even in the later part of the twentieth century, have had to struggle to gain respectability for their profession. But what about their rural counterparts, hailing from economically marginalized families, particularly the women of the *nachni* tradition popular in the Manbhum area of the country? While I knew of the existence of the *nachni*, these women were not spoken about in the circles that formed my community in my growing years: the bhadralok circles or even in the political circles where dance, like other aspects of cultural production, was a tool in the class struggle. Research about this group of women has gained much momentum in the last few years and particularly since 1995 when the West Bengal Government honored the octogenarian retired *nachni* Sindhubala Debi with the Lalon Purashkar Award for her dedication and contribution to the cultural life of the country. I arrived at Sindhubala Debi walking backwards, trying to trace a line of women dancers as professionals in the field of cultural work.[21]

Nachnis are different from *baijis*, who are spoken about in connection with the Babu culture of Kolkata and the Zamindari culture of Bengal in general. Whereas *baijis* were supposedly trained in the performing arts, particularly those recognized as prestigious (such as Kathak, popularized and patronized by Nawab Wajad Ali Shah of Lucknow), and, proficient in courtly etiquette, expected generous fees for their performances, the *nachni* were village women, who could

sing and dance, without necessarily having much training. A phenomena on the decline as movie theaters bring different kinds of
entertainment to the village commons, the *nachni* culture originated
probably with the zamindari system in the sixteenth century. The
zamindars, or feudal lords, charged initially by the Mughal emperors
and later by the British to collect taxes from the agricultural laborers in their constituency, entertained themselves through performances by village *nachnis* on some occasions and by the much more
exalted *baijis* on more prestigious ones. Denied both the cachet and
the financial compensation that accrued to the *baiji* through the artistry of her practice on one hand and the patronage of the temple and
the raja that were mandatory for the *devadasi* on the other, the *nachni*,
usually hailing from desperately poor homes, found themselves at
the mercy of a rasik, who is usually credited for having 'discovered'
them. The rasik has his own family and home, and the *nachni*, who
is understood to be under his total control once he has initiated her
into the profession, is a totally marginalized part of his household.
He is generally talented as a madol drummer, often a composer of
songs, and sings the celebrated romantic jhumur songs of Bengali folk
culture with her, as she sings and dances, for different village audiences, night after night. As can be expected in this situation, he also
controls her financially.

The poetry of jhumur songs, written in particular dialects of Bengali,
have enchanted well-known poets such as Kazi Nazrul Islam, who wrote
several songs based on the jhumur style. But there is little written about
the stylistic particularities of the dance of the women who were the
mainstay of these performances. Still, Tripti Biswas, in her field study
of the *nachni*, clearly indicates that this is a competitive profession, and
the women vie with each other in terms of their skills in dancing, the
arch of their eyebrows, the rhythmic tappings of their feet. She also
writes hauntingly about their desire to please audiences with popular
jhumur songs, matching the sentiments of the crowds on specific occasions, as their exhaustion mounts. Biswas exclaims about their little-
acknowledged labor: why do they work so hard, dance out their hearts,
when no acclaimed reviewer will mention their names in the next
morning's newspaper? (Biswas, 2003: 44, my transliteration).

Recently recognized as a 'folk dance' form, a necessary classification
if the state is to allocate any resources to it, is this rural entertainment
form going to be appropriated by city women searching for a 'new' form
that will mark their dancing careers? Will it be cast as a little-known
village form that needs to be 'cleansed' and 'sophisticated' to become

acceptable? Aforementioned scholar Mahua Mukherjee, in her efforts to legitimize the *nachni* tradition as part of the *Gaudiya Nritya* form, performed the *nachni* dances she had learned from her guru Sashi Mahato, in Rabindra Sadan Prangan in Kolkata on 17 February 2007. I cannot help but remember how 'classical' dances were repeatedly legitimized through appropriation by the urban elite, and how ultimately these forms, instead of simply becoming accepted in the public domain as performance traditions, really entered the cultural market as representations of 'tradition' that could be brokered primarily by performers from the upper classes. Can we witness the performances of such subalterns on their own terms? I remember the haunting tones of Postobala *nachni* singing her rasik Bijoy Karmakar's jhumur composition (2007), which urges recognition of the desperate poverty and indignity in this situation: *Puruliar nachni ki jhamp dibek jaley, budhhijibi, samajsebi, dao na kene bole?* (O intellectuals and social workers, tell us, must the *nachnis* of Purulia drown themselves in the river?). I was deeply moved by this stark reminder that little of the gains of the women's movement and of the government's development schema have reached this community, but I wondered how much of the celebration of physical and sexual love, central to the jhumur tradition, would have to disappear as their struggle becomes drawn into the rhetoric of human rights? (I am approaching this from thinking about a dilemma of GLBTQ communities in Bengal, who have, since 2003, organized a pride march in Kolkata. Some organizers have objected to the 'flamboyant' performative participation of the hijra community and other cross-dressers, which, they argue, spectacularizes the march and distances it from the 'serious' demand for rights. I wonder if, within such movements, given the necessary emphasis on the violations of rights and restorative justice, it might be productive to actively theorize excess, particularly in relationship to performative stagings of sexualities, as a strategy that provokes and mobilizes without necessarily distracting from the focus on legal and social justice?)

Of other women professionals in performance, those who are closest in lineage to the *nachni* though different, are the women entertainers of urban sites such as Kolkata and Dhaka known as the *khemtawalis*, who came from the lowest rungs of the socio-economic ladder and often were the neighbors of the *baijis* in the red-light areas of these cities in the early nineteenth century. Sumanta Banerjee, who has written much about the ways in which these entertainers, singers, and dancers came to be constituted as prostitutes extradited from social recognition in the colonial era, describes the khemta as a 'strongly rhythmical dance form set to lively music accompanying equally ebullient love songs. Practitioners of this dance form [...] harked back to the vivacious folk dances and songs that had been traditionally popular in the country-side of western Bengal, like jhumur' (2000: 12). A more typical opinion of the times is found in the Bengali journal, *Banga Darshan*, edited by novelist Bankim Chandra Chattopadhyaya, who in 1873 deplored the khemta dance, linking its origin to vulgar Tantric practices, describing it as 'marked by "abominable contortions of the middle part of the body"' (in Banerjee, 2000: 14), which indicates the earthy lusts and desires articulated in the khemta. In contrast, the dance of the *baijis* claimed aspirations to the kind of thought and spirituality that was seen in older Hindu scriptures, and the artistic refinement that flourished under the patronage of the Mughal courts, the latter being where this tradition was centered.

As Banerjee has demonstrated, although all of these professional entertainers were linked to sexual availability and promiscuity, and often prostitution, the class-consciousness among their clientele was an important factor in determining the socio-economic status of the women who entertained them. For instance, referring to the popularity of the *baijis* among the Bengali babus – the English-educated middle class – and their English associates, Banerjee writes:

> There was a somewhat sneaking attraction for the baijis – who evoked the ambience and charm of the feudal aristocracy of the Moghul era – among the newly arrived British settlers in Bengal who were enamored of the exotic Orient, the members of the old Bengali aristocracy who inherited the pre-British cultural norms and love for North Indian classical music and dance, and the new class of parvenu banias and dewans who wanted to impress their British patrons by flaunting their patronage of the baijis.
>
> (2000: 14)

Banerjee's substantial examination of the reconstitution of the courtesan, and of the professional entertainer as prostitute only, also allows us to trace how the categorization and containment of sexualities were a historical legacy of colonial rule. For example, regulatory measures, such as the Cantonment or the Contagious Diseases Act of 1864, were introduced by the colonial government apparently in order to protect the several different classes of British soldiers posted in India from sexually transmitted diseases. These diseases were supposedly acquired through contact with native women, whose glamour and allure, emphasized through their skills as 'dancing girls,' were almost impossible to resist. Such measures had various economic and political impacts and were key in repositioning different classes of women performers as colonial subjects in ways that vitally marked their bodies and histories.

Even as the lines are blurred, I want to draw attention to the disjunction between the pre-colonial courtesan, the *devadasi*, the concubine, all of whom, through the Mughal times, were recognized as part of the state machinery, 'required to serve the public, and enjoying in return certain privileges and protections from the state' (Banerjee, 2000: 19), and the later, different classes of performers, such as the *baiji*, the *khemta-wali*, the *nachni*, and traveling entertainers loosely grouped together as the *nautch* girls. Colonial regulations were often key in morphing these latter figures into a general category of sex workers, operating in an uncanny foreshadowing of today's free trade zones, where no government owed these women anything. Crucial to this history is the distinction British colonial rule introduced: though all of these roles were inscribed in patriarchal systems, the colonial regime introduced the angle of 'morality by attaching a stigma to prostitutes, and banishing them from society' (2000: 23).

> *How do I watch Posto's quick-moving dancing feet,*
> *where the alta and blood mix freely?*
> *Posto, can there be any pleasure in this flow of red?*[22]

Increasingly shorn of claims to artistry, those positioned on the lowest rungs of entertainment work, the *khemtawalis* and other urban cousins of the village *nachnis*, who mostly came to this work out of economic desperation, found themselves with fewer and fewer resources. They became women workers in a field singular for its erasure of their labor and societal function. In a strange looping back of history, the *nachni* are currently assisted in forming their own Federation by Durbar, a Kolkata-based forum of sex workers, which is branching out, with its work on the *nachni* women, to organizing women in the entertainment industry.

The critique of capitalism

One of my most fulfilling memories of dancing is at a Radical Humanist Conference in Kolkata in 1984. I did not understand then the possible import of the philosophy celebrated at this conference.

I only knew that we, a small ensemble of dancers, singers, and musicians, who often worked together and believed we were committed to a leftist ideology in our artistic work, were invited by famous songwriter and conference participant, Hemango Biswas, to perform at the end of the conference. Held in a small, disheveled, broken-down performance space of a local school, and attended by some leading thinkers of this movement, the performance consisted of a series of dances and songs based partly on folk traditions. These dances spoke generally of the struggles of the laboring masses and the impending revolution. I loved performing the pieces that formed the repertory of this group, where I functioned as choreographer and dancer. I found them exhilarating largely because, different from the classical repertoire, there was indeed the promise that dance can bring on the revolution, albeit with the help of powerful lyrics and music. There was also the possibility of strong and vibrant movement, dancing alongside a male colleague without playing a traditional 'female' role, and the euphoria of participation in a social change movement. However, by the time I left Kolkata in search of reunderstanding the possibilities of dance, this ensemble had pretty much petered out. And, struggling with lack of resources and with audiences who were unwilling to forsake the glamour and prestige that accrued to other mainstream performances, the participants had become disillusioned about the power of their work.

And at the time of writing this chapter, nearly two decades later, the visionaries of a movement inspired by the same leftist ideologies are working incessantly to try to halt the corporatization of a government initially elected by the working classes. In this resistance movement, urgently articulated to critique recent atrocities committed by Bengal's left-front government in the context of land rights violations, there is a lot of theater (such as the work of director Suman Mukhopadyay), film (documentaries by Ladly Mukherjee), music (the CD 'Nandigram' recorded by Kabir Suman), and literature (several pieces published by veteran writer Mahasweta Devi), but little dance. What about the incredible power of dancing bodies to stage protest? Is this the power of capital to subvert and co-opt? or the numbing effect of a cosmetic 'beauty'?

Nonetheless, I want to claim this movement, which has its roots in the Indian People's Theatre Association (IPTA) activities, as a vital piece of Bengal's performance culture, one in which several women played an important part. The IPTA was formed in 1942, and its constitution framed at a conference held in Bombay in 1945. Reportedly, the goals of this organization were:

(i) To foster the development of the theater, music, dancing, and other fine arts and literature in India, as an authentic expression of the social realities of our epoch and the inspirer of our people's efforts for the achievement of peace, democracy, and cultural progress;

(ii) To provide healthy and educative entertainments to the people in India, through all available forms of art;

(iii) To organize schools, lectures, libraries, and exhibitions, and to print and publish magazines pamphlets and books and other literature for the purpose of training artists and imparting education to the public on all matters pertaining to Indian culture.
(qtd in Pradhan, 1985, vol. 1: 253)

The potential impact that performing and other arts could have on an active agenda of social change was clear to the delegates gathered at this conference, as was the alignment of 'authenticity,' whatever that might mean, with an artistic practice that reflected the 'people's' realities. What I want to draw attention to is precisely that, although the language references Marxist ideas of false consciousness in the conceptualizing of a 'people's' art without any nuance in understanding 'authenticity,' what is unmistakable throughout the document is the conviction about the power of a 'committed' artistic practice. Moreover, although there is absolutely no attempt at actively dismantling patriarchal formations or constellations of power, my interest lies in examining whether this movement and its endorsement of a 'committed' practice might have offered some women dancers the possibility to reimagine their dance, and their dancing bodies as empowered and articulate.

Sudhi Pradhan's remarkable work, which compiles documents pertaining to the Progressive Writers' and IPTA initiative, sheds much light on the way in which work was received and critiqued at this time by the artists who were part of this movement. There seems to be a questioning of the idealization of the body through a practice of technique for its own sake (often aligned with classical practice) and a clear preference for representations of 'folk' life – which come to stand in for the life of the 'people' in a country where agriculture was still one of the most dominant livelihoods. The Annual Report filed in 1946, in fact, reports on activities over the past several years and describes performances by the Bengal squad of IPTA at a time when the famine was raging in that state – performances arranged as fund-raisers to relieve the misery of the peasants.[23] The report talks about the 'Hunger and Epidemic Dance' created and performed by Usha Datta and Panu Paul in 1943, which moved audiences deeply with its depiction of the plight of the starving people's of Bengal, so much so that audience members rushed to donate rupee notes and women's gold bangles to help in the relief efforts. Usha Datta and Panu Paul are, in fact, much mentioned performers of IPTA at this time, but there is little recorded beyond their names and stirring performances.

When the Bengal squad toured Bombay in 1944, there is mention of 'Starvation and Epidemic,' a ballet choreographed by Panu Paul, possibly a different version of the duet danced by Paul and Datta the previous year. This was presented along with the 'Famine Ballet' choreographed by Santikumar Bardhan, who worked with Uday Shankar. Both of these won much acclaim, and one of the press clippings cited in the report is quoted as having applauded the program thus: 'Here is art frankly utilized for the depiction of contemporary social reality – the plight of Bengal. Every song, every dance, every play is focused on this theme. And yet there is nothing cheap, nothing banal, nothing inartistic in the whole programme' (qtd in Pradhan, 1985, vol. 1: 295). There is little other information about the dance specifically, and with Bengal being a strong site for a progressive theater movement with groundbreaking plays such as *Nabanna*, it is theater that grabs the major share of attention in remaining records. I have tried many times to conjure up these dances in my mind's eye, particularly to imagine what the women looked like: clearly it offered artistic possibilities not totally subsumed under political propaganda. Clearly, too, all of the primary choreographers were male and enjoyed obvious creative agency. But did the women mark their performances in particular ways, details that might be attributed to their personal artistic style?

Pradhan's compilation also contains a critique written in 1952–53 by Hemango Biswas of the work of choreographer Uday Shankar, who had a relationship with IPTA from 1944. Biswas's essay suggests that Shankar's early work held a promise and was based on a sense of 'humanism,' different from the religious base of so much other dance. He applauds Shankar's early pieces such as *Peasant Couple* and *Grasscutter Girl*, which celebrate the dignity of the working classes despite the intensity of labor and paucity of resources. But he makes a clear distinction between these and Shankar's later major work, *Labor and Machinery*, where 'he drew our sympathy towards the exploited workers and roused our wrath against their exploiters, even though his characters were divorced from the social context and free from its struggles and consequently somewhat idyllic' (in Pradhan, 1985, vol. 2: 458). Biswas laments this disjunction and also that Shankar's work became increasingly romantic and distanced from the urgency of the class struggle. He argues that Shankar's later work came to focus increasingly on technique for its own sake, and presented fantasy and spiritual release beyond life as alternatives to successful class struggle. *Labor and Machinery*, for instance, has an elaborate dream sequence, which might be argued to distract from the focus on working-class life conditions.

I read in this critique hints about the unarticulated ideologies that framed the dancing bodies, particularly women's dancing bodies, which inhabited stages marked as socially progressive spaces, in mid-century. It suggests the ambivalences that might have haunted these performers, and possibly their unannounced efforts to body forth feminine subjectivities: navigating away from the idealized romantic figure of the emerging classical category, the sexualized fleshy bodies of the entertainers, and even the cleansing that was coming to mark forms that could be claimed as different forms of 'tradition' – could it be that these women's performances veered towards some idealized notion of 'pure' energy marking laboring bodies? I suggest that these ambivalences and others, imperatives and influences from Western modern dance for instance, sit on the shoulders of dancers and choreographers even now, particularly as they negotiate their way to a 'contemporary' aesthetic that can beckon to a feminist politics.

Looking for a 'new'

This part of the *kantha* must remain etched in broad outlines only due to limitations of space, but the availability of much more literature on more recent phenomena can perhaps allow readers the opportunity to fill out the map here. *Kantha* stitchers typically used old threads from the saris to embroider, threads that had stood the test of wash and wear. I suggest that readers might think similarly here, interpreting this section in the light of the questions I have tried to ask in previous sections.

On 15 August 1983, Manjusri Chaki-Sircar, recently returned from Nigeria and the United States where she had lived for the past several years, founded the Dancers' Guild in Kolkata, a choreographic laboratory whose main focus was movement experimentation. She and her daughter, Ranjabati Sircar, led an ensemble of dancers in exploring different vocabularies and the articulation of different ideas. With this group of dancers they also began to articulate their concept of Navanritya, literally new dance. Navanritya referred primarily to a new mode of training that enabled the dancers to deconstruct traditional vocabulary in order to articulate different ideas. Manjusri Chaki-Sircar's impatience with the patriarchal stranglehold on classical training struck a cord with many young dancers and they embraced the 'new' of deconstruction.[24] In an interview in 1990, she told me: 'We need an ideological revolution: new dancers need to challenge the ethos of dance tradition impressed upon them' (Chaki-Sircar, personal communication 1990).

> *No alta marked these dancers' feet: they marked their feminine, feminist aesthetics through loud footwork, jumps, and yogic extensions.*

Chaki-Sircar and Sircar were instrumental in inaugurating a feminist body consciousness at least in the urban landscape of Kolkata. But their untimely deaths (Sircar in 1999 and Chaki-Sircar in 2000) meant that they were unable to establish navanritya as a sustainable model. The Dancers' Guild continues to perform, led by a new Artistic Director, Jonaki Sarkar, sometimes staging revivals of the former's works, but it has ceased to make much of a mark. For one, the clear feminist imagery that Chaki-Sircar brought to the stage has dissipated almost completely, rupturing the brilliant fusion of a soft femininity of line and body attitude and boldly feminist sexuality and thematic focus that had been the particular accomplishment of Chaki-Sircar's choreography.

What red is possible?

Tomar payer talaye jeno go rang laagey. A love song from Tagore's illuminating dance-drama *Taasher Desh* (Land of Cards), which encourages communities to break through inherited customs and conventions, the lyrics suggest that the red touching the soles of the heroine Haratani's feet heralds the possibility of romance, imagination, and new ways of inhabiting spaces. This song has haunted me throughout the writing of this chapter: when did the possibility of reddened feet become hardened lines of alta that necessarily lined the feet of professional women dancers? When did it become inextricably mixed up with the blood oozing from their torn feet? Postobala *nachni* was complaining one day, as she finished dancing, that her feet hurt from a glass shard wedged in her sole. When I urged her to take care, her rasik, possibly stung by my unnecessary intervention, told me firmly that, in their community, the people's feet are hardier than I could ever imagine, even with my years of dance training.

Thinking of how I fumbled to answer his retort, I realize that the possibility of concluding is here precluded. I have been unable to separate out the alta from the blood, from romantic red hues, or to trace how and when they have transformed into each other in this chapter, but this I have learned: the feet of dancing women in Bengal now, even when casting marvelous creative hues, still fall on ground bloodied and marred with glass from broken bottles of alta and the spilt dye itself. The best I can do is to align my musings here with Kumkum Sangari's mode of mapping the possible: 'A method that could acknowledge the weight of relationality and make theoretical space for more than it demonstrated' (1999: xlviii). It is my hope that, by indicating the uneven and sometimes indeterminate ground of dancing, I have been able to nudge open some spaces where we can conjure up the many bodies whose dancing did/does not make it into the historical record.

Notes

1. Alta is a red dye, used traditionally by women in Bengal to line the edges of their feet. Originally made from crushed hibiscus petals, it is currently factory produced with chemical dyes and, particularly in Bengal, is a small-scale cosmetic industry. Alta has also been used by dancers across India to draw attention to their feet.
2. The ground-breaking work of Dr Amrit Srinivasan about *devadasis*, locating the dance at the intersection of several social, political, and economic formations, is an example to the contrary in this field.
3. See, for instance, my essay, 'Contestations: Constructing a Historical Narrative for Odissi' (2004).
4. These are both forms that gained stature through the complicated politics of naming and claiming during the period of cultural revivalism (mid-twentieth century), and importantly through the interventions of diasporic communities thereafter.
5. I am grateful to dance scholar Urmimala Sarkar-Munshi for helping me articulate this distinction clearly (Personal Communication, December 2007).
6. Gurusaday Datta, collector par excellence of folk arts and crafts of Bengal describes the kantha as 'a poor man's blanket made of old pieces of cloth patched and sewn into a single whole' (1954: 104). However, his collection, exhibited at the Gurusaday Museum, demonstrates the imaginary range of the women who crafted various objects of daily use, handkerchiefs, scarves, bed sheets, as extensions of the kantha.
7. I am referring here to the concept of the rhizome as a mode of knowledge production, as articulated by philosophers Deleuze and Guattari, particularly in *A Thousand Plateaus: Capitalism and Schizophrenia*, as a way of knowing that works through horizontal and cross-lateral connections, and through principles of heterogeneity.

8. Historian Bernard Cohn analyzes that the British codifications were rent with reductionisms and misnamings: 'In the conceptual scheme which the British created to understand and to act in India, they constantly followed the same logic; they reduced vastly complex codes and their associated meanings to a few metonyms [...]. India was redefined by the British to be a place of rules and orders; once the British had defined to their own satisfaction what they construed as Indian rules and customs, then the Indians had to conform to these constructions' (1996: 162).

9. *Gaudiya Dance, A Collection of Seminar Papers*, edited by Pallab Sengupta, Manabendu Banerjee and Mahua Mukherjee, was published by the Asiatic Society, Kolkata in 2005. Mukherjee (2004) also attempts to relate the *devadasis* of yore to the *nachni*, once again seeking to establish a respectable lineage.

10. Much of this discussion draws on personal communication with Mukherjee in Kolkata in December 2007.

11. Bishnupur was the capital of the Malla kingdom, which flourished in the seventeenth and eighteenth centuries, with temples such as Shyamarai, Jorbangla, Madanmohan, and Radheshyam being built in that period.

12. Scholars like John Hawley, Graham Schweig, and Norvin Hein have written about the *ras leela*, though their focus is not on the Gaudiya schools. Their work, in fact, is much cited by historians of the classical form, Kathak, where the myths of Radha and Krishna have inspired much of the choreography.

13. *Devadasis* are traditionally women dedicated to a particular deity at a young age, and remain employed at the temple in the service of that deity. A primary part of their work includes singing and dancing before the deity as spiritual offering.

14. I learnt Behula's dance from Shambhu Bhattacharya, a repository of folk dance knowledge, a song collected by famous folk poet Hemango Biswas: *O tomra dekho go chahiyaa, Behulaye netto korey chomkiya chomkiya* (O all, please watch how Behula dances with spirit and flair!).

15. While these views are expressed severally, the classic example is perhaps Lord Macaulay's, member of the Governor-General's Council of Bengal from 1834–38, description: 'The physical organization of the Bengali is feeble even to effeminacy [...] His pursuits are sedentary, his limbs delicate, his movements languid [...] Courage, independence, veracity, are qualities to which his constitution and his situation are equally unfavorable' (1843: 345).

16. See Rosselli (1980).

17. In *The Baratachari Synthesis*, published by the Bengal Bratachari Society in 1981, Datta (1937) emphatically claims the goals of the movement to be to revive a holisitic approach to life, which modernity has shattered. Re-establishing the connection of men and women to the indigenous cultural practices of their region is one of the key elements in this system.

18. See Datta (1934).

19. *Given To Dance*, produced and directed by Ron Hess, 1985.

20. This review is cited in Bangladeshi thinker Lubna Marium's essay 'Tagore's dance dramas,' in the Dhaka-based newspaper *New Age* (6 May 2005). I accessed it at: www.newagebd.com/2005/may/06/arts.html

21. Sindhubala's life is recorded by Tripti Biswas (2003). Another important sociological study of the life of the *nachni*, though it speaks little about their artistry, has been written by Dr Dipak Barapanda (2007).
22. A source of anger and pain for Postobala is that she can never have children. A previous rasik had had her forcibly sterilized when she was 16. She laments that her blood finds 'no fulfillment' (personal communication, December 2007).
23. That the performances and the formation of IPTA were sparked by the 1943 famine is significant because of the particular importance of the class oppression interwoven in this history. Economist Amartya Sen, among other scholars, has argued effectively that the famine was caused, not by a sudden huge shortfall in rice production, but by a huge discrepancy actively caused by manipulation and ineffective administration, marking a coalescence of the local land-owners and the colonial government. Thus the performances were critiques of such imbrications of power.
24. While I think the descriptor 'new' allies her politics to a modernist one, Manjudi's practice in fact problematized this name. Like the *kantha*, the new worked from what existed, dismantling what she deemed as patriarchal and problematic, and extending movements she felt had the potential for greater expressivity.

7

Artistic Utopias: Michio Ito and the Trope of the International

Yutian Wong

Michio Ito is often referred to as both an 'international artist' and 'the forgotten pioneer' in the canon of US modern dance. The coupling of these titles speaks to the multi-faceted contradictions found in the narration of his career by dance critics and historians. This chapter analyzes the political tensions of 'forgetting' Ito by revisiting narrations of his career in relationship to racialized understandings of the category – 'international artist' – in order to understand why Ito the 'international' must remain remembered as 'forgotten' within canonical narratives of early modern dance in the United States. Ito's status as an 'international artist' – a carefully honed, racially ambiguous, subjectivity – is disrupted upon the bombing of Pearl Harbor and US entry into World War II when subject to legal discourse (Executive Order 9066). His racially marked Japanese body becomes irreconcilable with an American modern dance history dependent upon narratives of US nationalism as a formative and productive means to achieve recognition for modern dance.

To understand how race functions in relationship to the contradiction between Ito's status as an international artist (his ubiquitous presence) and his status as forgotten pioneer (his absence), this chapter explores the case of Ito as an example for investigating the ways in which the trope of the non-white 'international artist' is often used to gloss the political exigency of racial, ethnic, gender, and class difference suggested by the term 'artist-of-color'. In the narration of socially decontextualized and personalized professional histories that span geographic regions including both Western and non-Western locales, the international artist has come to signify the utopian end of race as a highly politicized and polarizing category.

To rethink the complexities of Ito's career path and positioning in dance history I highlight seemingly insignificant moments in Ito's career that speak to the discrepancies between his past fame and his contemporary absence. I then situate his fame/absence within a career trajectory as it is commonly retold, in order to establish him as an 'international artist' while simultaneously offering an Asian Americanist critique. The chapter concludes by complicating notions of the international as both an erasure and inscription of race and ethnicity.

LOS ANGELES, April 1 (AP.) –

Michio Ito, widely known Japanese dancer, was divorced today by Mrs. Hazel Agness Ito, dancer, known professionally as Hazel Wright. Miss Wright said that Ito stayed out nights, was intoxicated frequently and was abusive. They were married in New York April 6, 1923, and separated Feb. 23, she testified.

(*New York Times,* 2 April 1936)

Reports of Michio Ito's divorce from Hazel Wright, a dancer in his company, appeared in major newspapers across the country. The *New York Times* attributed Ito's drinking and late-night carousing as the cause of the split, while the *Chicago Daily Tribune* reported a vague reference to Ito as having become increasingly Oriental after 13 years of marriage (*Chicago Daily Tribune* 1936). I include this high-profile gossip (if one can so call a by-line in the *New York Times*) as a testament to Ito's fame. The fact that the details of his personal life would make their way into the national news demonstrates the completeness to which Ito has been excised from US dance history. The reports of Ito's divorce also mark the conditions of his fame, under which he was framed as both 'abusive' and 'increasingly Oriental' in the years after the 1928 Denaturalization Act that stripped Asian Americans of their US citizenship and barred all Asian immigration. This framework, in which I read a moment in Ito's life through critical Asian American historicization, needs to be reconnected to the larger trajectory of Ito's career because it allows for an interdisciplinary rethinking of Ito's biography – his meteoric rise to international fame and his disappearance from dance history and the United States.

Accounts of this legendary rise to fame always begin with Ito at the age of 17 or 18 traveling to Germany from Japan to study at Emile Dalcroze's school in Hellerau. From Germany Ito traveled to London, where his mythic ascent is fully realized in true bohemian fashion when, as a starving young (dance) artist, he was discovered in a café by the poet Ezra Pound. Taken by the novelty of a French-speaking,

Japanese, German expressionist dancer, Pound took Ito under his wing and introduced the dancer to W. B. Yeats (Caldwell, 1977).

Here began the collaboration that would change Ito's life. As Yeats's storied muse, Ito would provide the inspiration for *At the Hawk's Well* while dancing his way into the hearts and salons of the European social elite, not unlike the way in which Isadora Duncan and Ruth St Denis enjoyed support from US and European socialites. By 1916, Ito had made such a name for himself in London that he was recruited to perform with the Ziegfeld Follies in New York City a decade after congress passed the 1907 Gentleman's Agreement Act. In response to anti-Asian sentiment on the part of the United States, and increasing reports of the exploitation and abuse of Japanese laborers in the United States, the Japanese government agreed to US pressures to end the migration of Japanese laborers to the United States. In exchange for Japan's 'voluntary' cessation of exporting Japanese laborers to the United States, the city of San Francisco in California would be required to allow the American-born children of Japanese immigrants to attend otherwise racially segregated, whites-only schools. In spite of this legislation, Ito was allowed in the country as a 'gentleman' – a category reserved for students, intellectuals, and other 'desirable' professionals.

After a brief stint with the Follies, Ito shook off the bonds of commercialism that they represented to pursue his 'art' again, much like the story told of Martha Graham's split from Denishawn and the Ziegfeld Follies. Less than three years after his arrival in New York City, Ito began teaching his own brand of 'modern dance technique' that coupled his reinterpretation of Dalcroze Eurythmics and the symbolic gestural qualities of Kabuki and Noh that had so fascinated Pound and Yeats. By the 1930s, Ito was a well-established modern dance choreographer and teacher. His contemporaries, Martha Graham, Doris Humphrey, and Charles Weidman would later become canonized as textbook examples of 'American choreographers.'[1]

In the late 1920s the city of Pasadena in Southern California recruited Ito to set up a school and stage mass-movement choirs for the newly built Rose Bowl. Upon his arrival in California, Ito was already considered a well-established artist who could propel the city of Pasadena towards its cosmopolitan dreams of becoming a world-class urban center by way of a thriving arts scene. Critics lauded Ito's dance spectacles, and work in the Hollywood film industry soon followed. Ito would remain in California until 1941, where his school provided the training ground for Georgia Graham (Martha Graham's sister), Lester Horton (Alvin Ailey's mentor), and Bella Lewitsky.

In September of 1929, Ito staged 'The New World Symphony,' a movement choir that included 200 dancers, a symphonic orchestra, and choruses for the first and last Pageant of Lights held at the Pasadena Rose Bowl in celebration of the installation of the largest sun arc ever used. Helen Caldwell, Ito's biographer and former company member, described the Dalcroze-influenced work as that which surpassed Dalcroze's ideas of music visualization, since Ito's choreography was entirely devoid of pantomimic gesture and narrative. The choreography featured groups of dancers in long dresses creating geometric patterns in space to represent musical themes (Caldwell, 1977: 86).

According to newspaper accounts, it was the most costly and elaborate pageant ever staged at the Rose Bowl with over 5000 people in attendance. The highlight of the evening was the 'Shadow Dance,' a solo in which Ito danced in front of a 40-foot gold screen illuminated by floodlights. Critics described Ito in the following terms:

> His dominance of the Bowl was the dominance of the artist. The dance in itself was extraordinary, with only the upper portion of the body, the arms and head serving as a medium of expression. Recalled to the stage he performed the dance a second time, and the audience gave every indication of being willing to see it as many times as he could be induced to perform it [...]
>
> (qtd in Caldwell, 1977: 9)

This review appeared in the *Pasadena Star News* in September 1929 and makes no mention of Ito's race or ethnicity.

The following year, Ito choreographed a production at the Hollywood Bowl that included Borodin's 'Prince Igor.' Staged during the Great Depression, Ito's productions drew praise from the press. Patterson Greene of the *Los Angeles Examiner* wrote: 'The Japanese director contrived a genuine symphony of movement, unconventional in its vocabulary of gesture and of absorbing, exciting interest. The whole spectacle was a triumph of gorgeousness that inspires the hope for others of the kind. Such an artist as Ito is an asset to the community' (16 August 1930, as quoted in Caldwell, 1977: 94). Although identified as 'Japanese,' Greene writes primarily about Ito as an artist. Characterizing Ito as an 'asset to the community,' he tacitly opposes the decades of escalating anti-Japanese sentiment in California that had resulted in the passage of a series of Alien Land Laws between 1917 and 1923.

The fact that the city of Pasadena recruited Ito to leave a successful career in New York City in 1929 is odd. During the late 1920s and early

1930s, the racial climate in California for its Asian-raced populations continued to deteriorate as efforts to foreclose all possibilities for people of Japanese ancestry to legally own land and run businesses reached an all-time high. White anxiety over interracial marriage between Filipino men and white women fueled the California senate's efforts to clarify its racial categories on who and what constituted Asianness, in order to strengthen and enforce its anti-miscegenation laws to ban all marriages between Asian men and white women. White women who married non-citizen Asian men were stripped of their US citizenship in an effort to curb the growth of an interracial population. These laws also closed a loophole in which non-white immigrant men could gain legal US citizenship through marriage.

In 1941 after the bombing of Pearl Harbor, the US Federal Bureau of Investigation investigated Michio Ito, along with hundreds of other prominent persons of Japanese ancestry then living on the West Coast of the continental United States, for espionage and treason. Ito was most likely targeted for his frequent lectures on the history and merits of Japanese art and philosophy – lectures that made Ito a darling of the cultural elite in London, New York City, and Los Angeles. Imprisoned in a detention camp in New Mexico where the US Justice Department and the US Army held individuals as 'troublemakers' and individuals of 'special interest' to the US government, Ito eventually chose repatriation to Japan rather than spend what, in 1942, would have been an indefinite amount of time living under the humiliating conditions of the internment camps.[2]

Ito also performed, in addition to his own modernist choreographies, Orientalized versions of various Asian dance forms and tangos popularized by white modern dancers Ruth St Denis and Ted Shawn. Ito taught at the Denishawn school where Martha Graham, Doris Humphrey, and Charles Weidman were former students. One of Graham's closest collaborators, the Japanese-Scottish designer/sculptor Isamu Noguchi, would help to change the aesthetics of what has become a uniquely American modern dance tradition over his 30 years of work with her. Noguchi's bust of Ito sits alongside the sculptor's set designs for Graham in the Robert Wilson-designed retrospective.[3] Ito, however, never achieved similar recognition, even though obituaries and memoirs of long-forgotten modern dancers all cite him as an influential teacher. Although Ito is entrenched both spatially and temporally amongst the players who would become the cornerstones of American modern dance history, he is always cast as an anomalous 'international' subject outside mainstream American (dance) history.

Since his death in 1961, Ito has been the subject of multiple retro-spectives, all with an eye towards integrating Ito 'the forgotten pioneer' into the canon of early twentieth-century US modern dance history. Despite the concerted efforts of Satoru Shimazaki in 1979, Repertory Dance Theater in 1991, Seattle's Chamber Dance Company in 2001, and Dana Tai Soon Burgess in 1996 and 2005, Ito continues to remain the obscure and 'all-but-forgotten' pioneer of early American modern dance (*New York Times*, 17 September 1979; Christiansen, 2001; Kaufman, 1996a,b; Littler, 1991; Traiger, 2005a,b). Even in the context of retro-spectives, revivals, and reconstructions, Ito remains in a state of per-petual 'all-but-forgottenness' which constitutes an integral part of his currency within each subsequent revival (Kauffman, *Washington Post*, 6 March 2006; Kisselgoff, 1978). For example, in her review of Dana Tai Soon Burgess's premiere of *Images from the Embers*, Sarah Kaufman refers to Burgess as one who has 'paid tribute to the outmoded and *all-but-forgotten* pioneer Michio Ito [...]' (Kaufman, *Washington Post*, 6 March 2006, my emphasis).

There is a melancholic aura surrounding the fate of Ito's 'forgotten' career. His biography as the celebrated Japanese-born, German-trained, London-approved, New York City-based, Los Angeles-relocated artist has been rehashed over and again. Most reviews of Ito's career, written in conjunction with the various reconstruction projects after his death in 1961, have privileged Ito the 'international artist.' Each time, the story emphasizes Ito as an artist so accomplished that at the height of his career in the 1930s, he was able to transcend the expected limits of inhabiting a racialized body. The circumstances around his arrest and deportation are either ignored or reported as an anomalous political quirk with little bearing on the rest of the modern dance world of the 1940s.

The desire to reclaim Ito is accomplished through the trope of inter-nationality as a process of deracialization overlaid with the desire to domesticate his racial otherness. This desire both distances Ito from the perceived limitations of race, ethnicity, or Japaneseness as a definitive qualifier of his artistic production, while assuming that the categories are in and of themselves limiting. The politics of whiteness, as that which remains invisibly central and absented from racial, ethnic, and national otherness, are never enunciated. In Anna Kisselgoff's review of the 1979 retrospective at the Open Eye featuring a program of Ito's early works with titles such as *Pizzacati* (1916); *Ball* (1928), and *Ave Maria* (1912), she situates Ito as a modern dance pioneer in the 1920s and 1930s alongside well-known modern dance icons such as Martha

Graham. Kisselgoff then proceeds to describe the Ito dance vocabulary in these terms:

> This emphasis on the upper body and arm gestures was the signature of the Ito style, and its influence today can be seen in the work of Mr. Horton. Yet Ito's esthetic was very much a marriage of East and West. He created his own movement vocabulary, discarding realistic gesture, and seeking to use symbolic gesture to convey dramatic ideas with universal resonance. The Kabuki and Noh traditions – with their own concentrated gestures – are not far away.
>
> (1979: C30)

After establishing the presence of East and West in Ito's work, she re-emphasizes the point made by the concert producers that Ito was 'not an "ethnic" choreographer' (Kisselgoff, 1979). Kisselgoff's observations reflect the conundrum posed by Ito, whose legacy escapes categorization.

Without confronting the role of aestheticized Orientalist discourse as the process by which Ito is able to achieve racial transcendence, the contrast between Ito's pre-World War II success and his disappearance from dance history appears to makes no sense.[4] Michio Ito begins his US career in the cradle of early modern dance, and ends up in an indefinable nowhere-as-elsewhere. Clearly not American, Japanese but not too Japanese, famous when most Japanese Americans were largely invisible, the instantiation of Ito's 'internationality' explains the validity and rightfulness of a retrospective, but it also sets into motion Ito's continued post-retrospective absence from US modern dance history.

The 'international'

Exceptionalized, the international artist is conceptualized as an individual who is simultaneously exotic in his/her worldliness and familiar in his/her exoticness. I argue that the appeal of the international artist lies in the execution of a balanced performance of social legibility and bodily difference. Internationality is evidenced by the perceived ability to transcend national borders while maintaining a reified point of origin. This movement back and forth between nation-states is couched in the discourse of world travel without the burdening affects of juridical discourses such as immigration and labor laws.

Described as making a contribution to cultural enrichment, cross-cultural/foreign exchange, or multicultural programming, I argue that the 'international artist' reifies stabilized notions of national narratives within a framework of 'moving across borders.' As a manifestation of the 'well-behaved' migratory body (in contrast to the illegal alien, the migrant worker, or the invading horde – terms that have been used to describe racialized forms of migration into the United States throughout the twentieth century), the racialized international artist's intervention on the international scene is still seen as sensational. However, the sensationality of the artist's artistic misbehavior is reconfigured through the polite terminology of neo-liberal usages of cross- or multiculturalism.

As mentioned earlier, Ito entered the United States as a 'gentleman' and, in this regard, insisting upon a stable place within national US polity, as in the case of the illegal alien, would not have provided Ito any advantage. His very ability to move into and within the United States was predicated on a brand of social mobility in which social mobility could translate into border crossings understood as glamorous travel as opposed to that which is threatening or invasive. Ito was part of a socially mobile upper-class constituency of Asian migrants whose entry into the United States was set apart from the racially contaminating anti-Asian immigration rhetoric. As a well-traveled, international artist invited to enter the United States, Ito possessed a class identity as well as an individual identity that could potentially separate him from the masses of migrant labor that US anti-Asian immigration rhetoric was attempting to hold at bay.

For Ito, mobility was such an important part of his international identity and artistic persona that it does not even matter if many of the travel narratives he recounted to family, friends, and students were either exaggerated or entirely made-up (Cowell, 1994). It is as if Ito's penchant for retelling conflicting stories is forgiven because the stories themselves are necessary for sustaining the investment in his internationality. Ultimately, cast as a European-Oriental, Ito's identity as an international artist situates him within the realm of an elite artist class, able to transcend racial boundaries through a geographically varied personal and professional history. The fact of his 'looking' Japanese situated him in the realm of the exotic, allowing him the cultural cache valued in a creative milieu invested in the consumption of Eastern philosophy, religion, art, and bodily practices (Desmond, 1991; Koritz, 1994; Yoshihara, 2003). But his international career as the fabled muse of Ezra Pound and W. B. Yeats, and darling of London society, garnered him even more exotic appeal as a Europeanized and thus culturally savvy individual.

Unlike Sadda Yacco who became a sensation in Europe and the United States from 1899–1900 by playing up her role as a former geisha who performed 'authentic' yet 'unintelligible' Kabuki dances, Ito drew from a specifically German movement vocabulary made more familiar to white American middle-class women through an early twentieth-century interest in physical culture and dance education. Early on in his career, Ito could perform a bodily language familiar in the living rooms of wealthy white American and European women while also remaining visually exotic. Much later in his career, work in the Hollywood film industry would have provided the financial means and social status to maintain his image (Cowell, 2001; Prevots, 1998).

The feted body of the 'international artist' masks the 'colored' side of globalization. Although globalization is often characterized in terms of economic progress that will ultimately result in a much-needed change in the social sphere, such progress is most often still defined in Western terms, informed by nineteenth-century stereotypes of non-white and non-Western backwardness and moral depravity (Sangari, 1990). Extending this argument to the dancing body, Ananya Chatterjea (2005) examines the conceptual impossibility of a postmodern Indian dance, given working (as in how it is circulated in dominant paradigms of institutionalized dance discourse) definitions of postmodern dance as a historical object that continues to inform present day conceptualizations of choreographic production.[5] Ito, as a historically global subject, is allowed to participate *as* a pioneer or *like* the other pioneers and benefit creatively from the tools of the West, but he can never *be* the pioneer. His synthesis of East and West remains identifiably syncretic whereas the acknowledged Orientalist appropriations of white modern dancers, such as Ruth St Denis, are narrated as necessarily American.

As an 'international artist' in the United States, Ito cannot be integrated into the canon of American dance history invested in maintaining its nativist origins for modern dance. Ann Daly's *Done into Dance* and Suzanne Shelton's *The Divine Dancer* both mark the path by which the idea of America could be claimed in the dance works of Isadora Duncan and Ruth St Denis, even as their works are redolent with reimagined Greek and Oriental antiquities. If the themes of the dances themselves were foreign, Americanness resided ultimately in the specificity of Duncan's and St Denis's dancing bodies – identifiably white and legally American.[6] Julia Foulkes (2001) identifies the 1940s as a period in which the Americanness of modern dance fully established itself after 'bourgeois' modern dance survived the Great Depression and could reap the unpredicted benefits of World War II. Ito's modern dance credentials are impeccable. Like Graham, Humphrey, and Weidman, his work was appropriately 'bourgeois' and, like St Denis and Duncan, his work was appropriately exotic and philosophical. However, Ito's racially marked dancing body, invested in social privileges allowed an 'international artist,' could never become an 'American.'

Racializing ethnicity

Dance historian Mary-Jean Cowell confronts the question of how Ito negotiated his racial difference in her essay 'Michio Ito in Hollywood: Modes and Ironies of Ethnicity' (Cowell, 2001). In the 1930s, Ito appeared in a number of Hollywood films in which he was cast in stereotypical ethnic roles. Cowell situates Ito within Asian American film history, such that Ito was not unlike other 'ethnic actors' relegated to a limited spectrum of acting jobs.

Cowell compares Ito's experience in the Hollywood film industry to that of the newly emerging modern dance scene in California. Without naming it as such, Cowell characterizes the modern dance community as colorblind – one that did not *see* Ito's ethnicity or *see* him as Japanese. The ways in which Cowells sets up Ito's position within these two communities presents a dichotomy between the film industry and dance community – both of which are predominantly white spaces – and fails to account for the racializing discourse of 'not *seeing* ethnicity' in the dance community.

I would argue that it is not the case that the dance community did 'not *see*' Ito's ethnicity, given that Ito's performance of ethnicity, his high class Japaneseness, was his currency. I would propose that Cowell's use of ethnicity as a mode of analysis cannot address how the dance community's investment in Ito's class identity as an 'international artist' allowed Ito to inhabit a temporary and contingent deracialized ethnic identity.[7] To extend Cowell's use of ethnicity as a framework in order to understand Ito's position within the film and modern dance communities, it is necessary to complicate 'ethnicity' because Cowell's description of Ito's negotiations of ethnicity within these communities more accurately describes a process of racialization. For Asian American subjects, the politics of ethnic identification are loaded and subject to misuse, and the terms 'ethnicity' and 'race' are frequently used interchangeably in the interest of tokenization and aestheticized multiculturalism (Lee, 2004: Lowe, 1996).

Cowell observes that Ito appeared in, or collaborated on, numerous films with imperialist themes, such as *Dawn of the East, Madame Butterfly,*

Boo Loo, and *Spawn of the North*, that employed a generically Oriental body that could read as East Asian, Pacific Islander, and Inuit on film. In comparing Ito's Hollywood projects to those of Lester Horton's, Cowell observes that Horton 'experienced none of the ethnically related circumstances, pro and con, that affected most of Ito's Hollywood assignments' (2001: 263). I would argue that under these circumstances, Ito's ethnicity, his Japaneseness, was secondary to his racialized Asian body. In focusing on ethnicity in her attempt to understand the psychology of Ito's relationship to the Hollywood film industry's casting practices, she fails to address the polite avoidance of the juridical consequences of *race* as an explanation for Ito's absence from US (modern dance) history at large.

Ethnicity operates as a racializing marker for the Asian American subject. In the United States, Asian and Asian American bodies are subject to a 'doubled racialization' – the first being that of visible racial difference and the second, that of assumed mandatory 'ethnic identity.' Mandatory ethnicity is used to describe Asian and Asian Americans, according to categories of nation, as that which is either 'known' by (intimate knowledge of national origins and family trees), 'seen' on, (the claim that one can identify bodily features), or 'performed' by the body (language, food, clothing, customs). Ethnicity, in its evocation of that which is both foreign and the racially other, is assumed present and available on the surface of the Asian-looking body. In contrast, white subjects in the United States must unearth ethnicities erased by twentieth-century melting pot rhetoric, while African American relationships to 'ethnicity' are always mediated through discourses of slavery and the politically transgressive recovery of ethnic identity.

Thus, I would argue that Asian and Asian American relationships to ethnicity are essentialized as always already present or waiting for the obvious to be claimed. In other words, Asian American formations of ethnicity are quite often created in response to US discourses of Asian as ethnic-as-racial-as-national difference. For the Asian subject in the United States, ethnicity is a matter of racial and latent national difference, whereas, for the white American subject, ethnicity is quite often a matter of proclaiming the invisible. The mass internment of Japanese and Japanese Americans during World War II is a case in point. Of the 110,000 people interned, two-thirds were legal American citizens and one-half were children and infants. Ito was detained in New Mexico, which also held Italian and German detainees; however, the United States differentiated between Italian and German nationals suspected of political ties with the German and Italian government and did not institute a program in which all Americans with Italian or German ancestry were interned.

In the case of Japanese Americans and Japanese immigrants, the US government conflated race with nationality such that all Japanese immigrants and Japanese Americans became 'enemy aliens.' It is also important to note that prior to the 1950s, Asian immigrants were barred from becoming naturalized American citizens. Legally, first-generation Japanese Americans were not American. The US-born children of Japanese immigrants also held legal Japanese citizenship since Japanese law dictated that all children of parents holding Japanese citizenship are automatically conferred Japanese citizenship at birth. The point here is that legal American citizenship, often considered the crown jewel of national belonging, is always contingent upon racialized readings of the law as demonstrated by Executive Order 9066.

Ito, the impossible subject

Cowell speculates that Ito's absence from modern dance history can be attributed to his move from New York City to California in 1930, which pre-dates John Martin's 1936 lectures – lectures sedimenting the canon of modern dance in the United States – at the New School (Kaufman, 1996a). Cowell's speculation implies that had Ito remained in New York City, he would no doubt have been included in Martin's lectures and duly canonized. This is an astute observation attesting to the legacy of John Martin's lectures, and it reveals the terms upon which US modern dance history has been constructed. I would also consider Cowell's speculation an optimistic view of dance history as a practice in terms of her faith in the translation of Ito's bodily presence in New York City into the written record. The scholarship on African American dance history unearths the ways in which presence does not necessarily translate into inclusion, how inclusion itself is always contingent and subject to racial formations (Gottschild, 1996; Green, 2002; Manning, 2005).

The lament over the fate of Ito's 'forgotten' career is useful for understanding the cultural logic of Ito's international persona as it skirts along the edges of canonical modern dance history. Ito's career is one that appears in dance history as isolated points of contact with the historically recognizable. The awkwardness of Ito is this: to connect these moments of isolated contact into a cohesive narrative feels like a project of rehabilitating a hanger-on. To ignore the mechanics of canonization and claim that one is working from another point of reference elides the conditions of Ito's disappearance from the canon and from the United

States. Take, for example, Mary-Jean Cowell's essay 'East and West in the Work of Michio Ito' (1994), in which Cowell compares Ito's movement vocabulary and choreography to that of Ruth St Denis, Isadora Duncan, Martha Graham, Doris Humphrey, and Dalcroze.

The tenor of Cowell's essay intimates that Ito's incorporation of Eastern aesthetics was more informed than that of St Denis, his music visualizations more rigorous than that of Duncan, his codified approach to teaching movement earlier than that of Graham, his abstract design on a par with Humphrey, and his reinterpretation of Dalcroze more creative than imagined. Cowell concludes that: 'Quite possibly the greatest tragedy in Ito's life may not have been his internment and subsequent deportation. Rather it was the general failure of critics and audiences to fully appreciate his effort to integrate East and West at a more profound level than that represented by contemporary Orientalia' (1994: 20). In this rehabilitative move, Ito is a choreographer worthy of canonization; however, Ito's exclusion from the canon is the responsibility of his contemporary critics and not the continued practice of writing dance history – a history that has yet to consider the significance of Japanese American internment as emblematic of US racial formations.

Historical reappearances: Asian American history

To understand Ito's continuous disappearance from dance history, I turn my focus towards Ito's reappearance into Asian American history. If Ito is to disappear literally from the dance scene (dance history), it is this disappearance (internment/deportation) that rematerializes Ito into Asian American discourse and places him within the matrix of US national discourse. Following Gottschild's reassertion of the centrality of Africanist aesthetics in US concert dance, I argue that Asian American discourse is central to US configurations of race within nationalist concerns. This move differs from Gottschild in that she argues that to see the presence of Africanist aesthetics is to see the presence of the African American subject in US dance history and not just 'African American dance.'

This is not my primary concern in relation to Asian American subjects, for Ito's Asianness and his Orientalist aesthetics are readily acknowledged. I am interested in recognizing Ito's materialization into Asian American history, a maneuver that could be read as a marginalizing one given the efforts by Caldwell and Cowell to situate him as a supranationalist artist. I argue that situating Ito within Asian American history is a centralizing move. It is central in terms of understanding why Ito's 'internationalism' becomes historically illegible within a modern dance history premised on neo-liberal understandings of multiculturalism when it comes to the dancing Asian American body.

An Asian Americanist reading of Ito's relationship to dance history allows for the close examination of the relationship between artistic discourse, class identity and how the subject position of the transnational or international artist is mythologized as a solution to racism. Ito and others like him have become symbolic of the multicultural universal subject, a floating signifier without race, nation, or culture, yet clearly marked as different and Other. In Alan Kriegsman's review of Astad Deboo's Washington DC debut, he compared Deboo's attempt to create a cross-cultural dance aesthetic with that of Asadata Dafora, Uday Shankar, and Michio Ito, who 'built international careers starting, so to speak from the other end and working their way westward' (1990). Mere mention of individuals like Dafora, Shankar, and Ito allows for multicultural inclusionism without a larger discussion of colonization, empire-building, and colonial attitudes towards non-Western artists.

As long as Ito was dancing, he escaped a threatening kind of racialization, but off stage, as in the newspaper reports of his divorce from Hazel Wright, Ito's racialized sexuality evoked a panoply of early twentieth-century stereotypes of Asian men as an economic and cultural menace to the Western world. On stage his single dancing body did not pose an immediate economic threat. In photograph after photograph, Ito is the one Asian body in a sea of white bodies. He is photographed partnering white female dancers and was himself married to a white woman. I would argue that in the wake of public concern over interracial marriage between racially marked men and white women, Ito was viewed as an acceptable 'Oriental' as long as he inhabited an attenuated masculinity.[8] Doubly effeminized as a male Asian dancer, Ito was also further asexualized through descriptions of his dancing. He was lauded by critics; however, a careful analysis of the language used to describe Ito's physicality and his dancing differed from the ways in which writers depicted other celebrated male dancers like Nijinsky and Ted Shawn. Rather than using language that emphasized virility, power, and dynamism, white writers used terms normally deployed in the depiction of female dancers to describe Ito – terms such as 'graceful,' 'gorgeous,' and 'beautiful.'[9]

Interestingly enough, it was the Japanese American community in Los Angeles who viewed Ito with suspicion. In the years preceding World War II, under the advisement of friend and collaborator, the photographer Toyo Miyatake, Ito began to teach dance in the Japanese

American community. Japanese mothers with daughters who wanted to study with Ito considered him morally suspicious. Not only was he a dancer who had worked in Hollywood, but Ito was not a part of the Japanese American community, subject to the forms of racialization that marked a community considered to be 'Japs.' Ito was not part of the working-class community of Japanese Americans who carved out livelihoods as gardeners, domestics, and grocers – jobs Japanese Americans were allowed to do.[10] Married to a white woman, Ito was in more ways than one an outsider to the Japanese American community. Ito was socially mobile in ways that other Japanese Americans were not. His studio in Hollywood required his Japanese American students to leave the racialized space of an ethnic enclave and travel across town to enter Ito's 'racially unmarked' studio. Ironically, Ito's Japaneseness, his knowledge of Japanese art and philosophy, allowed him entrée into spaces usually considered off-limits to his second-generation American-born Japanese students who lived in segregated neighborhoods.[11]

Asian American dance history

As I have tried to demonstrate, Ito is a problematic figure for American dance history. He was at the height of his career in California during the 1930s and embodied the qualities of what would now be recognized as the ideally acculturated immigrant subject as he circulated among his white colleagues and a Japanese American community. His internment and subsequent deportation pose a wrinkle in the otherwise smooth narrative of World War II as the watershed moment in American modern dance history when 'bourgeois modern dance' wins out over 'revolutionary modern dance.' At most this 'win' is attributed to censorship as the 'bourgeois modern dancers' responded appropriately to wartime patriotism by choreographing nostalgic and Americana-themed works such as Graham's 1944 *Appalachian Spring* (Foulkes, 2002).

Such a nationally appropriate response trumps homophobia and racism, and thus creates a space for Ted Shawn, Pearl Primus, and Katherine Dunham to remain in the picture (Foulkes, 2002). Ito on the other hand was literally removed from the narrative. Recasting American modern dance history within the context of the internment forces a rethinking of how this canonical history has made the practice of modern dance an autonomously enabling activity that can exist subversively outside of governmental regulation. Foulkes comes closest to articulating the relationship between the survival of 'bourgeois modern dance' and collaborations with the US state department, but like the speculation around Mary Wigman and Rudolf von Laban's collaboration with the Third Reich, making a direct connection between 'bourgeois modern dancers' and US wartime policies would be too embarrassing and considered extreme, as in the case of Marion Kant's work on Mary Wigman and Rudolf von Laban's ownership of fascist ideologies (Aloff, 2006).[12]

The mass evacuation and relocation of Japanese and Japanese Americans, Japanese Canadians, and Japanese Peruvians in the United States during World War II marks both a literal and metaphorical disappearance.[13] The bodies are both there and not there. Contained and out of sight in ten internment camps located in deserts and swampland, these camps were officially called 'concentration camps' by President Roosevelt. It was not until after the war, once the full impact of Hitler's Final Solution came to light that the Japanese American concentration camps came to be referred to as 'internment' camps. In the grand scheme of things the internment of Japanese Americans cannot be compared to the Holocaust, and thus it is viewed as an embarrassing glitch rather than an alarming failure of due process.

It is impossible to integrate Ito into a dance history that overlooks internment because his deportation does not coincide with the narrative that has been used to account for the integration of African aesthetics and African American choreographers into dance history – inclusion based on presence. Lumped under the historical rubric of 'Negro Dance' and the multicultural rubric of 'Black Dance,' the inclusion of African American modern dance choreographers in US modern dance history has continued to remain an elephant in the room, for its true inclusion requires a full recognition of the processes of exclusion – processes often considered tangential to modernist conceptualizations of what constitutes the parameters of the actual art work in of itself (DeFrantz, 2002; Gottschild, 1996; Green, 2002; Manning, 2004; Perpener, 2001).

If the inclusion of African American modern dancers and choreographers is based on the undeniable presence of black dancing bodies, Ito cannot benefit from the same logic for he literally disappears. It is at this moment of disappearance that Ito becomes legible within Asian American history because internment operates within the discipline as a central component in the formation of Japanese American identity. The same moment of disappearance marks Ito's illegibility within the context of US modern dance history. His internationality becomes his downfall, made especially acute by the fact that one of Ito's main supporters, Ezra Pound, was indicted by a US Grand Jury for making radio broadcasts promoting fascism from Rome during the war. Unlike Hanya

Holm, who managed to dissociate herself from Mary Wigman during the war, Ito could not escape his artistic past becoming more and more 'international' such that his 'internationalness' becomes 'alien.'

It is possible that thinking through Ito's 'internationality' as a form of national impossibility is the process by which Ito 'fits' into US dance history, thus acceding to the ways in which 'dance history' functions in everyday practice as an unacknowledged shortcut for a fixed and objectified canon. There is no question about Ito's past bodily presence. Every retrospective instance proclaims his 'thereness' when insisting upon his inclusion in the canon. I am less interested in seeking Ito's entry into the canon and more interested in understanding the ideological exclusion that the 'international' ultimately entails. The 'international' as it pertains to the Asian body is ultimately a racialized subject position in the face of a national crisis, and not the universal subject able to bridge the gaps of cultural misunderstanding.

What I have attempted here is to offer some ideas for re-examining the utopian rhetoric surrounding and justifying the necessity for inter-cultural or cross-cultural artistic collaborations that will in turn produce an international artist. The call for artistic collaborations has been used as a discursive antidote for racial conflict. Generally, the cross must be made between a Western and non-Western collaborator, preferably Asian (Jeyasingh, 1998). The idea that art can function as a cultural ambassador between people of differing ethnic, racial, and national identities as an attempt to bridge cultural divides was used by the US government during the Cold War when the Alvin Ailey Dance Theater was sent abroad to dispel criticism of white American racism against African Americans. The notion that the arts are able to transcend socio-political boundaries elides the ways in which the arts have been used by governments and artists to define categories of gender, race, and nation (Caute, 2003; Prevots, 1998). Artists themselves are viewed as cultural workers able to create 'alternative' worlds in which cross-cultural collaborations will promote peace and cultural understanding. The artist and particularly artists-of-color are cast in the role of 'cultural social-workers,' in the expectation that their work will 'uplift' 'assuage' and 'heal.' As a result, attempts to solve the problem of cultural difference become depoliticized and conflict is ignored in favor of displaying an idealized vision of resolution. The artistic space becomes romanticized as a safe harbor and the artistic product is envisioned as a sincere solution.

The utopian rhetoric of international collaboration has bled into historical readings of 'international artists.' It might be tempting to continue casting Ito's biography forward such that his articulated 'internationalness' enters contemporary discourses of the global or transnational subject, but Ito's story is a reminder of how easy it is to forget the conditions of migration or the conditional nature of racialized migrations. His deportation signals the failure of his body to overcome theoretical readings of his bodily history and body of work as an exemplary international (transnational) subject (Appadurai, 1996; Dirlik, 1994; Sandhu, 2007).

Notes

1. Mary-Jean Cowell writes 'During the early years of modern dance, Michio Ito was an older contemporary and sometime colleague of Martha Graham, Doris Humphrey, and Charles Weidman' (2001: 263).
2. Most accounts of Ito's career avoid mentioning where Ito was interned. Lisa Traiger, in her preview of the 2005 Ito, Horton, and Lewitsky retrospective, reports that Ito was detained in New Mexico (*Washington Post*, 3 June 2005a). New Mexico was not the site of one of the ten official 'War Relocation Centers' that became known as internment camps, where the majority of Japanese and Japanese Americans were detained during World War II. New Mexico was home to detention centers that held Italian, German, and Japanese prisoners singled out from the general population and considered dangerous or of 'special interest' to the US government or military.
3. 'Isamu Noguchi – Sculptural Design' at the Japanese American National Museum (JANM) 5 February – 4 May 2006 featured over 75 of Noguchi's works displayed in a series of dramatic installations conceptualized by Robert Wilson. The installations included a number of props and set designs created for Martha Graham. Conceived by a German design firm, the show traveled throughout Europe and the United States.
4. Helen Caldwell's biography *Michio Ito: the Dancer and his Dances* has been the primary English-language source asserting Michio Ito's ability to transcend his racial or ethnic identity.
5. Chatterjea (2005) offers an in-depth analysis into the ways in which the concept of contemporary Indian dance (as a definition of time not 'style') is forever caught in a post-colonial relationship with Western modern and postmodern dance aesthetics. Shobana Jeyasighn's autobiographical essay (1998) expresses a similar frustration with the inability to signify outside of this relationship as it is renamed as cultural difference. Modernism/postmodernism, unless specified, remains white. Thus 'cross-cultural' collaboration, which in and of itself does not name any specific aesthetic trajectory, is always assumed as West/non-West, with West meaning white.
6. Isadora Duncan's US passport was revoked in the 1920s; however, Duncan remains artistically American. The confiscation of Duncan's passport remains a historically legal issue that does not diminish her social status as a pioneer of American modern dance. If anything, Duncan becomes *socially* more American as both a political rebel and a victim of the government.
7. I emphasize the racialization of ethnicity, and in particular Asian ethnicity, because Cowell does not seem to investigate how certain ethnicities

are racialized. She draws on the work of Bernardi to understand ethnicity as how we 'see ourselves' and 'express ourselves.' Cowell uses this to infer Ito's ascription of his own ethnic identity, which seems highly problematic. Bernardi defines ethnicity as that which is expressed through a group, yet Cowell draws on materials in which he speaks as an individualist.

8. Ito and his relationship to Asian American masculinity deserve a much longer discussion which is beyond the scope of this paper. Orientalism in of itself is an effeminizing discourse which Ted Shawn transformed by combining Orientalist references with ancient Greek iconography to create a queer hypermasculine stage persona. See Foulkes (2001: 113–46).

9. In the 1920s and 1930s Asian men, particularly Filipino men, were fetishized as good dancers. The popularity of Filipino men among white women at taxi-dance halls gave rise to renewed efforts to ban interracial marriage between Asian men and white American women (Maram, 2006).

10. Personal interview with Amy Iwanabe conducted on 7 September 2001 with the assistance of Denise Uyehara. 'My mother didn't want me to study dance with him. She asked me, "what if he tries to do something [...] I said, "he's an old man, what's he going to try and do?" '

11. Both Caldwell and Cowell chronicle Ito's efforts at lecturing on the merits of merging Eastern and Western aesthetics.

12. Mindy Aloff's response to Marian Kant's (2005) review of *Liebe Hanya*, edited by Claudia Gitelman, takes issue with Kant's charge that Gitelman failed to emphasize Mary Wigman's affiliation with the Nazi regime. Aloff claims that Gitelman does address Wigman's relationship by reporting the scope of the controversy, and characterizes Kant's desire for dance history to recognize the extent of Wigman's collaboration with the Nazi regime as ridiculous. Aloff writes:

> It sounds to me that Gitelman records clearly and reasonably, leaving open the question of whether Wigman was 'really' a Nazi at heart, Kant would like to see chronicled from the presumption that Wigman's Nazi bona fides were unquestionable, that is, from the presumption that Wigman was more than a self-aggrandizing opportunist who had no compunction about expelling Jewish students from her school: that she would have been just as happy to see those students packed into the next boxcar for Auschwitz. Although Kant is welcome to make her argument, there is no reason why Gitelman should be forced to adopt it.
> (2006: 266)

Aloff's response reflects the polite avoidance of naming racism. For her racism is characterized as extreme behavior defined in ridiculously simplified terms – packing Jews into boxcars – rather than ideology that *governs* the seemingly mundane.

13. Not only did the US government intern its own citizens on the mainland, but the United States forced the Peruvian government to turn over its Peruvian citizens of Japanese descent. Japanese Peruvians were detained in separate detention centers run by the INS for the duration of the war. After the war was over, these Peruvian citizens were not allowed to return to Peru but were deported to Japan. See Fusao Inada (2000).

8
Worlding Dance and Dancing Out There in the World

Marta Elena Savigliano

Prompted by the late twentieth-century, and still growing, interest in World Dance evidenced by the emergence of this rubric in US college circles (including courses in Dance departments and newly developed academic jobs), bookings in performing venues (including World Dance festivals and shows), the support offered through funding agencies invested in arts and cultures, and the attention devoted by dance critics and scholars, as by dancers and dance lovers, I propose to consider some questions related to the discursive formation of this field. These questions are entangled with ethico-political concerns. What does 'world dance' actually represent at this historical conjuncture? What is the effect of imposing the 'world,' as a qualifying categorization, on 'dance,' as a set of aestheticized movement practices, in the era of so-called globalization? How does this totalizing framing (the 'world') work to supplement and expand the dance field as it fixes differentiations within it? How are dances from 'out there' selected to be included or excluded from 'world dance'? What kinds of institutional investments, technical knowledges, economic interests, aesthetic and ethical assumptions, political arrangements, pleasures and desires participate in the process of worlding Dance?

To world, to globalize [...] dance

Much like Global Culture, World Dance can be subjected to unsettling debates regarding its 'reality' or actual 'existence' out there, beyond academic and marketing arenas. Politically concerned scholars have to wonder also about the field's productive or expressive relationship to late capitalism's socio-economic and political structures. Regardless of the focus or position one might wish to assume, nothing is worlded without the intervention of an agential subject doing the worlding. Worlding amounts to inscribing what was presumed to be uninscribed (Spivak, 1985a: 243), naturalizing its inclusion in the world of the critic's text, thereby making it a part of a set (a whole) that derives from a privileged position and an all-embracing, proprietary viewpoint. The World is an outside that is taken in as territory and knowledge (Heidegger, 1993). And though 'worlding' is not unique to one culture or to this time in history, it does seem to coincide with moments of imperialist movement when circumscribing the world is possible and even necessary for the sake of managing populations and identities (Kadir, 2004; Radhakrishnan, 2001). Worlding within globalization or as a form of globalizing redoubles the all-encompassing emphasis beyond the metaphorical, deepening the pragmatic repercussions of control and, at the same time, eliciting local reactions that are always steeped in violence.

World Dance is a representation, a relatively new way of putting together, conceptualizing, and validating 'other' dances, rather than a plain discovery of their presence in the world. World Dance institutionalizes into the Dance field an enriching and disruptive flow of 'other' dances and dancers, imposing containment and order by framing some (not all) into the World. World Dance operates through disciplinary techniques that reshape the 'other' dances' presentational and pedagogical forms, along with the beliefs and values associated with them, their circulation and purposes, and the bodies and experiences of those who practice them. In order to get at 'what is World Dance?' one must pass through the theoretical entanglements that characterize discussions on Global Culture (Hall, 1997; Hannerz, 2006; Tagg, 1997; Wallerstein, 1997; Wolff, 1997, among others) concerning Marxist and neo-Marxist, deconstructivist, phenomenological, and 'postmodern' or post-structuralist viewpoints. The substantive make up of World Dance also requires us to address the condition of the 'others' through whom the field is constituted (Abou-El-Haj, 1997). What kinds of differences within or beyond the world of Dance does World Dance allude to and install? Are the 'others' in World Dance at the peripheries or at the metropolitan centers of the 'world-system'? Do they belong to the underdeveloped or developing 'third world' (*vis-à-vis* a developed 'first world') or to the 'local' in tension with the 'global'? Where does World Dance happen? Do the 'others' in World Dance practice World Dance before reaching the sites of World Dance selection, distribution, and validation? At what point and how do they become othered? Who among the 'others' participate in the making of World Dance and where does their status as World Dance practitioners become legitimated? How do some 'others' attain this status, through what practices and specific representations of 'otherness' *vis-à-vis* those who do not make it into World Dance? And what are the benefits and losses of participating as 'others' in the making of World Dance? Conversely are consumers of World Dance, especially when learning to practice World Dance themselves, 'others' to World Dance? What are the politics and the ethics involved in these multiplications of otherness? Does World Dance open a space for renegotiating 'otherness' as a site of 'neighborly' relations?[1] If so, who can afford to enjoy this privileged encounter of cosmopolitan bliss in globalization?

In order to work through these questions, I must add yet another set of reflections. World Dance, as a rubric, works at turning practices, those of dancing, into products (dances), and more precisely into a collection of products (World Dance). Dances rather than dancers make up World Dance, as if dances could be disassociated from their practitioners. Dance, however, is an art form that, unlike painting, music, writing, or film, requires an enactment, an embodied practice and a labor of performance, in order to be. There is no dance outside the practice and event of dancing, but dancers can be severed from where a particular dance is located in the world as they enter World Dance. World Dance, not unlike Dance, installs the possibility of creating a market for the consumption of aestheticized moving bodies, both as spectators and as invested, even identified, practitioners. World Dance thus expands the market of sanctioned and practiced pleasures, offering disciplined movement techniques of the body, access to the spectatorship and the embodiment of the beautiful and the exotic, and even options for the care of the self.

World Dance represents others' dancing as it designates a specific market for the consumption of a particular kind of dances that work at fascinating with difference as they elicit culturally progressive cosmopolitan values. Scholars, critics, professional artists, and presenters work transnationally as 'cultural intermediaries,' selecting and shaping the kinds of dancers and dancings that constitute World Dance (Bourdieu, 1985; Haynes, 2005; Negus, 2002). All dancing (that 'thing' that dancers do) obviously takes place in the world, but not all of it amounts to World Dance. I am calling attention to this obvious fact because World Dance, as a rubric, has the effect of putting together dancers who do not identify as 'world dancers,' and of piling up dance practices usually unrelated to each other. World Dance, thus, as a category of dances, denotes a specific 'worlding' of dancers and dance practices that are being newly incorporated into the world of dances that deserve the

Dance field's attention – a field sustained by scholars, critics, presenters, sponsors, practitioners, and spectators/consumers of dance primarily located in the United States and Europe. World Dance is a *classification* applied to newly 'discovered' dances and dancers who, while all along doing their dancing thing out there in the world, now have been *worlded differently* so as to fit the Dance collections under globalization. World Dance reframes difference as a political resource and allows us to imagine a globality of multicultural harmony that transcends boundaries of nationality, ethnicity, and race.

World Dance thus responds to an expansionist imperative of the Dance field immersed in the cultural politics of globalization. World Dance is a discursive practice that should be addressed along Foucauldian lines, 'ordering things' and 'disciplining' bodies and pleasures; World Dance is an effect of complex criss-crossings of social forces and constellations of interests and desires. Which dances practiced out there in the world qualify as World Dance responds to decisions concerning financializations of knowledge: the dynamics of recognition and legitimation that validate inclusions and exclusions of peoples and their practices (Spivak, 1993). There are gains and losses, enmeshed in material, ideological, and affective dynamics, wrapping up dancing bodies, and forcing them into new connections and unmoorings, at stake in World Dance. Rather than talking about World Dance as a thing or phenomenon in itself, we should zero in on the parameters of capital and war that dictate the practice of 'worlding' dances at this time in history: World Dance as aestheticized biopolitics.[2] World Dance seems to be inaugurating a vast 'new world' of dancing possibilities for the contemplation, consumption, and revitalization of dance scholars, artists, practitioners, and audiences. At the same time, World Dance enables selected dancers and dancing, previously outside the knowledge and awareness of presenters, funding agencies, teaching positions, and scholarly interests, to join Dance (the 'field') under certain conditions and adjustments. World Dance also carries promises to capture a wealth of mobility and mobilization capabilities (people dancing out there in the world) running subversively and/or unproductively in the wild. World Dance, from this viewpoint, is truly the promise of a New World.

Old and new World Dance encounters

World Dance designates more of a collision of dancing worlds than a smooth merging of dances and dancers. World Dance signals an addition, something new coming to the field of Dance – as dance scholars, presenters, practitioners, and audiences *qua* collectors knew it. World Dance expands the Dance field as it inaugurates a new axis of competition over resources available to those in the Dance field. From a professional practitioners' perspective, World Dance potentially offers recognition and the possibility of new jobs for newly selected World Dance representatives. At the same time, it posits a challenge for the established tenants of Dance knowledges and training.

Although World Dance is loosely defined in opposition to Western or Westernized dance forms, World Dances, in themselves, denote *fusion* and the challenges of articulating the aesthetics and pedagogies of other dance practices with those already established in the world of (Western or Westernized) Dance. World Dance therefore points to encounters of 'old' and 'new' dance genres and practitioners, where 'old' refers to the dance knowledges well established in the Dance field and 'new,' to the newcomers, regardless of their historical depth as practiced or as valued in their rooted geopolitical locations. As a matter of fact, 'traditional' dances – rather than 'modern' (i.e., Western-influenced), hybridized versions – are more apt to become a part of the World Dance market. Only some dances taking place out there in the world attain the status of World Dance. They are 'other' dances that have the capacity to be assimilated to the Dance field: Exotic, and yet disciplined enough to be incorporated through translation into what counts as Dance. Exoticism here is qualified as virtuosic difference, an otherness capable of being appreciated within the Dance field's parameters; discipline here refers to the actual or potential systematization of the dance form and its ensuing replicability and pedagogical implementation within the established parameters of the Dance field. These reconfigured encounters of 'old' and 'new' dances taking place in World Dance, in themselves, offer valuable clues for understanding the process of worlding dance that concerns us here.

A paradoxical and tense play between the 'old' and the 'new' characterizes the World Dance encounter with the established Dance field. 'New,' as in a new approach, announces a transformation that could potentially become a break, like a breakthrough, but that also retains continuity with what it proclaims to supercede. 'New,' far from a description, is a proclamation. The 'new' belongs to what it qualifies (and as such it is an addition, an expansion, here regarding the 'world' of dance) as it identifies the risk of a contending force, or even of inaugurating a replacement of the old by the new. Following Austin and Benveniste, 'new' is a performative utterance, an enunciation that creates what it names (Austin, 1961; and Benveniste 1971). In thinking about World Dance, a 'new' world of dances opens up as an unforeseen space, a 'world' that is a new space full of possibilities. At the same time, in announcing World Dance, quite like announcing a New World, Dance (the 'old,' established field) is claiming ownership over its discoveries. In this regard, World Dance makes little sense (except for the possibilities of financial support) for those dance practitioners who are discovered – by the tenants of the Dance field – dancing out there in the world.

I am trying to put together here a counter-narrative of dance trafficking, capable of accounting for the emergence of World Dance in the Dance field. International and intercultural encounters of dancers and dance knowledges have been taking place and reported for centuries. This traffic, however, did not amount to the reconfiguration of the Dance field, as defined in the West. Other dances and their practitioners were quite seamlessly assimilated into the Dance canon, often as contributing exotics, and welcomed as enriching innovations. World Dance announces a qualitative reconfiguration of this geopolitical traffic, a response to a quantitative upsurge of 'other' dances and dancers within the territorial boundaries as well as within the aesthetic boundaries of Western Dance and its outreach throughout the world. As such, World Dance is an acknowledgement of the limitations of Western Dance knowledges, a recognition of the relevance of otherness within the Dance field, and an awareness of the possibilities opened up by including 'otherness,' in itself, as an addition or supplement – rather than a set of discrete traits that can be assimilated into the Western/ Westernized Dance field.

World Dance is a collection of new discoveries in Dance, where Dance stands for the 'old world' of dances. And yet, World Dance brings the newness of other, old-rooted dance traditions that – unlike classical or modern Western dances – have not lost their cultural moorings and social functions. This discovery of the new (but traditional) world by the old world of Dance (although the 'world' has been implicit and the 'old' disavowed throughout this expansionist maneuver) is a territorial expansion coded as aesthetic discovery. The 'world' pops up as new dances make their appearance as World Dance *within* the Dance field (which I insist on calling the 'old world' of dances in this encounter.) This territorial-aesthetic discovery of dances will unfold, like all discoveries of 'new worlds,' through practices of occupation, which themselves are markers of time, of history. As a spatialized enunciation of time under the announcer's control (the announcer of the discovery here being the 'old world' Dance collectors), this pronouncement of a 'new world' of dances installs a progression, leaving behind a past that now appears as 'old,' and that questions the 'classic.' World Dance is thus a troubling addition in that, through its annexation to the established Dance field, it introduces a 'newness' that works as a spatio-temporal unmooring operation; it indicates moving forward, leaving plain 'Dance' (without the 'World') behind, and it qualifies the benefits of the conquest. World Dance enriches, renovates, and surpasses Dance through its pristine additions.

World Dance as a symptom

World Dance, made up of newly discovered dances, is an addition that challenges the Dance field as we know it, rendering it 'old,' and situating it in the world – and down from its 'outworldly' position as Art. The encounter between new World Dances (and their historical depth in 'other' locations) and the old (and taken for 'canonical') field of Dance has the potential effect of installing all dancing *in* the world, *in* geopolitics, and of provoking a reassessment of Dance as a universal aesthetic expression, above and beyond politics. World Dance adds to the (now old) Dance world, but it also re-worlds it by locating it in the world. The Dance field, however, has been struggling to neutralize the impact of World Dance by way of two maneuvers: first, introducing a cultural relativism borrowed from the field of Anthropology (establishing that cultures are 'different but equal,' and thus ignoring the fact of the forced articulations through colonizing globalization); and second, installing Choreography as a universal strategic tool for making dances.[3] The rest of this chapter will be devoted to exploring these maneuvers in an attempt to understand the worlding of World Dance.

World Dance is a symptom, as it were, of Dance under globalization. It conceals as it reveals the integration of newly discovered dancing territories into the world of Dance as we know it, opening the (old) world of Dance to revitalization but also to the risks of the new, namely the risk that new dancing and dancers will contend for legitimacy and resources in the expanding field of dance. Re-worlding Dance allows for the mobilization of others (other dancers and their dances) as they enter a dance world ruled by 'the' Dance: Ballet, of course, but also Modern, Postmodern, and above all, Choreography. How wild can this newly found world of dances get? What if that dancing taking place out there in the world is not easily accommodated to the Dance World and its rulings? Imagine if their accumulation (a process that occurs simultaneously with dance worlding's expansion) would activate chaotic disruptions in the field, question its worlding, and lead them into alliances with decolonizing or post-colonial critical factions. World Dance might develop a resistance to globalism. It might be that differing positionalities, those established under 'subaltern studies,' 'post-colonial studies,' 'minorities discourses,' or 'subjugated knowledges,' could sustain their critical force under the umbrella field of World Dance studies or histories without being recuperated into a relativistic collection of 'different perspectives' on 'different dances.' I hope World Dance can move away from reproducing differences and the endless replication of the same (i.e., danced otherness). Under what conditions would World Dance undo the obsession with the otherness of the other? I would like to envision World Dance as a radical rubric, capable of taking over and replacing Dance as a field, but World Dance might be confined by birth to represent the Other of Western or Westernized (i.e., Western assimilated) Dance.

A cartography of dance knowledges

Two ways of worlding have been at play in bringing 'new' and 'other' dancing into the Dance field. Dance scholarship has developed inside and outside dance departments, following a fracture established by the archival location of its chosen objects of study. The fracture does not necessarily follow the objects' sites of 'origin' (claimed belonging) in geopolitical terms such as West and non-West; First and Third World; or North and South. Two different 'archives,' as it were, have housed collections of movement practices, following differing paths as they identified, categorized, and analyzed their findings: One is 'the' Dance archive in the Arts; the other, the archive of 'dancing' (socially structured and meaningful movements)[4] in Anthropology.

   Scholars at the Dance-Arts archive primordially have documented, historicized, and critiqued professional artists and performers, their works, schools, and lives, most but not all stemming from hegemonic centers of art production with noticeable international impact. The cosmopolitanism and *déclassé* status (here meaning beyond/above class distinctions) of these professionals of aestheticized, presentational movement practices reached selected international (world) audiences and created an international network of collaboration with creative and promotional criss-crossing, transnational effects.[5] This collection has been kept in the Arts under the rubric of Dance. Dance historiography worked at accommodating all information pre-dating these artists (from Greek mythology to court dances, and their ritual and symbolic powers) as conducive to the artists' works. Any other dancing occurring along-side these artists was addressed either as a nostalgic remnant of the past (festivals and folk dances), as recreation of the masses (ballroom, social dances), or as entertainment for the masses (can-can, vaudeville, cabaret, music-hall). Aside from perfunctory entries, especially when artists used these 'less artistic' dances as sources, this vast diversity of dancing practices was to become the object of study in Folklore collections or Social History collections, finding a difficult fit in the Dance collections of the Arts. Evolution (of the Dance form) and evaluation (of the dancing qualities conducive to their stratification with 'the' Dance as the measure) served as the organizing criteria of the Dance collections and as the tools for the narrativization of Dance as history.

Curt Sachs's *Eine Weltgeshichte des Tanzes* published in 1933 (translated into English as *World Dance History* in 1937) broadened the scope of Dance by reaching into yet other dancing, that of (selected) non-like-us peoples from past and present. His cross-over move was made possible by extending the diffusionist evolutionism of Schmidt and Graebner's *Kulturkreis* school to accommodate dancing from all over the world to a World Dance History consistent with a primitive-to-civilized scale of progress. Sachs's is thus a worlding that enriches the Dance archive in the Arts, without disturbing its organizing principles, as he slips into the Archives of Anthropology – which leads into the second set of dancing collections (Kaeppler, 1978; Youngerman, 1974) under consideration.

Anthropology has served as an archive for 'other' dancing, dances outside Dance or loosely connected to Dance mainly as a source of inspiration. These collections have moved, following Anthropology's dilemmas of affiliation, between the Social Sciences and the Humanities. As part of the doings of people without history (cold history or eternal present),[6] dancing out there in the world was worlded as a signifying human behavior (a universal trait) and as a cultural expression of social organizations. Texts often cited as enabling this incorporation of dancing in anthropological discourse include Marcel Mauss's '*Les techniques du corps*' of 1936, published in *Sociologie et Anthropologie* in 1950 and translated into English as 'Techniques of the body' in 1973, and Franziska Boas's *The Function of Dance in Human Society* of 1944, an edited collection of ethnographic studies of dances in Bali, Haiti, and African 'primitive' societies together with an essay by Franz Boas, her father, on dance and music among the Kwaikutl of British Columbia. Franz Boas had been collecting data on dances among the Kwaikutl since at least 1888, and requested his daughter's assistance in analyzing filmed footage taken in 1930. Reportedly, he had great interest in the dancing, but no available tools for its analysis (Ruby, 1980). These inaugural works on dancing, supplemented by a long list of anthropological works on the social import of physicality and expressive culture, are narrativized through two strands of interests (and concomitant schools of thought): On the one hand, they conform to the scientific collection of empirical data on gesture, postural habits, physical behavior, motor habits, and non-verbal communication dating since at least the 1940s,[7] and, on the other hand, to the socio-cultural collection of ethnographic data on patterns of movement, movement structures, and other symbolic and semantic interpretations of embodied social action since at least the late 1920s.[8]

These collectors of other moving bodies coincided in the common goal of understanding the operation and social function of diverse physical actions and ways of performing across cultures. An interest in universals of the human body and universals of human behavior, and their possible linkages, can be traced throughout the discussions that incessantly seek to anchor their findings in terms of cognition and of communicative abilities, of behavioral patterns, of social structures established by collective human needs (functions) or deeply set through the universals of human language.

Preoccupations over establishing a progression in human historical development vary, and give rise to paradigmatic debates between evolutionists of different kinds as well as cultural relativists. As these researchers reached out to a world made up of different ways of living together (other societies with 'cultures' of their own), regardless of these scholars' intentions, their efforts had the effect of lumping humankind into a single population (a shared biological and social base) while simultaneously installing questions of discrimination (given that their socio-cultural arrangements were different, and that, in the last instance, some were better than others). Proof was to be found in the very enterprise of the archives, begging the question: Who is collecting whom?

Arm-chair anthropology such as Frazer's (1927/1966) (comparative works on world civilizations worlded on the basis of secondary data collections supplied by colonial administrators, priests, merchants, and travelers and interpreted at the monopoly's distant desk) was discredited in favor of extensive fieldwork (a scholar's immersion in the field of ethnographic study) as championed by Malinowski (1922) and Boas (Stocking, 1982). However, the colonial encounter in itself that provided the opportunity, if not the sponsorship, for these systematic collections of artifacts and customs was not as routinely critiqued. The 'primitive,' as a placeholder of difference on the scale of progress and civilization, served as a justification for conquest and for the ensuing studies. Race figures prominently as an organizational tool in these collections, and its biological, psychological, and social moorings often slip into one another by way of 'culture' and observations on 'cultural difference.' Franz Boas, who trained more than a dozen prominent American anthropologists (including those first writing on dance), wrote endlessly and critically about race, conducting research in all fields of physical, linguistic, and cultural anthropology, debating the complexity of racial differences, racial intermixing, and racial antagonism.[9] If 'culture' and later on 'ethnicity'[10] displace 'race' (and 'tribal') as the paradigmatic units of anthropological study, the biology/social ambiguity is retained and unresolved. Heredity and descent, and their close, murky link to 'tradition' make a quasi automatic connection to the racialization of cultures and racism. Difference is thus reinscribed in culture as more than distinction, race (by way of tradition) being the unmentioned supplement. This is, I believe, the biopolitical paradigm at work through anthropology.

Other dancing bodies are redundantly othered in this scheme of anthropological things. Bodies (already implicated in 'culture') are brought back as 'embodied culture,' calling attention to the doubled-binding of bodies as pertaining to a specific 'culture' and as subjected to a world politics that colonizes as it turns peoples into population.[11] The 'dance problem' in anthropology was not solved by Joanne Kealiinohomoku's renowned article on ballet as an ethnic dance (1983), although she successfully calls attention to the paradox of the two archives – the Dance in the Arts, with a supplement of Social History (turned into Dance History, and more recently into Dance Studies[12]), and the dancing in Anthropology, with its Social Science and Humanities divides (turned into Dance Ethnology, Dance Ethnography, and more recently into Cultural Studies of Dance). Her followers in Anthropology celebrate the triumph of 'cultural relativism' as ethnography makes its entry into the Dance/Arts archive, but ethnographic democracy stops with the ethnographers who claim to represent the 'native point of view.' Re-worlding Dance by including other dancing as collected by dance ethnographers expands the holdings of the archive, but leaves a multitude of doubly removed others (the objects and subjects of ethnographic study) out, doing their dancing thing. Again, the ethnographic encounter remains to be accounted for, even when it is being reflected upon and critiqued.

The fact is that our collecting continues, perhaps because, para-phrasing Baudrillard, in the last instance collectors collect themselves (Baudrillard, 1994: 12). We should address what, specifically, we are try-ing to collect, if other(ed) dancing seems to help us collect ourselves. I am tentatively proposing that dancing out there in the world – the 'opening' that as of yet has not been collected and, by extension, not worlded – points at an inoperative,[13] an excess of life still available for the revitalization of collector's worlds – and Archives. World Dance is another collection, an addition to the two main archives (Dance/Art/ Dance Studies and 'other' dances/Anthropology/Dance Ethnography) I have been discussing. It is housed at the thresholds, moving in between the two as the collection of other(ed) artistic dancing. Under archival efforts (which attempt to represent, replicate, protect, and save dances from their practitioners' ongoing innovations), World Dance works at capturing that dancing that occurs out there in the world.

At the World Dance collections

What composes the World Dance collections? How do these distinct dancing 'cultures' and 'subcultures' get to be identified, coded, and brought together, and to what effect? The maneuver of their inclusion into World Dance entails an exclusion that needs to be addressed. There is a Dance master who makes World Dance possible, who worlds dances as a set while establishing the master's own position outside the set, passing a discriminating judgment, as it were, on the nature of the col-lection by identifying what does and does not belongs in it, under what requirements and conditions, submitted to what kinds of treatments and adaptations.

World Dance happens in globalization, meaning that the power grip is dislocated and dispersed but also unprecedentedly forceful, perva-sive, and uncontested. War and Capital move together, indistinguish-ably as means and ends in themselves beyond ideological requirements of coherence. The world is undergoing a process of total domination, an unrestricted Empire that claims all space and all life for its own sur-vival. World Dance is an effect of these globalizing biopolitics and their regulations.

In globalization there seems to be an increasing awareness of untapped, intangible sources of wealth that pertain to the mobiliza-tion of life, that follow collective arrangements according to techniques and disciplines working outside or beyond established institutions, that strangely generate vitality as they consume energy, that require little or no investment or compensation beyond that of their own practitioners and their particular negotiations, that disappear as they happen, but that, unlike labor, result in nothing, no product – they run on account of desire, belief, and life itself. Some of these sources have been recuperated as Art, but a large number run wild in the unwelcoming Anthropology Archive as 'popular culture,' 'ritual,' or simple 'tradition.' Dances (a category not necessarily assumed or accepted by their practitioners) are detected out in the open of mobilized/mobilizing life, at the margins of state apparati or within these apparati but not exhausted by them, crossing over nationalist, classist, and racist borders, negotiating resignifications.

World Dance is an institutionalizing project that organizes, according to UNESCO's recommendation adopted on 15 November 1989, this 'intangible patrimony of humanity,' establishing administrative and scholarly order in its collection. Not all dancing will attain the status of collectible, much less UNESCO's legitimation and support. But World Dance as a new field and collection at universities and at UNESCO does work as a tantalizing archivist-driven net that, from the outset, places these allegedly 'vulnerable' practices into a framework of competition – for survival, for appreciation, for conservation through documentation and research, for preservation through education, and for dissemination through sponsored national and international tours and presentations (see UNESCO's Recommendation on Intangible Cultural Heritage in www.unesco.org/heritage/intangible/recommendation/html accessed 2/13/2004).

Choreography, at a distant privileged position, as the creative, innovative, progressive dance-making force, the truly artistic undertaking that makes dances happen, excludes as it includes world dances serving as the threshold's operator. Choreography is beyond dance, in the sense that it has no particular form to keep, and yet it makes dances possible. Moreover, Choreography can make anything into dance by capturing its constitutive movements, and it can set anything to dance by instilling mobility. Given these astonishing capabilities, Choreography, a strategic tool systematically developed in, and claimed by, the Western dance tradition, can accommodate World Dances as technical and inspirational sources. It, however, handles with difficulty its own integration into World Dance as one among other practices for decision-making concerning movement composition. Choreography stands out as a *processor of differences* in World Dance's inclusive thrust. Choreography determines how World Dance will incorporate a compound of cultural relativism values and collectionist interests (of old and new, aristocratic or popular, classy or rowdy, theatrical, club, slum or street, ritualistic, sacred or profane, group, partnered or solo, homo-, hetero-, trans- or a-sexual, erotic, puritanical or blasé – and all of the above, according to continents, nations, regions, as well as global trends, and foremost of ethnic but once again culturalized and racialized dances)[14] *and* of preservationist interests. Here the category of the 'traditional' introduces a new set of contested and overlapping distinctions into the worlding of World Dance.

As such, Choreography allows for the emergence of fusion dances and other 'misfits' that could eventually make their ways into World Dance such as spoken dances; balletic tangos (Julio Boca) and contact improv tangos (see Festival Cambalache); postmodern aboriginal dance/rituals; Butoh Ritual Mexicano (Diego Piñon); Chinese-Hip Hop (see HipHop Dance Fest); Senegalese-Butoh (see Acogny/Yamasaki Fagaala); and Modern Indian dances, to mention a few. Choreography enables a world-traffic of, and a trafficking in, dances, much like the English language (which cross-cultural and intercultural choreographers tend to use in their creative communications), and as such operates as an exclusion (from World Dance) that includes all dances, and as an exception (in the collection) that rules the dance archive. World Dance is thus composed of traditional, ethnic, and some fusion dances, 'other' to Ballet, Modern, and Postmodern (traditionally Western but practiced worldwide). World Dance, however, is not restricted to dances untouched by Western-inspired dance forms. The World Dance collections also house those fusion dances that, while borrowing from 'participatory' or 'presentational' and mostly Western forms, retain the signature elements of 'cultural' difference – showing their resilience to transformative forces, be it local or foreign, but usually attributed to Western modernity and its polluting influence. The World Dance collections, like all sponsored archives and collections, must be exhibited to the public.

Displaying and preserving World Dance

Exhibiting an intangible collection, like the World Dance collection, is not impossible but it is definitely challenging. Museums open their collections to public view by working at contextualizing their objects, following carefully selected narratives in terms of scientific classifications, aesthetic affiliations, thematic affinities, geopolitical and historical frames, structures of production, author's *oeuvre qua* creative development, and so on. Presenting world dances requires a similar work of reconfiguration that entails fetishizing movements, selecting, fragmenting, recomposing, and reinterpreting them and then also disa-vowing the operation. Take, for perfunctory examples, the staging of a ritual dance (i.e., the danced aspect of a ritual, excluding its constituent efficacy at conjuring something) or a street dance (i.e., the most striking moves, excluding its openness, improvisational, competitive, and fleet-ing bond-making capabilities). Staging, regardless of the format, intro-duces a context that excises the impetus for, and nature of, mobilization (the 'how these dances come to be') by installing a performer/audience structure in a venue or space charged with differing significations and established requirements. These signifying requirements (virtuosity, compositional intelligibility, interesting variation in terms of phrasing, sequencing, and group formations, flux in energy levels, spatial cover-age, defined trajectories) are impositions already installed with a Dance audience that the world dance performer must address whether s/he chooses to make them present or absent.

Audiences already have been trained for what to expect and how to evaluate a dance performance according to their familiarity with the (choreographically crafted) Balletic, Modern, and Postmodern dance forms designed for stages (Foster, 1986). This unavoidable framework for World Dance, whether performers welcome it or not, transforms the alluded world dance (as it is practiced out there in the world) into a World Dance that points at it, like a placeholder in the intangible col-lection. This complex maneuver cannot be undone or compensated for through lectures or informative theater notes.

Teaching, in order to revitalize the World Dance collection, follows a similar path, this time in terms of pedagogical adaptations: adjusting to the space of a studio; to the time frames and frequencies established in schedules; to the lack of available musicians/accompanists; to defining a vocabulary and systematizing signature moves, steps, phrases, sequen-cing; to 'counting' movement progressions; to the one-instructor-per class model even if multiple instructors teaching simultaneously are key to the form; to grade-format evaluations, and so on. This excruciating process conducive to World Dance preservation *at the archives* could be addressed as 'cultural' translation, but it would be a misleading (and lazy) euphemism.

This is not to say that World Dance at the archives is fake or lacking in quality, and even less an admonition that 'it shouldn't be done.' I'm not prepared to make this judgment. What I am interested in getting across is that World Dance is a practice in itself. And that under the guise of Dance (Choreography and the Ballet/Modern/Postmodern continuum) World Dance is always already fusion. World Dance is happening at that threshold where mobilized/mobilizing life (as it occurs out there, in the world) is processed for recuperation, and in order to revitalize Dance. Processing here means enabling as well as disciplining; producing and repressing. Recuperating here means giving a set form: institutionalizing, organizing, administering, accounting, mapping, classifying, framing into intangible production something out there that is tangibly unproductive; and turning a source into a resource.

Worlding Dances as desire

Towards what ends should we invest knowledge/learning about that intangible called World Dance? Framed in these terms, desire is co-opted into justification; pleasure into legitimation. Dance studies, as a discipline, must face these entanglements of knowledge and desire in general and more so when it comes to World Dance. I am making an effort to stay out of 'exploration' and its associations with occupation, invasion, expansion, globalism. But if globalism (the process of globalization, of encompassing the world as a site of a coherent machine of capital) dictates our efforts at (finally) coming up with 'new' studies of World Dance, the project should focus on what is suddenly justifying this effort, this interest. What is legitimating this object, and the ends (justifications) inscribed in it? What is arranging this desire to learn, and learn about world dances? We must admit that we are in the machine of global capital, that our learning is being financed (see Spivak, 2004: 557 *et passim*). The hard questions rush in: Who benefits from introducing a World Dance perspective into Dance Studies? Dance is a wild field when it comes to getting away with unchecked pervasive ideologies structuring difference (racism, sexism, classism, culturalism), and dancers and dance scholars enjoy the privileges of sanctioned ignorance – the pleasures of toying, irresponsibly and unaccountably, with carefully disciplined bodies as if they were to be found in nature, with sentient embodiments as if founded in trained yet intractable memories, with displacements of identities onto bodily movements severed from subjectivities, with access to imagined exotic otherness as if it were actually the embodied essence of dancing others.

These licenses to play with world dances are serious, not so much because of culturalist ethical concerns (lack of respect for others' traditions, cultural appropriations, cultural fetishizations or misrepresentations). Focus on these kinds of concerns, when addressed formally as in 'anti-racialism,' elicit moral responses (shame and guilt) that obscure serious political 'anti-racist' reflection and action.[15] Seriousness here concerns the distribution of resources, the pay-checks: *the directionality of the pay-checks in World Dance as it circulates in globalization.* Opening up the Dance field to World Dance does not automatically beget the necessary material shifts that would enable institutional access and support the necessary competition for resources that would transform power relations in Dance. Who keeps the World Dance collections? Who finances World Dance in globalization? Who owns the modes of production of World Dances? Who gets to decide which dances and dancers qualify as worldly? Who gets to present World Dances, where, and for the spectatorial pleasure of whom? Who provides the dancing labor? Who migrates with little more than world dancing labor to sell for his/her subsistence in the World Dance metropolis of the world? Who has no choice but to dance their way into the world and who World Dances for the heck of it? And who gets to write the stories about how this is happening, choosing what to tell and what to ignore? Framed in terms of 'otherness,' world dancers' aspirations (the Other's desire) remain unaddressed and even enigmatic to those running the Dance field – and, presumably, to the others themselves.

Dancing into World Dance

Still wondering about what is at stake in World Dance and its connections to globalization, I would hope that world dancers would jump into the conversation. Here we face a problem from the outset: 'World dancer,' anyone? Let me rephrase: do any dancers, whether in Dance or out there in the world, identify as a *world dancer*? I haven't located a single one. Not yet. Practitioners of a World Dance form, yes; applicants to World Dance teaching positions, yes; World Dance scholars, maybe – especially when pushed into territorial feuds within dance studies; but world dancers *per se*, no. World Dance is something we do – under duress (i.e., within the confines of Dance Festivals, Dance Departments, Dance Anthologies), but the rubric, as of yet, has not entered the complex realm of subjective formations. World Dance remains exogenous to dancers, who practice and hold the knowledges that compose this threshold in between the Dance/Art/Dance Studies archive and the dancing/Anthropology/Cultural Studies of Dance archive. World Dance is a collection of discrete, rare objects (specific 'other' dances) that materialize only through the labor of selected dancers (chosen out there in the world) who perform within the parameters of the Dance field. Entering World Dance entails considerable maneuvers in terms of translocation and translation.[16]

How do 'world dancers' operate so as to be included in the Dance archives and collections of World Dance? How do they frame their dancing so that producers, scholars or critics, and students engage with their work? We are back into rearranging desires. Dancers who wish to (make a living by) enter(ing) World Dance must learn to accommodate to the dictates of the World Dance pedagogical and presentational formats, and to the parameters of World Dance promoted aesthetics and values. A myriad of translations take place in this process, as well as endless validating voyages between 'home' and 'abroad.' I cannot do justice to the specificities of each case here, but I will mention two recurrent (and thus apparently) necessary efforts: first, the work of teaching how to 'read' and, hopefully, appreciate the particular (aspiring) World Dance form; and second, the job of tailoring the given World Dance form to the requirements of the (well-established) pedagogical and presentational settings.

Aspiring 'world dancers' (identified by specific World Dance forms such as Odissi, Hula, Samba, or Sabar; or by geopolitical identifiers such as Balinese dance, Senegalese dance, Cambodian dance, or Mexican dances; or by a combination of national and socio-functional markers such as Javanese court dance, Tibetan temple dance, or Brazilian Orixa dances; or by referencing dance practices pertaining to minorities such as North American or South American Native and Tribal Dances – criteria which are duly specified when specialists and practitioners find it pedagogically and promotionally convenient) must *talk* willing dance students and curious scholars *into* valuing and recognizing the form that they embody and practice. (Practitioners and scholars who travel abroad or translocate, and immerse themselves or witness dancing out there in the world assist the imported professionals in fitting in and translating dancing skills.) As a result, teaching how to appreciate and/ or practice a world dance requires one to ascribe to a worldview composed of culturalist interpretations imposed from above (those of the Dance field) that, while representing the triumph of the global, always re-installs a reconfigured local call. This relocalization of difference (into 'native,' 'courtly,' 'sacred,' 'Senegalese' (as if representing a whole nation), or alluding to renowned localized, rooted sensibilities such as 'tango' and sexualized passion or 'samba' and racial democracy) builds up a fascinating (exotic), diverse (multicultural), and politically correct (leveling and all inclusive) world buffet of dancing choices catered to anti-racialist whiteness with recruitment of people of color. There is no visibility and no chance of landing a position or a job in World Dance without learning these relocalized translations and without, in turn, owning and teaching them back.

Added to this formalist requirement for entering World Dance, successful 'world dancers' must agree to accommodate themselves to the available presentational spaces, the rehearsal and teaching studios, and the expected pedagogical formats of dance classes. The pace at which a world dance is taught and the judgments on the results of world dance classes, as well as the tensions between the validation of creative *vis-à-vis* preservationist concerns attached to particular world dance forms, impose technically frustrating and often irreconcilable conditions upon teachers and students alike. Transmitting World Dance in globalization entails a process of loss-in-translation, even when that knowledge is imparted by expert teachers. The losses are both qualitative and political: teachers in World Dance are required to fetishize the dance form, the culture it stands for, and even themselves as representatives of both. Importing dancing bodies and knowledges as World Dance does not amount to articulating the Dance field to the 'dancing happening out there in the world.' World dancers incorporated as scholars and practitioners in small numbers, as enriching supplements, with few resources at their disposal, and under exigencies of assimilation frequently coded as 'professionalism' while retaining 'authenticity' (the allure of differently rooted 'traditions'), are unable to bring the outside and rupture the terms of incorporation into the Dance world.

World Dance is a site of convoluted 'otherness' in other regards as well. Not all professional 'world dancers' are racially or ethnically 'others'; some practice World Dance forms as a choice. These dancers, frequently but not exclusively, cosmopolitan, white women, are driven by modernist sensibilities to search for a cultural elsewhere either to question their own socio-ideological positionings or to expand their aesthetic and even ethical horizons (Hannerz, 2006; Nava, 2002). They enter World Dance as 'others' to racially, ethnically, and thus more 'authentically' validated 'world dancers' – the ones practicing the dances of the cultures where they belong. Entanglements in terms of otherness here multiply as dances, the practices, intersect with physicalized, racist readings of embodiments as well as with issues of access indicating the interventions of class and geopolitics. World dancers practicing dances other than those culturally, nationally, or racially ascribed to them, follow 'elective affinities' made up of identifications and follow desires, in conjunction with opportunities to enact these cross-overs. They enter conflictively into World Dance on at least three accounts: as others to more 'authentic' world dancers, as not other enough to Dance, and as (especially when racial identifications intervene) the wrong others to World Dance. Ethics and politics here encounter a complicated terrain where misrecognitions confront misappropriations and formal distinctions collide with uneven access to resources. Competition for a World Dance, already diminished, status ensues, coded in essentialist figures of distinction. How to navigate these ruptures within World Dance, fueled, on the one hand, by formal racialisms and culturalisms, and on the other, by substantive racism and classism?

Belonging, in World Dance as in Global Culture, is a murky issue. In globalization, roots (those of the 'authentic' world dancers) are transportable and transported, affinities (those of the 'wannabe' world dancers) are available, consumable, and subject to choice. Dictates of 'legitimate' representation are installed as part of the marketing of differences, summoning some into translatable (and thus assimilated/assimilatable) 'nativism' and others into tasting, and even serious practicing of 'multiculturalism' with certain restrains. These World Dance populations, however, are required to maintain their differences under the peril of canceling out World Dance as a supplement to Dance. In sum, these misunderstandings are encouraged and, at the same time, repressed in World Dance, given that World Dance works under the assumption that there are 'real' differences out there, that are brought into Dance in pristine form and without causing deformations – the assumption being that hybridization and fusion come later, as creative and exploratory exercises under Dance-Choreographic control.

As in Anthropology, 'going Native' disrupts the arrangements of the discipline by breaking its protocols (which include preserving the view from above or, in Geertz's terms from 'over the shoulders of those to whom they [the texts] more properly belong' (Geertz, 1973: 452)). But also as in Ethnomusicology, and its more recent offspring of World Music, World Dance permits a permeability affordable specifically to artists with ethnographic inclinations as well as to ethnographers with artistic interests (Feld, 2000), who, given certain conditions of marketability, collaborate on uneven footings and with uneven results. The resources available to professional 'world dancers,' however, are scarce when compared to those of World Music, whether they are 'natives' or 'native-inspired,' and the necessary embodiment of World Dance performances, unlike the disembodied circulation of World Music recordings, establishes a permanent demand for the physicalized performance of perceived differences. In this sense, 'native-inspired' world dancers, no matter how authentically other they perform, are required to include physically authentic (or perceived as such through racialized traits) 'Natives' in their presentations and forced to share recognition, resources, and opportunities – not necessarily equitably.

This is a condition imposed by Dance as a restrictive marketable art: World dancers on both sides of the 'native'/ 'native-inspired' divide, in order to succeed, must collaborate as they transmit World Dance, co-operatively traversing assimilation and translation, and dissimulating these impositions.

This is the World Dance scenario onto which we are thrown as world dancers and cultural intermediaries, worlded differently and yet encountered in the process of making World Dance. An ethics should be shaped in terms of World Dance (not in general terms, but in terms of a practice like Lacan's ethics *of* Psychoanalysis) where we make decisions, decisions to recognize our worlded differences and to act upon them, implying not only formal acknowledgements – as in anti-racialism – but also the redistribution of resources (knowledges, opportunities, jobs, to name a few) – as in a committed anti-racism (Goldberg, 2004).

World Dance as neighboring

In this final section I propose to immerse World Dance into the so-called critical turn, into ethics and the renewed discussions on identity and otherness as challenged under globalism and Empire. Post-colonial critics and political philosophers, stemming from Emmanuel Levinas's works on ethics that privilege intersubjectivity in identity formation, have launched debates applicable to World Dance. Levinas's proposition (in a broken nutshell) to foster the decentralization of the self as it foregrounds the care of the other in relationality, could attract those concerned with the ethics of the encounter with 'otherness' as it occurs in World Dance as a set within Global Culture.

The main horizons of discussion pertain to the nature and status of otherness and responsibility towards the Other. Understanding difference and the consequences of its reinscriptions into identitarian communalities, from the 'cultural' and its multiple enmeshments to the biopolitical in the forms of 'race,' 'ethnicity,' and 'nationality,' has become an urgent task in the face of upsurging fundamentalisms and devastating enmities. Simply put, identity politics has turned from a source of organization and mobilization for those disempowered into a dangerous ideological device in the hands of Empire. Thus, figuring out how to undo the premises of identity politics while recuperating the force of contestation to global capitalism is crucial and urgent.

After Althusser and Foucault, it seems impossible to conceptualize a subject outside subjectification and the disciplinary introjection of the juridico-ethical machine. After Deleuze's denunciations of the ideological and corporeal grips of capitalism, and Lacan's and Derrida's elucidations of the linguistic structuration of the phallo(logo)centrism that rules sociality, a number of quasi-messianic efforts are being made in political philosophy to theoretically elaborate ways to break out of a deadly worlding system now globalized without contenders (Agamben, 2005; Badiou, 2006; Hardt and Negri, 2000). I have chosen to address here, briefly and experimentally, the notion of *vecinos* (neighbors) and *vecindad* (neighborliness) as instances of proximity – which do not constitute an idyllic relationality, but rather a permanent negotiation based on the encounters among others, without (and outside) the 'same' as an identitarian foundation. These negotiations would set into motion the constitutional threshold of difference (Badiou, 2001; Reinhard, 2005).[17] Would 'neighbor-ing' help to rethink issues of 'collecting otherness,' of appropriation and fetishization in World Dance? How would 'neighboring' reconfigure the World Dance encounters as we reconsider identity and belonging in globalization? I am starting an awkward conversation here since, let's admit it, dancers have not been invited to these heady discussions.

Žižek, Santner and Reinhard co-authored *The Neighbor*, a psychoanalytic investigation into 'what is happening when we enter into the proximity of the other's desire' (2005: 4). In addressing the biblical commandment to love thy neighbor, in the context of a critique of political theology, the authors aim at entertaining what is at stake in neighbor-love: 'does the commandment call us to expand the range of our identifications or does it urge us to come closer, become answerable to, an alterity that remains radically inassimilable?' (2005: 6). Following Reinhard's reading of Derrida (1997), the figure of the neighbor would allow for locating a politics that is beyond the friend/enemy opposition, a binary bound to the 'drive or decision of death,' to destruction. Neighbor-ing would amount to a politics that is more and less than secular politics, a practice that would straddle the locations of the friend/family/self and the enemy/stranger/other (Derrida, 1997: 17–18). I wonder if this kind of 'neighbor-ing' could be rehearsed in the encounters, one at a time, taking place in what we are calling World Dance. This is not an interpretation of what is actually happening in World Dance encounters, steeped as they are in 'regular' identity politics, and producing an exploitative confusion of friends and foes, 'others' on both sides to each other, in an endless play of unequally broken mirrors. (On the flaws of the politics and ethics of difference, see Badiou, 2001: 18–29). To neighbor is a decision followed by a careful practice that takes many risks and gives up privileges for the sake of neighborliness. Not tolerance for differences but '*recognizing the Same*,' in Badiou's words recognizing that 'infinite alterity is quite simply *what there is*' (2001: 25, emphases in the original). The ethics of difference contemplated in multiculturalism and human rights poses the problem of accepting as differences only those compatible with, or assimilated to, 'acceptable' differences – the parameters of acceptability being defined by those who rule. Like cultural relativism, the ethics of difference dictates 'become like me and I will respect your difference' (2001: 25). In World Dance the politics of identity and the ethics of difference translate as recognition and validation of aesthetics, pedagogies, and skills and even manners and motivations that are compatible (i.e., assimilatable) to the established Dance field under the parameters established by Choreography.

However, when it comes to 'neighbor-ing' and the encounter of multiplicities in their indifferent singularities (and not as groups of different ones), Žižek points out yet another problem. 'Loving' the neighbor, in a one to one scene, is not so difficult – the challenge is to respect and accept, beyond 'understanding,' precisely those not known. 'Others are primordially an (ethically) indifferent multitude, and love is a violent gesture of cutting into this multitude and privileging a One as the neighbor, thus introducing a radical imbalance into the whole. In contrast to love, justice begins when I remember the faceless many left in the shadow in this privileging of the One. Justice and love are thus structurally incompatible [...] The primordial ethical obligation is towards this Third who is *not* here in the face-to-face relationship' (2005: 182). It could be argued that art is not a proper site for justice, but if World Dance is offered as a symbol and laboratory of multicultural global harmony, reproducing culturalism and its racist connotations, and thus masking alliances of cosmopolitan artistic elites joined in classist and gendered exploitations that ultimately feed nationalist projects as well as international dance markets across the centers and peripheries of Empire, then the politics of World Dance needs to be addressed as an ethics of art-making.[18] Can we get used to the now seemingly awkward idea of discussing the rights or attending the truths of those dancers we don't even name 'world dancers'? (Badiou, 2001; Reinhard, 2005; Žižek, 2005).

Having dancers partake in reconfigurations of culture and subjectivity from the outside (Foucault, 2004), the not-yet (Agamben, 1998), and the not-All (Badiou, 2001), would amount to an invitation to make decisions on incorporations into modes of worlding. What if dancers out there in the world decide to reserve the right to not enjoy the privileges of entering World Dance as others, refusing, as it were, to participate (Hardt and Negri, 2000) as dancers encoded through sovereign trans-coders of the Dance field? I am thinking of dancers giving up translatability as practitioners of different dances, and instead establishing their presence in the world as neighbors rather than as 'others' or as 'the same.' These dancers would install partially articulated neighborhoods of movements rather than discrete dance forms and traditions or dance entities *qua* things. Dancers invested in outdoing the New Age attitude that reduces the Other to a mirror-image or to a means of self-realization and self-enrichment. And on the other side of the World Dance divide, dancers who refuse to represent 'otherness' as they seek to enter the Dance field, with its hold on knowledges and resources as well as its troubles and lacks. This encounter would not amount to a unity or a synthesis of conflicts, but 'to *a mode of sustaining conflict in politically productive ways*' (Butler, 1997: 269, emphasis in the original). In a discussion of identity politics and social movements, Butler indicates that:

> New political formations do not stand in an analogical relation with one another, as if they were discrete and differentiated entities. They are overlapping, mutually determining, and convergent fields of politicization. [...] Here difference is not simply the external differences, understood as that which differentiates them from one another, but rather *the self-difference of movement itself*, a constitutive rupture that makes movements possible on non-identitarian grounds, that installs a certain mobilizing conflict as the basis of politicization.
> (1997: 269, emphasis in the original)[19]

Butler is proposing to develop a sense of alliance, a new kind of conflictual encounter that would stay away from reinscribing and resubordinating differences to a politics of 'inclusion.'

Neighboring? In World Dance, as we currently know it, differences are recognized and incorporated as 'other' (other dances, other dancers). A politics of permanently negotiating alliances would entail re-establishing the parameters and methods of the whole Dance field. Obsession with difference coupled with peaceful coexistence will not deliver more than excessive, sentimentalized empathy (Kamboureli, 2007).

Although renowned political philosophers and influential post-colonial critics have not taken up dance as a field of inquiry or object of serious interest, dance as corporeal movement and mobilization offers the possibility to encounter a wild outside to Empire's sovereign rulings. World Dance, in particular, can be thought of as an open-ended, unlimited possibility of movements, dancers entering one by one, as singularities that amount to a 'not All' (Reinhard following Lacan, 2005) or to the 'multiple without One' (Badiou, 2001). Rather than a form of classification and an emergent discipline, World Dance would thus participate in the making of an untotalizing alternative to globalism, based on *decisions* (not on observations or accommodations to prescriptions) to expose our movements to the world.[20] These ethico-political decisions would entail dismantling otherness and differences as sources of identity and belonging, risking explorations into dissolution and betting on chosen, eventful reconstitutions. World dancers affiliated as neighbors, neighboring as we move each other into dancing, outside rubrics, disciplines, traditions. Beyond difference, otherness and marginality, dancing as moving the outside.

Notes

1. These thoughts have been prompted by recent attention on the part of philosophers such as Derrida (1997) and Badiou (2001) to rethink 'otherness' and what in the Humanities has come to be termed the 'ethical turn' (often linked to the thought of Levinas) in the face of the violent, catastrophic conflicts experienced in the twentieth century and their current escalations.
2. I am attempting to apply Foucault's (2004) and Agamben's (1998) teachings on biopolitics to World Dance.
3. For a much needed historical analysis of the term, see Foster, Chapter 5 in this volume. I use Choreography with a capital 'C' to connote the privileged status given to the ability to create or read meaningful and/or effective configurations of movement based on abstract notions such as space and time. In this sense, when applied to World Dance, Choreography assumes the role of a universal translator of dance traditions while positioning itself outside of history, beyond any particular cultural moorings. Choreography and choreographers thus are taken for exceptional operators that rule (create and interpret) the 'movement system' as a whole from outside the system, and yet make the system possible. Choreography clearly plays this paradoxical part in academic dance settings where specific dance traditions, including World Dances, are taught as techniques, while Choreography is imparted as a set of strategic tools capable of managing any specific technique, including their combinations. For an insightful discussion of the role of the choreographer in modern dance, see Martin (1992).
4. This is a compound definition that tries succinctly to reflect dance anthropologists' efforts to find a way to critique the imposition of the view of a eurocentrically informed observer (who would see and interpret all cultural complexes involving dancing as only 'dance' or as not dancing) over the Native's point of view. The terms 'patterned' and 'structured' appear frequently so as to show that this is not a purely emotional and volatile expression of individuals or of social haphazard frolicking (but then, what about improvisation among Natives?), as well as 'symbolic' or 'meaningful' to stress their social relevance and even their capacity to reflect, reaffirm,

or reconfigure the deep structure of a given culture. Legitimizing studies of 'bodies in movement' in the field of anthropology is an explicit concern that redefining 'dance' seeks to address. Historical accounts of dance anthropology repeatedly point out the methodological difficulties of fitting studies of 'dance' into the scientific paradigm guiding comparative studies of culture: reliable observation techniques; establishment of variables and parameters of classification; coherent interpretive frameworks for evaluating social relevance. Much of the discipline has been devoted to providing answers to these questions in terms of universal human behavior, of reflection of social structures, and of symbolic potency. For discussions of divergent terminology and ensuing perspectives in dance anthropology (which some refuse to call dance, favoring 'human movement', 'moving bodies,' etc), see, for example, Castaldi (2005), Farnel (1999), Kaeppler (1978), Reed (1998), Williams (2005).

5. Wong (Chapter 7) and Hammergren (Chapter 1) in this volume address such complex cases of 'international artist.'

6. See Levi-Strauss's argument in favor of cold versus hot history societies (1966) and Fabian's critique of the ethnographic present (1983).

7. See Efron (1942) *Gesture and Environment* and La Barre's (1947) *The Cultural Basis of Emotions and Gestures*. Comparative studies on gestures and sign language among North American Indians had been developed previously by Mallery (1881).

8. See Mead's (1928) *Coming of Age in Samoa*, Benedict's (1934) *Patterns of Culture* and Bateson's (1936) *Naven*, as well as Mead and Bateson's photographic study of Balinese dance, *Balinese Character*, of 1942.

9. See Boas's collections of essays from the 1890s to the 1930s in *Race, Language and Culture* (1982), and in *Anthropology and Modern Life* (1962).

10. For an informative discussion of the uses of 'ethnicity' in Anthropology, see Cohen's essay 'Ethnicity: Problem and focus in Anthropology' where he notes that 'the terms "ethnicity" and "ethnic" have come to refer to what was before often subsumed under "culture," "cultural," and "tribal" [...] Almost any cultural-social unit, indeed any term describing particular structures of continuing social relations, or sets of regularized events now can be referred as an "ethnic" this or that' (1978: 379).

11. See Foucault's extensive discussion of biopolitics and race in *Society Must Be Defended: Lectures at the College de France 1975–1976* (2003)[1997], and Giorgio Agamben's *Homo Sacer: Sovereign Power and Bare Life* (1998) [1995].

12. For a discussion of these 'archival' reinscriptions, see Reed's *The Politics and Poetics of Dance* (1998).

13. On the concept of the 'inoperative,' see Agamben (1998) following J. L. Nancy's *The Inoperative Community* (1991).

14. Note that this list *qua* catalogue is tellingly incomplete and it should be, given the nature of collections.

15. For a discussion of the distinctions between 'anti-racialism' (concerned with the categories and concepts of 'race') and 'anti-racism' (focusing on removing the structures that reproduce the conditions of racism), see David T. Goldberg, 2004.

16. Srinivasan's (Chapter 3) and Chatterjea's (Chapter 6) contributions to this volume extensively address the labors of translocation and translation that world dancers must undergo both as practitioners and as scholars.

17. Following Badiou's discussion in 'Does the Other Exist' (see *Ethics*, 2001), to the point to which I am capable, the 'same' sets up a paradox in that, on the one hand, sameness as identity should be dismantled given that 'infinite alterity is quite simply what there is' (every being is nothing other than an 'infinite deployment of differences'); and, on the other hand, the 'same' (i.e., what there is not) is 'what comes to be' through processes of truth, 'the labor that brings some truths into the world.' In his view, 'it is our capacity for truth – our capacity to be that *"same" that a truth convokes to its own sameness*' – that deserves our attention given that 'only a truth is, as such, *indifferent to differences.*' However, a truth that is *'the same for all'* does not follow the logic of cultural differences – which he provocatively renders 'insignificant as they are massive,' and whose basis he traces to 'vulgar sociology, directly inherited from the astonishment of the colonial encounter with savages,' including savages among ourselves, and to 'tourist's fascinations for the diversity of morals, customs, and beliefs.' Rather than an ethics of difference, invested in recognizing the other so as to respect 'differences' – and the consequent reproduction of identities based on the 'same' principle of differentiation (which is nothing other than the identity of the wealthy West) – Badiou proposes to focus on the problem of recognizing the 'same,' and on elaborating an ethics of 'truths in the plural' which should be, simultaneously, specific: ethics *of* politics, *of* love, *of* science, *of* art. For a helpful, critical discussion of Badiou's tendency to fall back into a universalism of sameness by foregrounding the power of thought to produce equality and cast off differences, see Santner 2005: 125–129. Making use of Agamben's proposal of an entirely new sort of logic that stresses the noncoincidence of every identity with itself (and thus avoids operating in terms of memberships in bounded sets of totalities set against each other), Santner introduces new ways to conceive of ethical responsibility.

18. Kraut, Chapter 4 in this volume, explores these issues specifically in relation to the pitfalls of choreographic copyrights.

19. On the Derridean underpinnings of the concept of *différance* as 'the active moving discord of different forces' that intervenes in the 'worlding of the world,' an active movement of cutting and inscribing that also brings together, producing new arrangements and organizations, see Grosz's (2005) lucid discussion.

20. Stressing the possibility of intervening by way of decisions does not amount to simple voluntarism. We are immersed in a social world, structured and overdetermined. However, a new conceptualization of subjectivity that highlights, following Agamben, the noncoincidence with oneself, coupled with the emergence of an eventful situation (a situation that provides new possibilities but that cannot be produced at will) allows for agency. Agency here would be the decision to not follow the socially scripted and to open up to the unknown. Badiou theorizes this possibility in terms of 'truth-processes,' that is for taking advantage as it were of a sudden rupture, a disonnance, a contradiction in the social fabric interpellating us into

being as members of a totalizing set in confrontation to other totalizing sets. Fidelity to this disorganizing event and experience, keeping close to its materiality and uniqueness, amounts to a decision to risk recognizing the tears and engaging in the processes of their elaboration. In Santner's terms, 'one cannot give oneself the possibility of new possibilities. Something must *happen*, something beyond one's control, calculations and labor, something that comes from the locus of the Other' (2005: 123).

Works Cited

Abou-El-Haj, B. 'Languages and Models for Cultural Exchange.' In *Culture, Globalization and the World-System: Contemporary Conditions for the Representation of Identity*, ed. A. King (Minneapolis: University of Minnesota Press, 1997), 139–44.

Abu-Lughod, L. *Remaking Women* (New Jersey: Princeton University Press, 1998).

'A Dull Season in Paris.' *New York Times*, 17 March 1878: 6.

Agamben, G. *Homo Sacer: Sovereign Power and Bare Life*, trans. D. Heller-Roazen (Stanford, CA.: Stanford University Press, 1998).

——. *State of Exception*, trans. K. Attell (Chicago: University of Chicago Press, 2005).

Allen, C. *Blood Narrative: Indigenous Identity in American Indian and Maori Literary and Activist Texts* (Durham, NC: Duke University Press, 2002).

Aloff, M. 'Letter to the Editors.' *Dance Chronicle*, 29.2 (2006): 265–6.

'A Play to Run Six Months.' *New York Times*, 30 October 1882: 5.

Appadurai, A. *Modernity at Large: Cultural Dimensions of Globalization* (Minneapolis: University of Minnesota Press, 1996).

——. 'Grassroots Globalization and the Research Imagination.' In *Globalization*, ed. A. Appadurai (Durham, NC, and London: Duke University Press, 2001), 1–21.

Arcomano, N. 'Choreography and Copyright, Part One.' *Dance Magazine*, 54.4 (April 1980): 58–9.

Ashcroft, B., G. Griffiths and H. Tiffin. *Key Concepts in Post-Colonial Studies* (London and New York: Routledge, 1998).

Atkins, C. and J. Malone, *Class Act: The Jazz Life of Choreographer Cholly Atkins* (New York: Columbia University Press, 2001).

Au, S. *Ballet and Modern Dance* (London: Thames & Hudson, 1988).

Austin, J. L. *How To Do Things With Words*, 2nd edn, ed. J. O. Urmson and M. Sbisá (Cambridge, MA: Harvard University Press, 1961).

Badiou, A. *Ethics: An Essay in the Understanding of Evil*, trans. P. Hallward (London: Verso, 2001).

——. *Metapolitics*, trans. J. Barker (London: Verso, 2006).

Banerjee, S. *Dangerous Outcast: The Prostitute in Nineteenth-Century Bengal* (Kolkata: Seagull, 2000).

Barapanda, D. *Nachni Katha* (Kolkata: Pustak Bipani, 2007).

Bateson, G. *Naven* (Stanford, CA: Stanford University Press, 1958).

Baudrillard, J. 'The System of Collecting.' In *The Cultures of Collecting*, ed. J. Elsner and R. Cardinal (Cambridge, MA: Harvard University Press, 1994), 7–24.

Beckley, P. V. 'Choreography Is Copyrighted for First Time.' *New York Herald Tribune*, 14 March 1952, Hanya Holm Clippings File, Dance Collection, New York Public Library.

Benedict, R. *Patterns of Culture* (New York: Houghton Miffin, 1934).

Benveniste, E. *Problems of General Linguistics*, trans. M. E. Meek (Coral Gables: University of Miami Press, 1971).

Bhabha, H. *The Location of Culture* (1994), with new preface (London and New York: Routledge, 2004).

Bhachu, P. *Dangerous Designs: Asian Women Fashion the Diaspora Economies* (New York: Routledge, 2004).

Biwas, T. *Sindhubala Jhumur o naachni* (Kolkata: Kobita Pakkhikh Desk, 2003).

Blue Spruce, D. (Ed.) *Spirit of a Native Place: Building the National Museum of the American Indian* (Washington, DC: National Museum of the American Indian, Smithsonian Institution, 2004).

Boas, F. *The Function of Dance in Human Society* (New York: Boas School, 1944).

———. *Anthropology and Modern Life* (New York: Norton, 1962).

———. [1940] *Race, Language and Culture* (Chicago: University of Chicago Press, 1982).

Bourdieu, P. *Distinction: A Social Critique of the Judgement of Taste* (Cambridge, MA: Harvard University Press, 1985).

———. *The Logic of Practice*. Trans. Richard Nice. (Stanford, CA: Stanford University Press, 1992).

Butler, J. 'Merely Cultural.' *Social Text*, 52/53 (1997): 265–77.

'Cal Performances.' Brochure for the 2007–08 Season of performances sponsored by the University of California, Berkeley.

Caldwell, H. *Michio Ito: The Dancer and his Dances* (Berkeley: University of California Press, 1977).

Caroso, F. *Nobilità di dame: A Treatise on Courtly Dance*. Translated from the printing of 1600. Ed. and with an introduction by Julia Sutton (Oxford: Oxford University Press, 1986).

Cass, J. *Dancing Through History* (New Jersey: Prentice Hall, 1993).

Castaldi, F. *Choreographing African Identities: Negritude, Dance and the National Ballet of Senegal* (Bloomington: University of Illinois Press, 2005).

Caute, D. *The Dancer Defects: The Struggle for Cultural Supremacy During the Cold War* (Oxford: Oxford University Press, 2003).

Chakrabarty, D. *Provincializing Europe: Postcolonial Thought and Historical Difference* (Princeton, NJ: Princeton University Press, 2000).

———. *Habitations of Modernity: Essays in the Wake of Subaltern Studies* (Chicago: University of Chicago Press, 2002).

Chakravarti, U. 'Re-Inscribing the Past: Inserting Women into Indian History.' In *Culture and the Making of Identity in Contemporary India*, ed. Kamala Ghosh and Usha Thakkar (Delhi: Sage, 2005).

Chakravorty, P. *Bells of Change: Kathak Dance, Women and Modernity in India.* (Delhi: Seagull, 2008).

Chatterjea, A. *Butting Out: Reading Resistive Choreographies Through Works by Jawole Willa Jo Zollar and Chandralekha* (Middletown: Wesleyan University Press, 2005).

———. 'Contestations: Constructing a Historical Narrative for Odissi.' In *Rethinking Dance History*, ed. A. Carter (London and New York: Routledge, 2004), 143–56.

Chatterjee, Partha. *Nationalist Thought and the Colonial World: A Derivative Discourse* (Minneapolis: University of Minnesota Press, 1986).

Chatterjee, Piya. *A Time for Tea: Women, Labor, and Post/Colonial Politics On An Indian Plantation* (Durham, NC: Duke University Press, 2001).

Christiansen, T. 'Dance Kept from Becoming Footnotes.' *The Seattle Times Company*, 20 February 2001: F3.

Clifford, J. 'On Collecting Art and Culture.' In *The Predicament of Culture: Twentieth-Century Ethnography, Literature, and Art* (Cambridge, MA: Harvard University Press, 1988), 215–51.

Clifford, J. and G. Marcus. (Eds). *Writing Culture: The Poetics and Politics of Ethnography* (Berkeley: University of California Press, 1986).

Cohen, R. 'Ethnicity: Problem and Focus in Anthropology.' *Annual Review of Anthropology*, 7 (1978): 379–403.

Cohn, B. *Colonialism and Its Forms of Knowledge: The British in India* (Princeton, NJ: Princeton University Press, 1996).

Cohn, J. 'Grades/Groove: Students can release stress, get moving and get units in a variety of classes from hip-hop to salsa.' *UCLA Daily Bruin*, 29 February 2008: 1.

Comaroff, J, and J. Comaroff. *Of Revelation and Revolution*, Volume 1: *Christianity, Colonialism, and Consciousness in South Africa*. (Chicago, University of Chicago Press, 1991).

'Concerning George White and his "Scandals."' *New York Times*, 19 December 1926: X4.

Conner, L. *Spreading the Gospel of Modern Dance: Newspaper Dance Criticism in the United States, 1850–1934* (Pittsburgh: University of Pittsburgh Press, 1997).

Cook, M. 'Moving to New Beat: Copyright Protection for Choreographic Works.' *UCLA Law Review*, 24. 5/6 (June–August 1977): 1287–312.

Cook, W. M. '"Spirituals" and "Jazz,"' letter to the editor, *New York Times*, 26 December 1926: X8.

Coombe, R. J. *The Cultural Life of Intellectual Properties: Authorship, Appropriation, and the Law* (Durham, NC: Duke University Press, 1998a).

——. Response to Michael F. Brown, 'Can Culture Be Copyrighted?' *Current Anthropology*, 39.2 (April 1998b): 207–9.

'Copyright by Hanya Holm.' *Dance Magazine*, 39.7 (July 1965): 44.

Cowell, Mary-Jean. 'East and West in the Work of Michio Ito.' *Dance Research Journal*, 26.2 (Fall 1994).

——. 'Michio Ito in Hollywood: Modes and Ironies of Ethnicity.' *Dance Chronicle*, 24.3 (2001): 263–305.

Dagens Nyheter, 29 December 1958.

Daly, A. *Done into Dance: Isadora Duncan in America*. (Middletown: Wesleyan University Press, 1995).

'Dancing Wife Divorces Ito.' *New York Times*, 2 April 1936: 29.

Datta, G. *Bratachari sakha* (Kolkata: Bengal Bratachari Society, 1934).

——. *The Folk Dances of Bengal*. (Kolkata: B. S. Dutt, 1954).

DeFrantz, T. (Ed.). *Dancing Many Drums: Excavations in African American Dance* (Madison: University of Wisconsin Press, 2002).

Derrida, J. *The Politics of Friendship*, trans. J. Collins (New York: Verso, 1997).

Desmond, J. 'Dancing Out the Difference: Cultural Imperialism and Ruth St. Denis' "Radha" of 1906.' *Signs*, 17.1 (1991): 28–49.

Dickason, O. P. *Canada's First Nations: A History of Founding Peoples from Earliest Times* (Toronto: Oxford University Press, 1997).

Dilley, R. 'Introduction: The Problem of Context.' In *The Problem of Context*, ed. R. Dilley (New York: Berghahn Books, 1999).

Dirlik, A. 'The Postcolonial Aura: Third World Criticism in the Age of Global Capitalism.' *Critical Inquiry*, 20 (Winter 1994): 328–56.

Display Ad, *New York Times*, 22 November 1926: 29.

'Display Ad 112,' *New York Times*, 10 October 1926: X3.

Djebar, A. *Fantasia: An Algerian Cavalcade* (London: Quartet Books, 1997).

Doughty, H. 'The Choreographer in the Courtroom: Loie Fuller and Léonide Massine,' SDHS Proceedings, Fifth Annual Conference, Harvard University, 13–15 February 1982: 35–9.

Dutt, G. *Folk Arts and Crafts of Bengal* (Kolkata: Seagull, 1990).

Efron, D. *Gesture and Environment* (New York: Kings Crown, 1942).

Enloe, C. *Bananas, Beaches and Bases: Making Feminist Sense of International Politics* (Berkeley: University of California Press, 1990).

Erdman, J. L. 'Dance Discourses: Rethinking the History of the "Oriental Dance."' In *Moving Words: Re-Writing Dance*, ed. G. Morris (London and New York: Routledge, 1996), 288–305.

Ewen, D. *Complete Book of American Musical Theater* (New York: Henry Holt, 1958).

——. *New Complete Book of the American Musical Theater* (New York: Holt, Rinehart & Winston, 1970).

Eye on Dance: Yesterday Shapes Today: Tracing the Roots [videorecording]. Produced by ARC Videodance, Celia Ipiotis, and Jeff Bush, No. 160, 1985.

Fabian, J. *Time and the Other: How Anthropology Makes Its Object* (New York: Columbia University Press, 1983).

Fairfax, E. *The Styles of Eighteenth Century Ballet* (Lanhan, MD: Scarecrow Press, 2003).

Farnell, B. 'Moving Bodies, Acting Selves.' *Annual Review of Anthropology*, 28 (1999): 341–73.

Feld, S. 'A Sweet Lullaby for World Music.' *Public Culture*, 12.1 (2000): 145–71.

Fetterman, M. 'Yoga Copyright Raises Questions of Ownership.' *USA Today* online edition, 28 June 2006: http://www.usatoday.com/tech/news/2006-06-28-yoga-usat_x.htm, accessesed 5 July 2007.

Foster, S. L. *Reading Dancing: Bodies and Subjects in Contemporary American Dance* (Berkeley: University of California Press, 1986).

——. Introduction. In *Corporealities: Dancing Knowledge, Culture, and Power*, ed. S. L. Foster (New York: Routledge, 1995), xi–xvii.

——. 'Closets Full of Dances: Modern Dance's Performance of Masculinity and Sexuality.' In *Dancing Desires: Choreographing Sexualities on and Off the Stage*, ed. J. Desmond (Durham, NC: Duke University Press, 2001), 147–208.

——. *Dances That Describe Themselves: The Improvised Choreography of Richard Bull* (Middletown, CT: Wesleyan University Press, 2002).

Foucault, M. *The Order of Things* [1966]. (New York: Vintage Books, 1973).

——. *Society Must Be Defended: Lectures at the Collége de France 1975–1976* [1997], trans. G. Burchell (New York: Picador [St. Martin Press], 2003).

——. *El Pensamiento del Afuera*, [1986] trans. M. Arranz (Valencia: Pre-textos, 2004).

Foulkes, J. 'Dance Is for American Men: Ted Shawn and the Intersection of Gender, Sexuality, and Nationalism in the 1930s.' In *Dancing Desires: Choreographing Sexuality On and Off the Stage*, ed. Jane C. Desmond (Madison: University of Wisconsin Press, 2001), 113–46.

——. *Modern Bodies: Dance and American Modernism* (Chapel Hill, NC: University of North Carolina Press, 2002).

Frazer, G. J. *The Golden Bow: Studies in Magic and Religion* [1927] (London: Macmillan, 1966).

Freeman, W. M. 'Ann Pennington, Dancing Star, Dies,' *New York Times*, 5 November 1971: 46.

Fusao Inada, L. *Only What We Could Carry: The Japanese American Internment Experience* (Berkeley, CA: Heyday Books, 2000).

Gautier, T. *Gautier on Dance*, comp and trans. Ivor Guest (London: Dance Books, 1986).

'Gay Parisian Topics.' *New York Times*, 2 April 1882: 3.

Geertz, C. *The Interpretation of Cultures* (New York: Basic Books, 1973).

George-Kanentiio, D. *Iroquois Culture and Commentary* (New Mexico: Clear Light Publishers, 2000), 92–4.

Goldberg, T. D. 'The End(s) of Race.' *Postcolonial Studies*, 7.2 (2004): 211–30.

Golshani, F., P. Vissicaro and Y. Park. 'A Multimedia Information Repository for Cross Cultural Dance Studies.' *Multimedia Tools and Applications*, 24 (2004): 89–103.

Goldstein, Paul. *International Copyright: Principles, Law, and Practice* (New York: Oxford University Press, 2001).

Gopal, R. *Rhythm in the Heavens* (London: Secker & Warburg, 1957).

Göteborgs Sjöfarts- och Handels Tidning, 25 April 1968.

Gottschild, B. D. *Digging the Africanist Presence in American Performance: Dance and Other Contexts* (Westport, CT: Greenwood Press, 1996).

——. *Waltzing in the Dark: African American Vaudeville and Race Politics in the Swing Era* (New York: St Martin's Press, 2000).

Graham, M. *Blood Memory* (New York: Doubleday, 1991).

Green, A. and J. Laurie, Jr. *Show Biz: From Vaude to Video* (New York: Permabooks, 1951).

Green, R. '(Up) Staging the Primitive: Pearl Primus and "the Negro Problem" in American Dance.' In *Dancing Many Drums: Excavations in African American Dance* (Madison: University of Wisconsin Press, 2002), 105–39.

Grosz, E. 'Derrida and Feminism: A Remembrance.' *Differences: A Journal of Feminist Cultural Studies*, 16.3 (2005): 88–94.

Guest, A. H. 'The Golden Age of the Broadway Musical: A Personal Reminiscence.' *Dance Chronicle*, 16.3 (1993): 363.

Hall, S. 'Cultural Identity and Diaspora' (1990). In *Colonial Discourse & Postcolonial Theory: A Reader*, ed. P. Williams and L. Chrisman (Harlow: Pearson Educational, 1994), 392–403.

——. 'The Local and the Global: Globalization and Ethnicity.' In *Culture, Globalization and the World-System*, ed. A. D. King (Minneapolis: University of Minesotta Press, 1997), 19–40.

Hamera, J. *Dancing Communities: Performance, Difference and Connection in the Global City* (Basingstoke: Palgrave Macmillan, 2007).

Hammond, S. N. 'International Elements of Dance Training in the Late Eighteenth Century.' In *The Grotesque Dancer on the Eighteenth-Century Stage: Gennaro Magri and His World*, ed. R. Harris-Warrick and B. A. Brown (Madison: University of Wisconsin Press, 2005), 109–50.

Hannerz, U. 'Two Faces of Cosmopolitanism: Culture and Politics.' *Documentos CIDOB, Serie* Dinámicas Culturales, 7 (2006): 1–29.

Hanya Holm Papers, Dance Collection, New York Public Library.

Hanya: Portrait of a Pioneer [video], produced by Nancy Mason Hauser, Dance Horizons Video, 1988.

Hardt, M. and A. Negri. *Empire* (Cambridge, MA: Harvard University Press, 2000).

Harrison, D. D. 'She's Got a Mind to Ramble: Alberta Hunter.' In *Black Pearls: Blues Queens of the 1920s* (New Brunswick, NJ: Rutgers University Press, 1988).

Harris-Warrick, R. and C. G. Marsh. *Musical Theatre at the Court of Louis XIV: Le marriage de la Grosse Cathos* (Cambridge: Cambridge University Press, 1994).

Haynes, J. 'World Music and the Search for Difference.' *Ethnicities*, 5.3 (2005): 365–85.

H'Doubler, M. *The Dance* (New York: Harcourt, Brace, 1925).

——. *Rhythmic Form and Analysis* (J. M. Rider, 1932).

Heidegger, M. 'The Origin of the Work of Art' [1935]. In *Basic Works: From Being and Time (1927) to the Task of Thinking (1964)*, ed. D. F. Krell (San Francisco: Harper, 1993), 137–212.

Holm, H. '*Kiss Me, Kate*,' n.s. 23 September 1951, Hanya Holm Scrapbooks, Dance Collection, New York Public Library.

Horse Capture, G. 'The Way of the People.' In *Spirit of a Native Place: Building the National Museum of the American Indian*, ed. D. Blue Spruce (Washington, DC: National Museum of the American Indian, Smithsonian Institution, 2004), 30–45.

Horst, L. *Pre-Classic Forms* [1937] (Princeton, NJ: Princeton Book Publishers, 1987).

Humphrey, D. *The Art of Making Dances* (New York: Grove Press, 1959).

Hylland Eriksen, T. *Ethnicity and Nationalism: Anthropological Perspectives* (London: Pluto Press, 1993).

Idestam-Almqvist, B. (sign. Robin Hood), *Stockholms-Tidningen*, 9 March 1949.

Jaimes, M. A. with T. Halsey. 'American Indian Women At the Center of Indigenous Resistance in Contemporary North America.' In *The State of Native America*, ed. M. A. Jaimes (Boston, MA: South End Press, 1992), 311–44.

Jenyns, S. *The Art of Dancing, A Poem in Three Cantos* [1729], ed. Anne Cottis (London: Dance Books, 1978).

Jeyasingh, S. 'Imaginary Homelands: Creating a New Dance Language.' In *The Routledge Dance Studies Reader* (London: Routledge, 1998).

Jonas, G. *Dancing: The Pleasure, Power, and Art of Movement* (New York: Harry N. Abrams, 1992).

Jones, R. D. 'Modern Native Dance: Beyond Tribe and Tradition.' In *Native American Dance: Ceremonies and Social Traditions*, ed. C. Heth (Washington, DC: National Museum of the American Indian Smithsonian Institution with Stanwood Publishing, 1992).

Jowitt, D. *Time and the Dancing Image* (Berkeley: University of California Press, 1989).

Kadir, D. 'To World, To Globalize – Comparative Literature's Crossroads.' *Comparative Literature Studies*, 41.1 (2004): 1–9.

Kaeppler, Adrienne L. 'Dance in Anthropological Perspective.' *Annual Review of Anthropology*, 7 (1978): 31–49.

Kamboureli, S. 'The Limits of the Ethical Turn: Troping Towards the Other, Yan Martel, and Self.' *University of Toronto Quarterly*, 76.3 (2007): 937–61.

Kant, Marion. 'A Review of: "Mary Wigman and Hanya Holm: A Special Relationship."' *Dance Chronicle*, 28.3 (September 2005): 417–23.

Karina, L. and M. Kant. *Hitler's Dancers: German Modern Dancers and the Third Reich*, trans. Jonathan Steinberg (Oxford: Berghahn Books, 2003).

Kaufman, Sarah. 'Retracing Lost Steps; Japanese Dancer's Pioneering Works are Revived,' *The Washington Post*, 14 January 1996a: G01.

———. 'The Power of Michio Ito.' *The Washington Post*, 22 January 1996b: B07.

Kealiinohomoku, J. 'An Anthropologist Looks at Ballet as a Form of Ethnic Dance.' In *Moving History/Dancing Cultures: A Dance History Reader*, ed. A. Dils and A. Cooper Albright (Middletown, CT: Wesleyan University Press, 2001). Also in *What Is Dance? Readings in Theory and Criticism*, ed. R. Copeland and M. Cohen (Oxford: Oxford University Press, 1983), 533–49.

Kersenboom, S. *Nityasumangali: Devadasi Tradition in South Asia* (Delhi: Motilal Banarsidass, 1987).

Khokar, M. 'Western Interest, and Its Impact on, Indian Dance.' *Bulletin of the Institute of Traditional Cultures Madras*, 2 (1961): 203–17.

Kisselgoff, Anna. 'Dance View: An All-But-Forgotten Pioneer of American Modern Dance.' *New York Times*, 26 February 1978: D10.

———. 'Dance: Michio Ito Salute.' *New York Times*, 4 October 1979: C30.

Kiss Me, Kate. Dance Clippings File, Dance Collection, New York Public Library.

Kiss Me, Kate. Labanotated score, Dance Notation Bureau Library.

Koritz, Amy. 'Dancing the Orient for England: Maud Allen's "The Vision of Salome."' *Theater Journal* (March 1994): 63–78.

Krasner, D. *Resistance, Parody, and Double Consciousness in African American Theatre, 1895–1910* (New York: St. Martin's Press, 1997).

Kriegsman, S. A. *Modern Dance in America: The Bennington Years* (Boston, MA: G. K. Hall, 1981).

———. 'Dance: Deboo's Confluence of Cultures.' *The Washington Post*, 19 November 1990: D2.

Laban, Rudolf. *Choreutics*, annotated and edited by Lisa Ullman (London: McDonald & Evans, 1966).

La Barre, W. 'The Cultural Basis of Emotions and Gestures.' *Journal of Personality*, 16 (1947): 49–68.

La Meri (Russell Meriwether Hughes). *Dance Composition: The Basic Elements* (Massachusetts : Jacob's Pillow Dance Festival).

———. *Total Education in Ethnic Dance* (New York: Marcel Dekker, 1977).

Langer, S. *Feeling and Form: A Theory of Art* (New York: Scribner, 1953).

Lansdale, N. 'Concerning the Copyright of Dances.' *Dance Magazine* (June 1952): 21, 41.

Laurenti, J. N. 'Feuillet's Thinking.' In *Traces of Dance*, ed. Laurence Lope, trans. Brian Holmes (Paris: Editions Dis Voir, 1994), 81–103.

Lawson, F. I. *Only What We Could Carry: The Japanese American Internment Experience* (Berkeley, CA: Heyday Books, 2000).

Lee, B. *Dancing: All the Latest Steps* (Chicago: Franklin Publishing, 1926, 1927).

Lee, J. Kyung-Jin. *Urban Triage: Race and the Fictions of Multiculturalism* (Minneapolis: University of Minnesota Press, 2004).

Levi-Strauss, C. 'The Scope of Anthropology.' *Current Anthropology*, 7.2 (1966): 112–23.

Levine, L. *Highbrow/Lowbrow: The Emergence of Cultural Hierarchy in America* (Cambridge, MA: Harvard University Press, 1988).

Lieb, S. R. *Mother of the Blues: A Study of Ma Rainey* (Amherst: The University of Massachusetts Press, 1981).

Littler, W. 'History of Dance Lives Again via Utah.' *Toronto Star*, 7 November 1991: E4.

Lomax, A., I. Barinieff and F. Paulay. 'Dance Style and Culture.' In *Folk Song Style and Culture*, ed. Alan Lomax (New Brunswick, NJ: Transaction Books, 1968), 222–73.

Lopez y Royo, A. 'Classicism, Post-Classicism, and Ranjabati Sircar's Work.' *South Asia Research*, 23.2 (November 2003): 153–69.

Lowe, L. *Immigrant Acts: On Asian American Cultural Politics* (Durham, NC: Duke University Press, 1996).

Lynton, L. *The Sari* (London: Thames & Hudson, 2002).

Macaulay, T. B. 'Warren Hastings' (1843). In *Critical and Historical Essays* (London. Accessed through http://www.gutenberg.org/etext/2333).

Machan, K. 'Bending Over Backwards for Copyright Protection: Bikram Yoga and the Quest for Federal Copyright Protection of an Asana Sequence.' 12 *UCLA Entertainment Law Rev.* 29 (2004). Online. LexisNexis® Academic. 9 July 2007.

Malinowski, B. *Argonauts of the Western Pacific* (New York: Routledge & Kegan Paul, 1922).

Mallery, G. *Sign Language Among North American Indians Compared with that Among Other Peoples and Deaf-Mutes* [1881] (The Hague: Mouton, 1972).

Malone, J. *Steppin' on the Blues: The Visible Rhythms of African American Dance* (Urbana: University of Illinois Press, 1996).

Manning, S. *Modern Dance, Negro Dance: Race in Motion* (Minneapolis: University of Minnesota Press, 2004, 2005).

Maram, L.-E. *Creating Masculinity in Los Angeles's Little Manila: Working Class Filipinos and Popular Culture, 1920s–1950s* (New York: Columbia University Press, 2006).

Martin, J. 'Broadway on its Toes.' *New York Times*, 23 January 1949a: SM18.

——. 'The Dance: Debut,' *New York Times*, 30 January 1949b: X6.

——. 'The Dance: Broadway.' *New York Times*, 14 January 1951: X8.

——. 'The Dance: Copyright.' *New York Times*, 30 March 1952a: X10.

——. 'The Dance: Progress.' *New York Times*, 8 June 1952b: X2.

Martin, R. 'Dance Ethnography and the Limits of Representation.' *Social Text*, 33 (1992): 103–23.

Mauss, M. 'Techniques of the Body' [1936]. *Economy and Society*, 2.1 (1973): 70–88.

Mazo, J. *Prime Movers: The Makers of Modern Dance in America* (New York: Morrow, 1977).

McClintock, A. *Imperial Leather: Race, Gender and Sexuality in the Colonial Contest* (New York: Routledge, 1995).

Mead, M. *Coming of Age in Samoa* [1928] (New York: Morrow Quill, 1961).

——. and G. Bateson. *Balinese Character: A Photographic Analysis* (New York: New York Academy of Science, 1942).

Meduri, A. *Nation, Woman Represented - the Sutured History of the Devadasi and Her Dance: 1856–1960*. PhD Diss. (New York University, 1997).

——. *Transcultural Modernities* (Wesleyan: Wesleyan University Press, Forthcoming).

Mehta, S. 'A Big Stretch.' *New York Times*, 7 May 2007: A21.

Merleau Ponty, M. *Phenomenology of Perception* (New York: Routledge, 2002).

'Michio Ito to be Honored at Festival of His Dances.' *New York Times*, 17 September 1979: C15.

'Modern Dances Held to Mean a Modern Renaissance.' *New York Times*, 3 May 1914: SM5.

Mohanty, C., A. Russo and L. Torres. (Eds). *Third World Women and the Politics of Feminism* (Bloomington: Indiana University Press, 1991).

Money, K. *Anna Pavlova: Her Life and Art* (London: Collins, 1982).

Moore, F. B. 'Glorified Ballet Art.' *New York Times*, 24 December 1916: III1.

Mordden, E. *Beautiful Mornin': The Broadway Musical in the 1940s* (New York: Oxford University Press, 1999).

Morris, G. *A Game for Dancers: Performing Modernism in the Postwar Years, 1945–1960* (Middletown, CT: Wesleyan University Press, 2006).

Mukherjee, M. *Gourbanger Devadasi* (Kolkata: N. E. Publishers, 2004).

Nava, M. 'Cosmopolitan Modernity: Everyday Imaginaries and the Register of Difference.' *Theory, Culture & Society*, 19.1–2 (2002): 81–99.

Negus, K. 'The Work of Cultural Intermediaries and the Enduring Distance between Production and Consumption.' *Cultural Studies*, 16.4 (2002): 510–15.

Ness, S. *Body, Movement, and Culture: Kinesthetic and Visual Symbolism in a Philippine Community* (Philadelphia: University of Pennsylvania Press, 1992).

'Never the Twain....' *Chicago Daily Tribune*, 5 April 1936: B8.

'New Ballet Puzzles.' *New York Times*, 12 July 1913: 4.

'News and Gossip of the Rialto.' *New York Times*, 21 November 1926: X1.

Novack, C. *Sharing the Dance: Contact Improvisation and American Culture* (Madison: University of Wisconsin, 1990).

Noverre, J. G. *Letters on Dancing and Ballets* [1760], trans. Cyril W. Beaumont (Brooklyn: Dance Horizons, 1966).

Okazawa-Rey, M. and G. Kirk (Eds) (2004). *Women's Lives: Multicultural Perspectives*, 3rd edn. New York: McGraw Hill.

'OnStage: After 20 Years of Silence, Alberta Hunter Sings "Remember My Name" – and Memphis Gives her the Key to the City.' *People* n.d.: 118, Alberta Hunter Clippings, Theatre Collection, New York Public Library.

O'Shea, J. *At Home in the World: Bharata Natyam on the Global Stage* (Middletown: Wesleyan University Press, 2007).

Parker, A. C. 'Certain Iroquois Tree Myths and Symbols.' *American Anthropologist*, (1912): 608–20.

Perpener, J. *African-American Concert Dance: The Harlem Renaissance and Beyond* (Urbana: University of Illinois Press, 2001).

Pradhan, S. (Ed.). *Marxist Cultural Movement in India, Chronicles and Documents, vols I–III* (Kolkata: Pustak Bipani, 1985).

Prevots, N. *Dancing in the Sun: Hollywood Choreographers 1915–1937* (Michigan: UMI Research Press, 1987).

——. *Dance for Export: Cultural Diplomacy and the Cold War* (Middletown: Wesleyan University Press, 1998).

Radhakrishnan, R. 'Aesthetic Truth: Production or "Letting Be."' In *Arts and Mirrors: Topologies of Art and Politics*, ed. Steve Martinot (Evanston, IL: Northwestern University Press, 2001), 304–18.

Ramchandran, N. 'Bharata Natyam – Culture and Dance of the Ancient Tamils.' Paper presented at the *First International Conference Seminar of Tamil Studies* (Kuala Lumpur, Malaysia, 1966): http://www.tamilnation.org/culture/dance/index.htm#Dance%20and%20Music%20in%20Cilapathikaram

Randall, R. 'Thousands Never Get a Chance, Says Gifted Alberta Hunter.' *Daily Worker*, 3 November 1939: n.p., Alberta Hunter Clippings File, Theatre Collection, New York Public Library.

Reed, S. A. 'The Politics and Poetics of Dance.' *Annual Review of Anthropology*, 27 (1998): 503–32.

Reinhard, K. 'Toward a Political Theology of the Neighbor.' In S. Žižek, E. L. Santner and K. Reinhard, *The Neighbor: Three Inquiries in Political Theology* (Chicago: University of Chicago Press, 2005), 11–75.

Rose, M. *Authors and Owners: The Invention of Copyright* (Cambridge, MA: Harvard University Press, 1993).

Ross, A. 'Hip, and the Long Front of Color.' In *No Respect: Intellectuals & Popular Culture* (New York and London: Routledge, 1989).

Ross, J. *Moving Lessons: Margaret H'Doubler and the Beginning of Dance in American Education* (Madison: University of Wisconsin Press, 2000).

Rosselli, J. '"The Self-Image of Effeteness": Physical Education and Nationalism in Nineteenth-Century Bengal.' *Past and Present*, 86, February 1980: 121–48.

Ruby, J. 'Franz Boas and Early Camera Study of Human Behavior.' *Kinesics Report* (1980): 1–16.

Sachs, C. *World History of the Dance* [1937] (New York: W. W. Norton, 1963).

Said, E. W. *Orientalism*. (New York: Random House, 1979).

——. *The World, the Text, and the Critic* (Cambridge, MA: Harvard University Press, 1983).

Sandhu, S. '*The Guru* and the Cultural Politics of Placenessness.' In *Alien Encounters: Popular Culture in America* (Durham, NC: Duke University Press, 2007), 161–75.

Sangari, K. 'The Politics of the Possible.' In *The Nature and Context of Minority Discourse*, ed. Abdul Jan Mohamed and David Lloyd (New York: Oxford University Press, 1990).

——. *Politics of the Possible* (Delhi: Tulika, 1999).

Santner, E. L. 'Miracles Happen: Benjamin, Rosenzweig, Freud, and the Matter of the Neighbor.' In S. Žižek, E. L. Santner and K. Reinhard, *The Neighbor: Three Inquiries in Political Theology* (Chicago: University of Chicago Press, 2005), pp. 76–33.

Sassen, S. *Cities in a World Economy* (Thousand Oaks, CA: Pine Forge Press, 1994).

Saukko, P. *Doing Research in Cultural Studies* (London: Sage, 2003).

Savigliano, M. *Tango and the Political Economy of Passion* (Boulder, CO: Westview Press, 1995).

——. *Angora Matta: Fatal Acts of North-South Translation* (Middletown: Wesleyan University Press, 2003).

'Scenes from Paris Life.' *New York Times*, 7 March 1882: 7.

Scott, A. 'Spectacle and Dancing Bodies that Matter: OR If it don't fit, don't force it.' In *Meaning in Motion: New Cultural Studies in Dance*, ed. Jane Desmond. (Durham, NC: Duke University Press, 1997).

Segal, L. 'Looking at Postcards: World Dance on Western Stages.' In *Looking Out: Perspectives on Dance and Criticism in a Multicultural World*, ed. D. Gere et al. (New York: Schirmer Books, 1995).

Shea Murphy, J. *'The People Have Never Stopped Dancing': Native American Dance and Modern Dance History* (Minneapolis: University of Minnesota Press, 2007).

Shelton, S. *Ruth St. Denis: A Biography of the Divine Dancer*. (Austin: University of Texas Press, 1990).

Sinha, N. K. *The Economic History of Bengal – From Plassey to the Permanent Settlement* (Calcutta: Firma KLM, 1962).

Singer, B. A. 'In Search of Adequate Protection for Choreographic Works: Legislative and Judicial Alternatives vs. The Custom of the Dance Community.' *University of Miami Law Review*, 38 (1984): 287–319.

Six Nations of the Grand River, *Six Nations of the Grand River: Land Rights, Financial Justice, Creative Solutions*, November 2006, available at: http://www.sixnations.ca/LandClaimsUpdate.htm and http://www.sixnations.ca/Nov3ClaimsBooklet.pdf

Sklar, D. *Dancing with the Virgin: Body and Faith in the Fiesta of Tortugas, New Mexico* (Berkeley: University of California Press, 2001).

Smith, S. 'Kaha:wi: Cultural Transmission through Contemporary Iroquoian Song and Dance.' Major Research Paper for an MA in Dance, York University, 2004.

Sorell, W. *Hanya Holm: The Biography of an Artist* (Middletown, CT: Wesleyan University Press, 1969).

Spivak, G. A. 'Three Women's Texts and a Critique of Imperialism.' *Critical Inquiry*, 12.1 (1985a): 243–61.

———. *A Critique of Postcolonial Reason* (Boston, MA: Harvard University Press, 1985b).

———. 'Three Women's Texts and a Critique of Imperialism.' In *'Race,' Writing, and Difference*, ed. Henry Louis Gates, Jr. (Chicago: University of Chicago Press, 1986), 262–80.

———. *Outside in the Teaching Machine*. (New York and London: Routledge, 1993).

———. 'Righting Wrongs.' *The South Atlantic Quarterly*, 103.2/3 (Spring/Summer 2004).

Srinivasachari, C. S. *History of the City of Madras* (Madras: P.Varadachary, 1939).

Srinivasan, A. 'The Hindu Temple Dancer: Prostitute or Nun?' *Cambridge Anthropology*, 8.1 (1983): 73–99.

Srinivasan, P. *Performing Indian Dance in America: Modernity, Tradition, and the Myth of Cultural Purity*. PhD Diss. (Northwestern University, 2003).

———. 'The Bodies Beneath the Smoke or What's Behind the Cigarette Poster: Unearthing Kinesthetic Connections in American Dance History.' *Discourses in Dance*, 4.1 (2007): 7–47.

———. 'The Nautch Women Dancers of the 1880s: Corporeality, U.S. Orientalism, and Anti-Asian Immigration Laws.' *Women and Performance: A Journal Of Feminist Theory*, 19.1 (March 2009): 3–21.

Stearns, W. M. *Jazz Dance: The Story of American Vernacular Dance* (New York: Schirmer Books, 1968).

Stockholms-Tidningen, 16 October 1958.

Stockholms-Tidningen, 17 October 1958.

Stocking, G. 'From Physics to Ethnology.' In *Race, Culture, and Evolution: Essays in the History of Anthropology* (Chicago: University of Chicago Press, 1982), 133–60.

Surowiecki, J. 'Exporting I.P.' *The New Yorker*, 14 May 2007: 52.

Susman, J. Note, 'Your Karma Ran Over My Dogma: Bikram Yoga and the (Im) possibilities of Copyrighting Yoga.' 25 *Loyola L.A. Entertainment Law Rev.* 245 (2004/2005). Online. LexisNexis® Academic, 9 July 2007.

Svenska Dagbladet, 17 October 1958.

Tagg, J. 'Globalization, Totalization and the Discursive Field.' In *Culture, Globalization and the World-System: Contemporary Conditions for the Representation of Identity*, ed. A. King (Minneapolis: University of Minnesota Press, 1997), 155–60.

Taylor, D. *The Archive and the Repertoire: Performing Cultural Memory in the Americas* (Durham, NC: Duke University Press, 2003).

Taylor, F. C. with Gerald Cook. *Alberta Hunter: A Celebration in Blues* (New York: McGraw-Hill, 1987).

Taylor, T. D. *Global Pop: World Music, World Markets* (New York: Routledge, 1997).

Terry, W. 'Dance: Miss Holm and her Fine *"Kiss Me, Kate"* Choreography.' *New York Herald Tribune*, Hanya Holm Clippings File, Dance Division, New York Public Library.

Tharu, S. and K. Lalita. (Eds). *Women Writing in India: 600 B.C. To the Present*, Vols 1 and 2 (New York: City University of New York, 1991).

'Theater Dance.' Clipping from *PM Star*, 4 January 1949; Hanya Holm Scrapbooks, Dance Collection, New York Public Library.

The Baratachari Synthesis. (1937) (Kolkata: Bengal Bratachari Society, 1981).

The Dancing Times, June–August, 1963.

Todd, A. 'A Brace of Musicals This Season on Broadway.' *Dance* (March 1949): 28–9, Dance Clipping File, Musical Comedies, *Kiss Me, Kate*, New York Public Library.

Tomko, L. *Dancing Class: Gender, Ethnicity, and Social Divides in American Dance, 1890–1920* (Bloomington: Indiana University Press, 1991).

Traiger, L. 'Dance Masters from Coast to Coast.' *The Washington Post*, 3 June 2005a: T24.

——. ' "Facing West": Sizing Up L.A. Dance Pioneers.' *The Washington Post*, 13 June 2005b: C05.

Turner, D. *This is Not a Peace Pipe: Towards a Critical Indigenous Philosophy* (Toronto: University of Toronto Press, 2006).

Ulvenstam, L. *Nyfiken på, med Lars Ulvenstam*, interview with Lilavati Häger, Sveriges Television, 1984.

Vaidhyanathan, S. *Copyrights and Copywrongs: The Rise of Intellectual Property and How It Threatens Creativity* (New York: New York University Press, 2001).

Vail, J. 'What The Words Say: Watching American Critics Watch World Dance.' In *Looking Out: Perspectives on Dance and Criticism in a Multicultural World*, ed. David Gere (New York: Schirmmer Books, 1995), 165–79.

Van Camp, J. 'Copyright of Choreographic Works.' In *1994–95 Entertainment, Publishing and the Arts Handbook*, ed. Stephen F. Breimer, Robert Thorne and John David Viera (New York: Clark, Boardman & Callaghan, 1994), 59–92.

——. 'Martha Graham's Legal Legacy.' *Dance Chronicle*, 30 (2007): 67–99.

Varmer, B. 'Copyright in Choreographic Works,' Copyright Law Revision. (Studies prepared for the Subcommittee on Patents, Trademarks, and Copyrights of the Committee on the Judiciary, United States Senate, Eighty-Sixth Congress, 2nd session 28, 1961).

Venkataram, L. 'Ambassador of Indian Dance.' *The Hindu*, online edition, 24 October 2003.

Vissicaro, P. *Studying Dance Cultures Around the World: An Introduction to Multicultural Dance Education* (Dubuque, IO: Kendall/Hunt, 2004).

Visweswaran, K. *Fictions of Feminist Ethnography* (Minneapolis: University of Minnesota Press, 1994).

Vizenor, G. *Manifest Manners: Postindain Warriors of Survivance* (Hanover, NY: University Press of New England, 1994).

Wallerstein, I. 'The National and the Universal: Can There Be Such as Thing as World Culture?' In *Culture, Globalization and the World-System: Contemporary Conditions for the Representation of Identity*, ed. A. King (Minneapolis: University of Minnesota Press, 1997), 91–106.

Walton, L. A. 'Lucky Roberts Autographs Songs for the Prince,' n.s. 17 October 1926: 6, Black Bottom Clippings File, Dance Collection, New York Public Library.

Weaver, J. *Orchesography. Or, The Art of Dancing by Characters and Demonstrative Figures* (London: H. Meere, 1706). Reprinted in Ralph, Richard. *The Life and Works of John Weaver* (New York: Dance Horizons, 1985).

Westman, N. *Dans med Häger: En pionjär i den svenska dansvärlden* (Stockholm: Lind, 2006).

West, W. R. Jr. 'As Long as We Keep Dancing.' In *Spirit of a Native Place: Building the National Museum of the American Indian*, ed. D. Blue Spruce (Washington, DC: National Museum of the American Indian, Smithsonian Institution, 2004), 46–55.

White, H. 'The Value of Narrativity in the Representation of Reality.' *Critical Inquiry* (Autumn 1980): 5–27.

Wilder, L. 'U.S. Government Grants First Dance Copyright.' *Dance Observer*, 19.5 (May 1952): 69.

Williams, D. 'The Body, Dance and Cultural Theory.' *Journal for Anthropological Study of Human Movement*, 1 (Autumn 2005): 11.

Williams, R. *Culture and Society 1780–1950* (New York: Columbia University Press, 1983).

Wolff, J. 'The Global and the Specific: Reconciling Conflicting Theories of Culture.' In *Culture, Globalization and the World-System: Contemporary Conditions for the Representation of Identity*, ed. A. King (Minneapolis: University of Minnesota Press, 1997), 161–73.

Yoshihara, M. *Embracing the East: White Women and American Orientalism* (Oxford: Oxford University Press, 2003).

Youngerman, S. 'Review: Curt Sachs and His Heritage: A Critical Review of *World History of the Dance* with a Survey of Recent Studies that Perpetuate his Ideas.' *CORD News*, 6.2 (July 1974): 6–19.

Zieger, R. H. and G. J. Gall. *American Workers, American Unions: The Twentieth Century* (Baltimore, MD: The Johns Hopkins University Press, 2002).
Žižek, S. 'Neighbors and Other Monsters: A Plea for Ethical Violence.' In S. Žižek, E. L. Santner and K. Reinhard, *The Neighbor: Three Inquiries in Political Theology* (Chicago: University of Chicago Press, 2005), 139–90.

Index